T0166136

The Transmission of Old English Poetry

WESTFIELD PUBLICATIONS IN MEDIEVAL AND RENAISSANCE STUDIES

12

The Transmission of Old English Poetry

by

Peter Orton

WESTFIELD PUBLICATIONS IN MEDIEVAL AND RENAISSANCE STUDIES

12

BREPOLS

British Library Cataloguing in Publication Data

Orton, Peter
   The transmission of Old English poetry. – (Westfield publications in
   medieval and Renaissance studies ; 12)
   1.English poetry – Old English, ca. 450-1100 – Criticism, Textual
   2.Transmission of texts
   I.Title II.Queen Mary and Westfield College
   821.1'09

   ISBN 2503510728

© 2000, Brepols Publishers n.v., Turnhout, Belgium

D/2000/0095/88

Printed in the E.U. on acid-free paper.

In Memoriam

Archibald Frank Orton
1908–1989

Contents

viii

Preface

I am grateful to the staff of numerous libraries for supplying me with reproductions of the manuscript texts of Old English poems included in this study, often with useful information about them. I should mention particularly Ms Mary L. Robertson, Associate Curator of the Huntington Library, San Marino, California; Mr Georges Dogaer, Curator of Manuscripts at the Bibliothèque Royale, Brussels; Canon F. Bussby, Librarian of the Cathedral Library, Winchester; Mr T. Kaye, Sub-librarian of Trinity College Library, Cambridge; Mr Conrad Swan, York Herald of Arms, London; and the staff of the Bodleian Library, Oxford. Mr Neil Ker and Professor R. I. Page kindly answered my queries by letter. The staff of the British Library Students' Room and Exeter University Library responded to my requests with efficiency and courtesy. Michael Swanton of the University of Exeter supervised the research upon which this book is based, patiently easing the difficulties I encountered, and providing a steady flow of encouragement. I am most grateful for all his help. An even older (though no lighter) debt is to Donald Scragg of the University of Manchester, who first aroused my interest in the transmission of Old English poetry by setting me to work on *Soul and Body*. I am also grateful to Tom Shippey of the University of St Louis, who read the original typescript and made many valuable suggestions for the book's improvement. Finally, I would like to thank my partner, Dr Felicity Rash, not only for much unpaid copy-editing work on my typescript, but also for unobtrusively smoothing my path in all sorts of ways while I was writing this book during the summer vacation of 1999.

Abbreviations

acc.: accusative
And: Andreas
ASPR: The Anglo-Saxon Poetic Records
Aza: Azarias
BCr: The Brussels Cross
BGDSL: *Beiträge zur Geschichte der deutschen Sprache und Literatur*
Brb: The Battle of Brunanburh (937)
Bwf: Beowulf
c.: century
Cæd: Cædmon's Hymn
Cæd1: Cædmon's Hymn (Northumbrian version)
Cæd2: Cædmon's Hymn (West Saxon version)
CFB: The Capture of the Five Boroughs (942)
Chr: Christ
Crd: The Creed
Dan: Daniel
dat.: dative
DEw: The Death of Edward (1065)
DrR: The Dream of the Rood
EEMS: Early English Manuscripts in Facsimile
EETS: Early English Text Society

EgC: The Coronation of Edgar (973)
EgD: The Death of Edgar (975)
EHR: *English Historical Review*
Ele: Elene
ES: *English Studies*
Exo: Exodus
F: Fragments of Psalms
f(f).: folio(s)
fem.: feminine
FtM: The Fortunes of Men
Gen: Genesis
gen.: genitive
GfM: The Gifts of Men
Gl1: The Gloria I
Gl2: The Gloria II
Glc: Guthlac
Gmc.: Germanic
HbM: The Husband's Message
imp.: imperative
indic.: indicative
inf.: infinitive
instr.: instrumental
Jg1: The Judgement Day I
JEGP: *Journal of English and Germanic Philology*
Jln: Juliana
Jud: Judith
Kt.: Kentish
LdR: The Leiden Riddle
LP1: The Lord's Prayer I

LP2: The Lord's Prayer II
MÆ: *Medium Ævum*
masc.: masculine
MB1-MB31: The Meters of
Boethius 1-31
MCh1-MCh12: The Metrical
Charms 1-12
Merc.: Mercian
Mld: The Battle of Maldon
Mnl: The Menologium
MP: *Modern Philology*
MS: manuscript
Mx1: Maxims I
Mx2: Maxims II
N&Q: *Notes and Queries*
neut.: neuter
nom.: nominative
North.: Northumbrian
OE: Old English
OEG: A. Campbell, *Old English
Grammar* (1959).
OrW: The Order of the World
P: The Metrical Psalms of the
Paris Psalter
p(p).: page(s)
part.: participle
PCE: The Metrical Epilogue to
the Pastoral Care
PCP: The Metrical Preface to
the Pastoral Care
Phx: The Phoenix
pl.: plural
Pnt: The Panther
Pra: A Prayer

Pre: Precepts
pres.: present
pret.: preterite
Prim. Gmc.: Primitive
Germanic.
PMLA: *Publications of the
Modern Language
Association of America*
R1-R95: Riddles 1-95 (cited by
number and line)
r: recto
RCr: The Ruthwell Cross
RES: *The Review of English
Studies*
Rsg: Resignation
Rui: The Ruin
Run: The Rune Poem
SB1: Soul and Body I
SB2: Soul and Body II
Sfr: The Seafarer
SFt: The Seasons for Fasting
sg.: singular
SN: *Studia Neophilologica*
SnS: Solomon and Saturn
subj.: subjunctive
TPS: *Transactions of the
Philological Society*
W-S: West-Saxon
v: verso
XSt: Christ and Satan
ZDA: *Zeitschrift für deutsches
Altertum und deutsche
Literatur*

Sigla and Manuscripts

Aza: Exeter, MS Cathedral Library 3501 (Ker 116, s. x^2)
Dan: Oxford, MS Bodleian, Junius 11 (Ker 334, s. x/xi)

Brb A: Cambridge, MS Corpus Christi College 173 (Ker 39, s. x med.)
Brb B: London, MS British Library, Cotton Tiberius A. vi (Ker 188, 977-9 A.D.)
Brb C: London, MS British Library, Cotton Tiberius B. i (Ker 191, s. xi med.)
Brb D: London, MS British Library, Cotton Tiberius B. iv (Ker 192, s. xi med.)

Cæd B: Cambridge, MS Corpus Christi College 41 (Ker 32, z. xi^1)
Cæd Br: Brussels, MS Bibliothèque Royale, 8245-57 (Humphreys and Ross 1975, 53).
Cæd Bu: Bury St. Edmunds, MS St. James's Cathedral Library, now San Marino, MS Huntingdon Library HM 35300 (Humphreys and Ross 1975, 53, c. 1400 A.D.)
Cæd Ca: Cambridge, MS Univ. Lib. Kk. 3. 18 (Ker 23, s. xi^2)
Cæd Di: Dijon, MS Bibliothèque Municipale 574 (Ker, Appendix, 8, s. xii)
Cæd H: Oxford, MS Bodleian, Hatton 43 (Ker 326, s. xi^2)
Cæd Hr: Hereford, MS Cathedral P. v. I (Ker 121, s. xii^1)
Cæd L: Leningrad, MS Pub. Lib., Lat. Q. v. i. 18 (Ker 122, s. viii)
Cæd Ld_1: Oxford, MS Bodleian, Laud Misc. 243 (Ker 341, s. xii^1)
Cæd Ln: Oxford, Lincoln College, Lat. 31 (Ker 356, s. xii med.)
Cæd Lo: London, MS College of Arms M. 6. (Humphreys and Ross 1975, 53, s. xii)
Cæd M: Cambridge, MS University Library Kk. 5. 16 (Ker 25, s. viii^1)
Cæd Mg: Oxford, MS Magdalen College, Lat. 105 (Ker 357, s. xii med.)
Cæd O: Oxford, MS Corpus Christi College 279, Part ii (Ker 354, s. xi in.)

Cæd P: Paris, MS Bibliothèque Nationale, Lat. 5237 (Wuest 1906, 212-3, 1425-30 A.D.)

Cæd T: Oxford, MS Bodleian, Tanner 10 (Ker 351, s. x^1)

Cæd To: Tournai, MS Bibliothèque Municipale 134 (Ker 387, s. xii)

Cæd Tr1: Cambridge, MS Trinity College R. 5. 22 (Dobbie 1942, xcvii, s. xiv)

Cæd W: Winchester, MS Cathedral 1 (Ker 396, s. xi med.)

CFB A: Cambridge, MS Corpus Christi College 173 (Ker 39, s. x med.)

CFB B: London, MS British Library, Cotton Tiberius A. vi (Ker 188, 977-9 A.D.)

CFB C: London, MS British Library, Cotton Tiberius B. i (Ker 191, s. xi med.)

CFB D: London, MS British Library, Cotton Tiberius B. iv (Ker 192, s. xi med.)

Dan: see under Aza above.

DEw C: London, MS British Library, Cotton Tiberius B. i (Ker 191, s. xi)

DEw D: London, MS British Library, Cotton Tiberius B. iv (Ker 192, s. xi^2)

EgC A: Cambridge, MS Corpus Christi College 173 (Ker 39, s. xi^1)

EgC B: London, MS British Library, Cotton Tiberius A. vi (Ker 188, 977-9 A.D.)

EgC C: London, MS British Library, Cotton Tiberius B. i (Ker 191, s. xi med.)

EgD A: Cambridge, MS Corpus Christi College 173 (Ker 39, s. xi^1)

EgD B: London, MS British Library, Cotton Tiberius A. vi (Ker 188, 977-9 A.D.)

EgD C: London, MS British Library, Cotton Tiberius B. i (Ker 191, s. xi med.)

F: Oxford, MS Bodleian, Junius 121 (Ker 338, s. xi, third quarter)

Gll C: Cambridge, MS Corpus Christi College 201 (Ker 49, s. xi med.)

Gll J: Oxford, MS Bodleian, Junius 121 (Ker 338, s. xi, third quarter)

LdR: Leiden, MS Rijksuniversiteit, Vossianus Lat. 4° 106 (Ker, Appendix, 19, early 9th c.)

P: Paris, MS Bibliothèque Nationale 8824 (Ker 367, s. xi med.)

PCE D: Oxford, MS Bodleian, Hatton 20 (Ker 324, 890-97 A.D.)
PCE H: Cambridge, MS Corpus Christi College 12 (Ker 30, s.x^2)

PCP D: Cambridge, MS Corpus Christi College 12 (Ker 30, s.x^2)
PCP H: Oxford, MS Bodleian, Hatton 20 (Ker 324, 890-97 A.D.)
PCP T: Cambridge, Trinity College R. 5. 22 (Ker 87, s. x/xi)

Pra J: London, MS British Library, Cotton Julius A. ii, ff. 136-144 (Ker 159, s. xii med.)
Pra L: London, MS Lambeth Palace 427, ff. 1-209 (Ker 280, s. xi^1)

R30a, R30b, R35: Exeter, MS Cathedral Library 3501 (Ker 116, s. x^2)

SB1: Vercelli, MS Biblioteca Capitolare CXVII (Ker 394, s. x^2)
SB2: Exeter, MS Cathedral Library 3501 (Ker 116, s. x^2)

SnS A: Cambridge, MS Corpus Christi College 422 (Ker 70A, s. x med.)
SnS B: Cambridge, MS Corpus Christi College 41 (Ker 32, s. xi^1-med.)

Introduction

Approximately 185 OE poems (complete texts or fragments) survive in contemporary manuscripts of the Anglo-Saxon period,[1] amounting to about 30,535 long lines of alliterative verse (see Bessinger & Smith 1978: ix). Of these 185 poems or fragments, 20 survive, either wholly or in part, in multiple (two or more) manuscript versions. 20 out of 185, however (10.8%), gives an exaggerated impression of the amount of overlap: most of the poems in question are quite short, and the total number of overlapping lines is 679 or thereabouts, only 2.2% of the 30,535 lines in the OE poetic corpus as a whole.

The number of surviving versions of each poem varies between two and thirty, and the length of the overlap ranges from 3 to 120 lines. The following is a full list:

Poem	Number of manuscripts	Amount of overlap (lines)
Aza 1–75/Dan 279–364	2	73
BDS1/BDS2/BDS3	30	5
Brb	4	73
Cæd1/Cæd2	20	9
CFB	4	13
DEw	2	34
DrR 39–64/(RCr)	2	18*
EgC	3	20
EgD	3	37
F53.1-F140.2/P53.1–140.2	2	66
Gl1	2	57
LdR/R35	2	14
LEP	2	3
MCh5.3–5/MCh10.3–5	2	3
PCE	2	30

---

[1] I take P51-P150, MB1-MB31 and MCh1-MCh12 as three single poems, but R1-R95 as 95 separate poems, in arriving at this figure.

PCP	3	16
Pra 1–15	2	15
R30a/R30b	2	9
SB1 1–126/SB2	2	120
SnS	2	64**

* 18 lines or parts of lines (the text of RCr is fragmentary).

** not counting lines 1–29, for which the A MS is almost illegible.

This book is a study of the relationships between the manuscript texts of these poems, excluding only the three shortest texts (BDS, LEP and MCh5.3–5/MCh10.3–5).

The variant readings among the extant texts of these poems attracted little scholarly interest until 1946, when Kenneth Sisam used some of the variants from SB1/SB2, Aza/Dan and the A and B texts of SnS as evidence against the authority of late manuscripts of OE poetry (Sisam 1953: 30). Sisam's target was the easy assumption that the generality of OE poems (most of them surviving in a single manuscript) had been accurately transmitted by scribes since their composition. He questioned the logic of a stolid defence of the manuscript reading (even when it makes little sense) in these circumstances:

> [...] it implies that the extant manuscripts of Old English poetry represent the original compositions with a high degree of accuracy. Yet there seems to be no modern work which attempts to establish a thesis so fundamental. To say that 'an accurate scribe did not as a rule depart from the *wording* of his original except as a result of oversight' is begging the question, unless the editor goes on to inquire whether the scribes with whom he is concerned accurate in this sense, and whether, since the assumed date of composition, the transmission of the text has been entirely in the hands of scribes who aimed at copying what was before them.

Sisam's subsequent remark that the question of how accurately OE poetry was transmitted 'could well occupy a monograph' (Sisam 1953: 31) encouraged me to embark on the research which underlies this book (Orton 1981). I hope to offer here some general conclusions about the accuracy of OE scribes in copying poetry, and also address the more specific question raised by Sisam about whether scribes ever did 'depart' deliberately from their exemplars. I shall argue that they did, and suggest reasons why.

Sisam's attack was directed chiefly at an unquestioning conservativism amongst editors of OE poems surviving in single manuscripts, though his criticisms were not, perhaps, entirely fair. The editor of an OE poem surviving in a single witness is in an difficult position, especially if he feels forced to conclude that his text is corrupt. Not only will he have no support for this conclusion in the form of other, independent, more reliable witnesses to the text, but he will also have to rely on conjectural emendation in his edited text. No scholar likes to be reduced to guess-work, and an editor, whose first task is the establishment of the text, likes it less than most, because a bad, misguided, or doubtful emendation will prejudice other aspects of his edition. The emending editor will also leave himself vulnerable to the charge of claiming a better knowledge of OE than scribes who were native speakers of the language. No wonder, there-fore, that the feeling had arisen by the time Sisam was writing in the forties that the editor's duty was to defend the manuscript reading tenaciously against any charge of corruption. Editors of single-witness OE poems do not want to find corruptions in their texts because we have not developed any general procedure for dealing with them.

Other quite intractable problems of method follow on from this one. Anyone who has ever edited an OE poem will have tried to find ways of evaluating the condition of the manuscript text or texts in which the poem survives; yet a host of difficulties stand in the way. Each apparent corruption presents the editor with several more or less unanswerable questions. How deep-seated is the corruption? Is it a simple slip by the latest scribe, or has the extant reading evolved over several copyings? Perhaps a whole string of corruptions have compounded the original one. The editor will, of course, always prefer the 'simple slip' explanation because it keeps conjecture to the minimum. He knows, however, not only that the availability of an explanation of this kind in any given case is largely a matter of chance, but also that a textual 'restoration' based upon it has little real authority. To produce a palaeographically credible deduction about how a textual corruption arose is to suggest a possibility about the corresponding reading of the authoritative text, nothing more. For example, the sequence *in* may be substituted editorially for a manu-script's *m* (or vice-versa) if this improves the sense or removes a technical irregularity in the metre. This kind of emendation is regarded as permissible because the forms of these letters in Anglo-Saxon script create the potential for this confusion. This is the level of editorial action the editor prefers. Once he has edited the text, many other laborious and time-consuming jobs lie ahead. He therefore welcomes piecemeal solu-tions which involve a minimum of disruption to the received text. Such solutions are relatively easy to apply and relatively acceptable to users of editions. Sometimes they seem very convincing, though I think everyone recognizes (and excuses) the element of conjecture that they often involve.

When there are two or more independent witnesses to a poem, how-ever, the general evaluation of textual quality (in terms of fidelity to the work of the poet) comes closer to the editor's grasp. A scribal error, or other kind of mismanagement of the exemplar, in one extant version may be explicable on the basis of an alternative, apparently uncorrupted reading in another manuscript witness. The editor can compare the two readings and look for possible links between them; more specifically, he can seek an explanation of the error in terms of its supposed source in the uncorrupted version. The element of conjecture still remains, of course, but it is limited by the requirement to suggest a convincing relationship between two *witnessed* readings. In no single case can I ever actually prove that a bad reading in an extant text of a poem originated in the good reading I find in another witness to the same poem; but validating factors often emerge, sometimes unexpectedly. For example, a few poems sur-vive in three or more independent witnesses, which means that corrup-tions can often be identified as a matter of virtual certainty. Alternatively, we may find unexpected patterns of variation between texts: two texts of the same poem may (for example) show a pattern of variation in which one version's variants are consistently less convincing in some way than the other version's variants; or one version of a poem may show a general tendency to replace exclusively or largely poetic items of vocabulary with more generally distributed words. In this way the low evidential value of individual cases may be compensated for by the aggregated impact of many examples all pointing to the same kind of influence on OE poetry during transmission. Valuable guidelines for editors working with only a single witness could easily emerge from this collection of evidence. Armed with a broad idea of the kinds of corruption that Old English scribes were likely to introduce into the texts they copied, the editor of a single-witness poem such as *Beowulf* will be in a better position than before to identify, interpret and emend at least some of the corruptions in his text.

The word 'corruption' has become almost taboo in Anglo-Saxon tex-tual studies recently, reflecting a general revulsion against the whole notion of textual decay during transmission; and even the idea of 'trans-mission' has to some extent been undermined. These developments have arisen partly from a questioning of the idea that the modern editor or commentator is in a position to overrule Anglo-Saxon scribes in matters of OE poetic language or style; but a much more potent and far-reaching influence has been the idea, expounded by O'Keeffe, that Old English poems, even after they had been written in manuscripts, remained subject to free, creative transmission of an essentially oral nature (O'Keeffe 1990). I shall discuss O'Keeffe's ideas more fully in the concluding chapter of this book (below, §9.7). Here I shall only anticipate my conclusions to the extent of saying that scribes made all manner of mistakes in copying OE poetry, and it is clear that some copyists had a weak grasp of the language and expression of the texts they were dealing with. So I shall continue to use the word 'corruption' in this book in the sense of a reading which is not the poet's. We may identify a corruption by the fact that it makes no (or at least very poor) sense in its context, or seems impossible linguistically, based on what we know of the Old English language generally, or is formally irregular to a degree which could not credibly be attributed to the poet. A corruption in a text of a poem surviving in multiple manuscripts may or may not occur in other texts of the same poem. If another text has a better reading at the corresponding point, it seems natural to consider this better reading as the authorial reading from which the corrupt reading has, for some reason or other, deviated. It is, of course, always possible that a 'good' reading has resulted from the improvement during transmission of a 'bad' one; but there are, as we shall see later in this book, reasons for accepting the commonsense view that bad readings are the result of transmission and corresponding good readings belong to the poet. This conclusion is, for obvious reasons, crucial to any investigation of the variant texts of Old English poetry.

This book will therefore present an accumulation of information about the kinds of influence to which Old English verse was subject during its transmission, based on the general precept that good readings are earlier than bad ones and that bad readings derive somehow from good ones. It will deal with the kinds of error which tended to occur; the kinds of words and constructions that were open to misinterpretation; attitudes to metrical regularity, towards the spelling of items of the poetic vocabulary, towards punctuation, and so on. But I shall not be exclusively concerned with variations between the texts of these poems; I shall also try to define what aspects of Old English poetic texts were relatively resistant to alteration during transmission.

It is obvious that the only sound basis for this kind of information is poems for which a number of independent witnesses survive, providing the means of deducing the character of antecedent texts which have not survived, or of a common archetype from all the surviving witnesses ultimately derive. Poems surviving in a single manuscript cannot provide this kind of information, at least not very much of it and not of very reliable quality. It is sometimes said that *Beowulf* shows signs of having descended through several levels of transmission; but it is difficult to define the qualities of any of its antecedent versions with any degree of assurance, for obvious reasons. When, on the other hand, we have two or more manuscript witnesses to a poem, it is sometimes possible to identify correspondences between them which are unlikely to have arisen independently — an irregular pattern of punctuation or scribal vowel-accents, for example. Again, an aggregation of evidence of this sort may enable us to generalize about those textual characteristics which transmitters tended to preserve unchanged.

The question of 'oral transmission' will be addressed. It has been suggested (though not lately, so far as I know) that oral transmission accounts for the variations between some of the poems studied here (see Jones 1966). If it were possible to demonstrate literary connections between texts of the same poem — significant correspondences of a purely literary or presentational nature such as patterns of punctuation or capital letters or accents — it would be reasonable to conclude that oral transmission had played no part in producing any of the variations between them; that they all result from the activities of copyists. It is, on the other hand, difficult to imagine what kind of variation between texts could be explained *only* on the basis of oral transmission; but it should be possible to isolate those texts which show no indications of any literary connection with any others that survive. These, at least, may contain variants resulting from oral transmission, though it will obviously be impossible to be certain that they do.

I must here describe briefly the procedures followed in the research upon which my findings are based. In comparing the manuscript texts of the poems listed earlier, I took no account of line-division in the manuscripts. Old English poems are normally presented in prose format in the manuscripts, with no regular indication of line-endings or verse-divisions except (in a few cases) scribal pointing. The running-together by scribes of separate words and the separation of individual words into syllabic (or other) units were similarly ignored; but all other aspects of textual presentation were noticed, transcribed and compared: punctuation, capitalization, accenting, abbreviations and *signes de renvoi*. Letter-forms were given particularly close attention: þ and ð were distinguished and texts compared in their use. The more conspicuous formal variations in the shape of other letters, especially *s* and *y*, which show great variety of shape in Anglo-Saxon script, were treated in the same way. Scribal insertions, deletions and other alterations to words or letters were all examined in the hope that they might be informative about textual relationships or transmission.

Within each manuscript, the poetic text was examined, not in isolation, but in the context of any other texts that surrounded it, especially those copied by the same scribe as copied the poem. These other texts were identified with the help of Ker 1957. Any notable features of textual presentation were noted and compared across manuscripts. The scribe's use of variant letter-forms in the poem were compared in detail with his usages elsewhere in the manuscript. This line of investigation was pursued in the hope of finding evidence (in the form of variations in usage from text to text) of the condition of the scribe's exemplar. If, for example, a scribe was found to be consistent in his employment of variant letter-forms throughout his contribution to a manuscript, I had no option but to conclude that the consistency was attributable to the latest scribe; but if a poetic text differed from adjacent texts in its deployment of variant forms, I regarded this difference as a possible reflection of a distinction among the texts of the scribe's exemplar or exemplars which could take us one step closer to the archetype. If I found inconsistency of usage within the poetic text, I considered the possibility that some, at least, of the forms used might derive from the exemplar. Correspondences between two texts of a poem residing in forms which are unusual in the general context of both scribes' contributions to the manuscripts they worked on were of particular interest, because they could be used as evidence of a literary (i.e. non-oral) connection between the two texts. The study of unusual or distinctive letter-forms is also valuable because they can, if traceable to antecedent texts, help to explain corruptions or scribal slips. Abbreviated words and accent-marks were also investigated in much the same way as variant letter-forms, again in the hope of shedding light on the processes of transmission and the practices of scribes.

Every kind of variation and correspondence (with the exceptions already noted) between texts of the same poem were examined in detail, including variations and correspondences in the spelling of individual words. These phonological investigations were designed, like the study of letter-forms and other scribal impositions described earlier, to reveal as much as possible about the history of the text and its transmission. Spellings in the poetic text were therefore compared with the same scribe's spellings of the same (or phonologically comparable) words elsewhere in his contribution to the manuscript he worked on. The purpose of this line of investigation was to reveal significant linguistic correspondences between texts which might shed light on its transmission and on the linguistic character of lost antecedent versions of the text. A spelling which is usual in a scribe's work may well be his or her preferred spelling (though of course it could simply be an accurate and regular reflection of the exemplar text or texts); at any rate, it is impossible to maintain with any assurance that it derives from an antecedent text; but if a spelling is atypical of a scribe, it may be a chance survival from an antecedent text. Alternatively, it may be that the whole range of spellings of the word in question in the scribe's work, or his spelling of words of the same general phonological type, reflects the condition of his exemplar. If two texts correspond in such isolated spellings, the chances are that the connection between them is literary, not oral, and we may learn something about the transmission of distinctive linguistic forms. One can sometimes see evidence of earlier impositions of forms belonging to particular Old English dialects or periods; and it sometimes happens that words found only in poetry tend to preserve archaic or dialectal (non-standard-W-S) spellings; or that corruptions may be explained on the assumption that a non-W-S (and so perhaps unfamiliar) spelling appeared in an antecedent text.

More substantial variations between texts are of many different kinds. Transpositions, substitutions, and omissions or additions of letters, words or sequences of words are often to be explained as the result of error, but not always; such differences may have arisen as a result of a conscious decision on the part of a transmitter of the text. Differences in vocabulary, word-order, syntax or inflection, or in the presence or absence of verses and lines, or even, in a few cases, whole sequences of lines, are also open to these two kinds of interpretation.

The question of how best to classify these variations in a general account of them in many different poems is clearly a crucial one. To present them in purely descriptive terms would mean (for example) placing what there are good reasons for believing were additions to poems in the same category as what seem to be omissions in another (or the same) poem. Large and relatively unmanageable collections of raw, unprocessed data would accumulate in this way, which would then need to be interpreted and divided up into other categories according to the likely causes of the differences, such as mechanical error, ignorance, or some more constructive attitude to the received text. This would make a very long book; and in view of the amount of technical and linguistic detail which is inevitable in a study of this kind of material, I have chosen an overall classification of variants according to their probable causes. Part 1 of the book deals with changes imposed on the texts of poems during transmission, Part 2 with the preservation of existing features of the text. In Part 1, Chapter 1 deals first with the scribal imposition of standard spellings; Chapter 2 is concerned with mechanical errors;[2] Chapter 3 deals with copyists' treatment of existing corruptions in their exemplars in cases where these are detectable; Chapter 4 with modifications to the text that seem to have arisen from various kinds of misunderstanding of the exemplar text; Chapter 5 with changes that were probably deliberate and appear to be based on a sound grasp of the meaning of the exemplar; and finally Chapter 6 identifies interpolations and extensions — major modifications of the text effected by scribes of their own free will. Thus the succession of Chapters 2 to 6 shows a progression in the degree of conscious involvement on the part of scribes with the texts they were copying: the mechanical errors of Chapter 2 are unthinking, unconscious slips, whereas the interpolations and extensions of Chapter 6 are deliberate, creative responses to the received text. In Part 2, Chapters 7 and 8 look at the texts of these poems from a different angle, examining them for indications of the preservation by copyists of exemplar forms and features, some of which may go back as far as the original composition. Finally, Chapter 9 offers some general conclusions about the effects of transmission on OE verse texts and the strengths and weaknesses of the scribes who copied them.

---

[2] Although I felt that linguistic standardization and mechanical error could not be neglected in a study of this kind, they undoubtedly represent the drier end of my topic. Some readers may therefore prefer to skim or skip Chapters 1 and 2.

Part 1:

Changes Resulting from Transmission

Chapter 1. The Language of the Scribe and the Language of the Text

§1 The scribal imposition of preferred spellings

§1.1 STANDARD FORMS

The political power and influence exercised by the kingdom of Wessex during the late Anglo-Saxon period gave rise to a standardized written dialect or koine with its phonological basis in Wessex speech, known to scholars as late W-S. Most OE literary texts copied during the second half of the tenth century or later are preserved in this form of OE, irrespective of whether or not they were originally composed, or first preserved in writing, in one of the other OE dialects that are distinguishable in the written records of the time. The best-attested of these are the two Anglian dialects, Northumbrian (hereafter North.) and Mercian (Merc.), and the Kentish (Kt.) and early W-S dialects.[1] The impressive series of texts of Cæd, ranging chronologically from the first half of the eighth century to the twelfth,[2] provide the clearest available illustration of the West-Saxonization of a text originally composed in a different dialect. Cædmon, to whom the poem is attributed by Bede, was a seventh-century Northumbrian, a Whitby monk, and the two earliest surviving texts of the poem, M and L, both from the eighth century, are preserved in a literary North. dialect. Cædmon himself, who according to Bede composed Cæd orally, would have spoken North., but

---

[1] See Campbell 1959: §§1–22, hereafter referred to as *OEG*.

[2] Two texts from the fourteenth century survive in Tr₁ and Bu, and P is fifteenth-century, but in none of these cases is the language of the text that of the time it was copied; all three texts show a level of error which suggests that they were reproduced mechanically, with little, probably no, understanding of the meaning.

the language in which the M and L texts of the poem are written is more safely interpreted as the language, not of the poet himself, but of the Northumbrian scribes who preserved the text; for both the M and L manuscripts were written in Northumbria, M certainly not long after Bede's death in 935.[3]

The West-Saxonization of the phonology of Cæd over the course of its transmission is illustrated below by a comparison of the earliest North. text of Cæd, M, from the first half of the eighth century, with two of the later W-S versions, T and H, from the tenth and eleventh centuries respectively.

Cæd M

Nu scylun hergen[a] hefaenricaes uard
metudæs maecti end his modgidanc
uerc uuldurfadur sue he uundra gihuaes
eci dryctin or astelidæ
5   he aerist scop aelda barnū
heben til hrofe haleg scepen.
tha middungeard moncynnæs uard
eci dryctin æfter tiadæ
firum foldˇ frea allmectig

Notes on the text: 1 *hergena* with second *e* underdotted, *a* added super-script. 4 *dryctin* with original *in* altered to *yc*. 7 *middungeard* with first *d* adapted from original *n*. 8 *tiadæ* with *ti* originally written *d*. 9 *foldˇ*: the superscript mark does not resemble *u*.

Cæd T

nu sculon herigean heofonrices weard
meotodes meahte & his modgeþanc
weorc wuldorfæder. swa he wundra gehwæs
éce drihten ór onstealde.
5   he ærest sceop eorðan bearnū
heofon to hrofe halig scyppend.
þa middangeard moncynnes weard

---

[3]   See Ker 1957: 38, who dates the M text to the first half of the eighth century. There has been a revival of interest recently in the idea that the version of Cæd that has come down to us is a translation of Bede's Latin paraphrase back into OE (see Frantzen 1990: 146). However, even if this were the case (and no evidence either sustains or refutes it), the question does not impinge on the history of the poem's transmission since Bede's lifetime (or shortly after his death). A recent discussion of the text's history is Orton 1998.

éce drihten æfter teode
firum foldan frea ælmihtig.[4]

Cæd H

Nu we sculon herian heofonrices weard.
metudes myhte. & his modgeþanc.
wurc wuldorfæder. swa he wundra gehwilc
ece drihten ord astealde.
5 He ærest gesceop ylda bearnū
heofon to hrofe. halig scyppend
middangearde mancynnes weard
éce drihten. Æfter tida
firum on foldum frea ælmyhtig

Notes on the text: 3 *wuldorfæder* with *o* originally written *u*.

T shows the substitution of W-S forms in 9 *ælmihtig* with *i* in the stem
from earlier *ie* the W-S *i*-umlaut of *ea* (*OEG* §§200.3, 300, 301, 316).
The *e* of M's *allmectig* is the non-W-S *i*-umlaut of *ea* (*OEG* §200.3). T 2
meahte, with *ea* preserved, is probably also W-S but could also be Kt.,
whereas the *ae* in M's *maecti* derives from *ea* by Anglian smoothing
(*OEG* §§145, 204.5, 223). The *ea* in T 4 *onstealde* (by fracture of *æ*
before *l* plus consonant) is either W-S or Kt. (*OEG* §143), whereas the *e*
in M's *astelidæ* results from the *i*-umlaut of unbroken *æ* (*OEG* §§143,
194, 752) and is not in itself a distinctive dialectal feature, though the
form is unique. Another general W-S spelling (early or late) in T is 1
herigean with -*ig*- by parasiting (*OEG* §365). The corrected form in M is
probably intended to be *hergan* which, though not a typical early North.
form, is certainly not a typical W-S one either. Specifically late W-S
forms in T are 5 *sceop* with *eo* (which could also possibly be late North.,
though this seems unlikely here; see *OEG* §§179–183; M has *scop*) and 6
scyppend with *y* (*OEG* §§185, 201(4), 301). The derivation of the *e* in the
stem of M's form *scepen* is obscure, but the form is non-W-S (*OEG*
§188; Smith 1968: 30, §9).

In the eleventh-century H we find again *eo* in 5 *gesceop*, 6 *scyppend*
with *y*, and 5 *ylda* with *y*, all late W-S forms (*OEG* §301 covers the
development of the stem-vowel in *ylda*), plus 2 *myhte* and 9 *ælmyhtig*,
both with late OE *y* for earlier *i* (*OEG* §§317–18). T and H also contain a
number of general OE forms in places where M's forms are specifically

---

[4] The Tironian sign used by OE scribes for 'and' is here replaced in all quotations from
OE with the ampersand, as in line 2.

North., e.g. 1, 7 *weard*, 5 *bearnū*, both with *ea* by fracture of *æ* before *r* plus consonant, beside M's *uard*, *barnū* showing typically North. retraction of *æ* to *a* before fracture has had a chance to affect the vowel (*OEG* §144).

We do not have as plentiful evidence as this for most of the OE poems which survive in multiple manuscripts; Cæd is exceptional in this regard. But although the effects of standardization are easily demonstrated, one would like to be able to observe the process itself at closer quarters. Would a text composed in, say, an Anglian dialect, as Cæd evidently was, lose its distinctive linguistic characteristics only gradually, as copying succeeded copying, or was the transliteration from one dialect to another done at a stroke in the course of a single copying? The evidence here is very limited; but the condition of the O text of Cæd suggests that this poem, at least, did not lose its Anglian linguistic character overnight when scribes who customarily used W-S spellings began to copy it. The O text of Cæd was written at the beginning of the eleventh century. It is the second oldest of a group of four W-S texts, known as the W-S *eorðan* group (texts T, O, B and Ca), all of which survive as parts of the OE translation of Bede's *Historia Ecclesiastica* (hereafter referred to as the *OE Bede*). O is distinguished from its fellow-members of the group (in fact, from all other W-S texts of the poem) by a number of amendments that the scribe made to what he originally wrote. That these amendments were not all made to achieve conformity with an exemplar inaccurately copied in the first instance is suggested by certain correspondences between the text prior to correction with the authoritative T text, reproduced above (cf. Dobbie 1937: 26). Other forms in O link it with the earlier North. texts, represented above by M. Here is the O text, with notes on the corrections the scribe made to it:

> Cæd O
>
> Nu,^{we}sculan herian heofonrices weard
> metodes mihte & his modgeþonc
> wera wuldorfæder swa he wundra gehwæs
> ece dryhten oór^{d}, onstealde
> 5 he ærest gesceop eorðan bearnum
> heofon to hrofe halig scyppend
> ða middongeard moncynnes weard
> ece dryhten æfter teode
> firum folda^{n}, frea ælmihtig.

Notes on the text: 1 *we*, 4 *d* of *oórd*, 9 *n* of *foldan* all added superscript above an insertion-mark (here represented by a comma, which this mark resembles). 3 *wera* with *a* altered from original *o*. 5 two or three letters erased after *bearnum*, with the last stroke of the *m* on the erasure. 8 *teode* with erasure of one letter, perhaps *d*, after *o*.

The insertion of the pronoun *we* in 1 brings the O text into conformity with all other surviving texts of the poem except T and the two very earliest North. texts, M and L, all of which omit the pronoun. In 3, *wera* was originally written *wero*, a form suggesting an error for an exemplar's *werc*, the Anglian smoothed form (*OEG* §§222, 227) which only the North. texts of Cæd exhibit (M, L *uerc*, much mangled as *puerc* or *peure* in the continental texts Di, P and Br). The W-S texts have mostly *weorc* or *wurc*. In line 4, the word originally written was *oór*, a form of *or*, 'beginning', a largely poetic word which appears in T and in all the North. texts but is replaced in all the other (W-S) texts by the synonymous *ord* (Frampton 1924: 6–7; Dobbie 1937: 29–30). In line 7, the form *middongeard* is unique: the general OE form is *middangeard*, used regularly elsewhere by the scribe of O in his copy of the *OE Bede* (Miller 1890: 320/28, 340/30, 346/5); *middongeard* is probably to be interpreted as a slightly modernized spelling of the *middungeard* of M (L has *middingard*, Di and P *middumgeard*, Br *middumgaerd*), also a unique form in OE (see Smith 1968: §11; Ross 1950: 93, 94, note 38; *OEG* §377).[5] 8 *teode* was probably originally written *teodde*. The unetymological doubling of consonants is typical of the North. dialect. Finally, 9 *folda*, before correction to *foldan*, shows the same loss of final *n* in weak nominal inflexion exhibited by the corresponding forms in all the North. texts (with M the only possible exception: the significance of the scribe's abbreviation is uncertain) but not in any of the other W-S texts.

What is the significance of these original (i.e. uncorrected) forms in the O text? They are too numerous to be dismissed *en bloc* as chance correspondences with the earlier, Northumbrian textual tradition of Cæd. The conclusions we are entitled to draw depend on the authority of the O manuscript. Although O is not, as I have already pointed out, the earliest member of the W-S *eorðan* group — that distinction belongs to T — there is nothing in either its uncorrected or its corrected state to suggest that it actually derives from T; in fact, O's corruption *wera* in 3 argues against derivation from T, in which the standard W-S form *weorc* is clear and unmistakable. O therefore has claims to be treated as an independent

---

[5] The Br text is printed, rather inaccurately, by Humphreys & Ross 1975: 53.

witness to the late-ninth- or early-tenth-century archetype of the W-S *eorðan* group; and if that is what it is, perhaps we are justified in regarding O as a rather clumsily West-Saxonized version of a prototype text which still retained some of its original Anglian colouring — colouring that the T text has rather more thoroughly obliterated. If this view is accepted, O provides the evidence we are looking for of a gradual eradication of one dialectal matrix in favour of another in the course of the transmission of an OE poem, though we cannot, of course, conclude solely on the basis of a single text that the process was always as gradual as it seems to have been here. Similar modernizations are observable here and there in other manuscripts of Cæd, an example being 3 *wuldorfæder* in H (above), where the unstressed parasite-vowel *o* in the first element was originally written as the *u* which is normal in early North. (see *OEG* §373) and in fact appears in this word in the two earliest North. texts of Cæd (M, L *uuldurfadur*; Di *puldurfudur* mistakes the OE runic letter *wynn* for *p*).

§1.2 NON-STANDARD FORMS

Generally speaking, the later a text is, the more likely it is to contain a preponderance of late W-S forms; but occasionally we find evidence of the imposition of dialectal (i.e. non-standard) spellings in late texts. The best body of evidence for this in a single text is the small group of Kenticisms in the T version of PCP. The T manuscript of the *Cura Pastoralis* translation was written in the late tenth or early eleventh century, though we do not know where. Sisam suggested Salisbury (Sisam 1953: 145). The forms with the best claim to be considered Kt. are 15 *ledensprœce* (H, D *lœdensprœce*), showing late Kt. raising of *œ* to *e* in the stem of the first element (*OEG* §288); 11 *ælfrœd* (H, D *ælfred*), in which *œ* for *e* in the final syllable is probably also a sympton of the Kt. raising of *œ* to *e* in stressed syllables and the general interchangeability of the *œ* and *e* graphs that resulted; and 15 *myahte* (H, D *meahte*), where the representation of the diphthong is an inverted spelling indicating the unrounding of *y* to *e* that is characteristic of late Kt. (*OEG* §§288, 298). 10 *merþum* (H, D *mærðum*), with non-W-S *e* in the stem from Prim. Gmc. *ǣ* (*OEG* §§128–29), could also be Kt.

The hypothesis that scribes sometimes archaized the spellings of their exemplars has been invoked (by Horgan 1980) to explain some of the instances of early W-S *ie* in the D text of PCE that are not matched in the earlier text H (5, 9, 10, 13, 18, 28 *hiene*, 7 *wætersciepes*, 10 *sieððan*, 11 *hieder*, 30 *liefes*). All of these forms are inverted spellings with *ie* for etymological *i* as a symptom of the monophthongization of *ie* to *i* in early W-S (*OEG* §300). With these forms we may compare those shared by H and D in which the *ie* spellings are direct reflections of earlier sound-changes in W-S: 10, 23 *gier(e)don*, *gegiered* with early W-S *i*-umlaut of *ea* (*OEG* §200), and 17 *giefe*, with W-S palatal diphthongization of earlier *e* (*OEG* §185). Although it is difficult to prove deliberate archaizing on the part of scribes in the absence of a firm dating of D's exemplar and of any independent knowledge of its linguistic character, the frequency with which these inverted spellings occur is very striking.

Chapter 2. The Pathology of Copying

§2 Mechanical errors

The term 'mechanical errors is used here for changes to the received text made without any conscious thought. Instances are divided below into four main categories: substitutions, transpositions, omissions and additions, with further sub-divisions of the evidence in cases where it makes a large number of examples more manageable.

§2.1 SUBSTITUTIONS

§2.1.1 Mechanical replacements of individual letters

Mechanical replacements of whole words are dealt with in a separate category below (§2.1.2).

§2.1.1.1 Misinterpretation of unusual letter-forms

We are occasionally in a position to offer tentative explanations of errors or unexpected spellings in a text on the assumption of scribal ignorance of unusual letter-forms in an exemplar. Such explanations must be tentative because we are almost never able to identify one extant text of a poem as the actual exemplar of another. One possible example of a mistake provoked by an unusual letter-form is Brb C 53 *negledcnearrum* (A *nęgledcnearrū*, B *nægledcnearrum*): C s *e* in the first element instead of the W-S *æ* we find in A and B is open to interpretation as a dialectal form (Merc. or Kt.; see *OEG* §§164, 288); but it may also represent a scribe s misinterpretation of the unusual form of *æ* — a hooked *e* — which occurs in A s version of this word. The C text of Brb certainly does not derive, even indirectly, from the A text, because A has several corruptions not repeated in C, for example A 13 *secgas hwate* for B, C, D

secga swate, and A 56 & *eft hira land* for B *eft ira* (C, D *yra*) *land*. A s
scribe does not employ this unusual letter-form anywhere else in his work
on the A manuscript and it may therefore be a chance survival from the
archetype from which C derives independently. In Cæd L 5 *aeldu* for
aelda (gen. pl.), -*u* may be the product of a confusion between *u* and the
'open *a* that the scribe sometimes employs in the text of the Latin Bede.[1]
Cæd Di 3 -*fudur* for -*fadur* may well result from the same conflation of
'open *a* with *u*.

§2.1.1.2 Confusion of minims

The letters *m* and *n* are sometimes confused, especially when other
minims are adjacent. SB1 48 *meda* for *nieda* (cf. SB2 45 *neoda*) is a clear
instance. The scribe of Brb in the C manuscript originally wrote *namū* for
nanu (dat. pl.), 'none , in 25 (A, B, D *nanum*), but corrected the error.
The three North. texts of Cæd which were copied on the continent (Di, P,
Br) all have 7 *middum-* in *middumgeard* (Br -*gaerd*), 'earth , presumably
an error for the form *middungeard* (as in M). The corruption evidently
derives from the archetype of the North. *eordu* group which these three
texts represent. The same error in reverse is exemplified by CFB C 4
hunbran for B *humbran*, 'of the Humber (A has *humbra*; on D s *himbran*
see below), and Gll J 43 *héah r nnesse* for the correct reading
heah rymnesse, 'great glory , in C. Confusion of the vowels *i* and *u* is
often to be explained in the same way, again, especially when other
letters using minims, such as *n* or *m*, are adjacent. Thus CFB D 4 has
himbran for *humbran*, and Cæd L 7 *middingard* for *middungard* may be a
second example, though the form has been defended as authentic.[2]

---

[1]   Anderson 1941: 78–80, considers analogy with *yldo*, 'age , possible here, comparing
Bwf 70 *yldo* (gen. pl.), 'of men , though the fact that the scribe of L confuses *a* and *u*
elsewhere in the manuscript makes the former explanation more credible.

[2]   Ross 1950: 93–4, explains *middingard* as an analogical formation in West Gmc.
involving such forms as Gothic *midjungards* and OHG *mittigart*. The late Br text of Cæd
(one of the three texts of the North. *eordu* group) exemplifies multiple confusions of this
kind, showing *n* for *u* in 1 *scinlun* for *sciulun*, *ui* for *in* in 1 -*ruicaes* for -*rincaes* (itself a
corruption; cf. Cæd P 1 -*rincaes*; of this group, only Di has the correct form -*ricaes*), and
un for *uu* in 2 *metundaes* for *metuudaes*; but the scribe of Br, like the scribes of the other
texts of the same group, was evidently unfamiliar with written English and it seems
inappropriate to classify his errors with those made by English scribes.

§2.1.1.3 Confusion of other letters

In SnS A 41 *gesylleð* (B *gefilleð*), the graph *f* has been misread as the tall *s* that it often somewhat resembles in Anglo-Saxon script. The same mistake is evident in Cæd Lo 9 *sysū* for *fyrum*, which also exemplifies the confusion of *r* and *s* that we find in Brb D 63 *æres* (before correction) for *æses*, 'carrion'.[3] In the two closely-related Ld₁ and Hr texts of Cæd (Ld₁, Hr and Lo make up the W-S *eorðe* group), we find the distinctive error *o* for *n* in 10 *scyppeod*. Lo has the correct reading *scyppend*.[4] The letter *h* seems to have been mistaken for *b* in Brb 47 D *hlybban* where A, B and C have *hlehhan* or *hlihhan*, 'to laugh'. In EgD 18 B *weard* for A, C *wearð*, the sense requires the verb *wearð* and we seem to be faced with a simple confusion of *ð* in an exemplar with *d*. Cæd Lo 3 *seorc* for *weorc* confuses *wynn* with *s*; Cæd Bu 1 *Hu* for *Nu* confuses *N* with *H*; and finally, DEw 30 D *heahðungena* (originally written *heahðungna*) in place of C's grammatically correct *heahþungenū* (dat. sg. masc.) is probably grounded in a misreading of an abbreviated form of final *-um* in an exemplar.

Mistakes involving the confusion of a letter in an exemplar with another of similar shape are simple errors of the eye; but their presence, if left uncorrected, indicate a copyist who is either taking no notice of the meaning of the text that is being reproduced, or does not understand it. SB1 48 *meda* for *nieda* is particularly revealing, for alliteration depends on the *n* of *nieda*:

SB1 48

ne generedest þurh þinra nieda (*MS* meda) lust

' [...] (you) did not defend (me), because of the pleasure of your desires'

The scribe responsible for such a mistake was probably working silently, with no sense of the text as a communicative utterance. Copyists working late in the OE period, or after the Norman Conquest, probably had very little idea of the meaning of the poetic texts they reproduced, and an error such as *sysū* for *fyrum*, as in Cæd Lo 9, may indicate, in a late (12th c.) text such as this, not simply ignorance of alliterative style and diction (*fir*,

---

[3] A third instance of *s* for *f* is Cæd Br 1 *hesun-* for *hefun-*, 'heavenly', though as we have already noted, the scribe of this text was evidently unfamiliar with written English. Br also has 8 *ciade* instead of *tiade*.

[4] In Ld₁, the *o* is partially erased or smudged near the writing line and perhaps this represents an attempt to correct it to *n*. Judge (1934: 91) regards this error as grounds for 'virtual certainty' that Hr is a copy of Ld₁; see further below, §3.3.

'man', is a poetic word, not found in prose), but a basic unfamiliarity with the normal shape of Anglo-Saxon letters. This is not to say, however, that all copyists throughout the Anglo-Saxon period were mechanical workers; later we shall find evidence of alertness, comprehension and considerable resourcefulness.

§2.1.1.4 The factor of poetic vocabulary

The mechanical replacement of a letter in an exemplar form with a different one was perhaps more likely to occur in unfamiliar words than in familiar ones. Exclusively poetic words, in particular, may have offered difficulties to scribes unused to the special vocabulary of verse. This section deals with cases of the simple substitution of letters in exclusively poetic words. We have just seen one example of this in Cæd Lo 8 *sysū* for *fyrum*. A second is DEw D 11 *orecmægcum* for *oretmægcum* (C *oretmægcū*), 'warriors', with *c* for *t*: the element *oret-* is chiefly poetic in OE; but *c* and *t* can resemble each other closely in Anglo-Saxon script, so this could be a case of simple misreading. A more clearcut example is Brb A 59 *hremige*, 'exultant' (B, C, D *hremige*), originally written *hramige* with *a* instead of *e* (on the phonology of this adjective, see Campbell 1938: 110, note to 39). Here too belongs SnS 60 A *dreoseð*, B *dreogeð* in the following context:

SnS B 59b–61	SnS A 59b–61
nænig monna wat	nænig manna wat
hæleða under heofnum hu min hige dreogeð	hæleða under hefenum hu min hige dreoseð
bisi æfter bocum	bysig æfter bocū

'No man, no warrior beneath the heavens, knows how my mind labours (*or* A fails), engrossed in books.'

The usual meanings of A's verb *dreosan* are 'to fall', 'to perish'; but Bosworth & Toller 1898: s.v. *dreosan*, III, cites SnS 60 as the sole example of the meaning: 'to fall, not remain alert, droop, fail, sink'. Intransitive *dreogan*, 'to be employed', 'to labour', is found only in verse (see Bosworth & Toller 1898: s.v. *dreogan*, IV; Toller 1921: s.v. *dreogan*, II(2)). In view of the fact that the mind is described in 61 as *bisi*, and then in 62 as surging near the heart (*hige heortan neah hædre wealleð*), there can be little doubt that B's *dreogeð* suits the context better than *dreoseð*. Copying error (*s* for *g*) may have been involved here.

A fifth example involving a poetic word is Dan 323 *me* for *in e-* of *in eare*, 'in the sea'. This reading is not confirmed by Aza, which has a different construction, albeit one involving the element *ear*, 'sea' (Aza 40 *yþe geond eargrund*, 'the waves throughout the ocean floor'); but *ear* in this sense is poetic and (in simplex form) rare, occuring elsewhere only in R3.22 *eare geblonden*, 'mingled by the sea'. In Dan 321 *brimfaro.þæs* we see a fairly clear case of the mangling of the gen. sg. poetic compound *brimfaroþes*, 'of the sea-shore', though the corresponding line in Aza (38) has *brimflodas*, and the presence in the next line in Dan (322) of *sæfaroða*, a compound with the same second element as *brimfaroþes*, makes one suspect some conscious modification of Dan 321 (see further below, §2.1.1.5.2); but in all these cases, it may well be that the scribe responsible for initiating these corruptions was affected by the unfamiliar character of the poetic words he misrepresented.

§2.1.1.5 Dittography.

§2.1.1.5.1 Retrospective

Dittography, writing twice what should be written once, is a common cause of false substitutions in OE poetic texts. Dittography may be retrospective, as when something (a letter, a sequence of letters, a word, etc.) which has already been written is repeated in place of something else, or prospective, as when something in the exemplar is anticipated and written 'early' as well as in the right place. Retrospective dittography is the commoner form in the OE texts examined here. An instance involving individual letters is CFB D 5 *burga gife* for A, B, C *burga fife*, 'five boroughs', in which the *g* of *burga* is repeated. Similar examples are SnS 43 B *ðu miht mih* (possibly *mib*), before correction, instead of *ðu miht mid* ('you might [...] with') as in A; SnS 84 B *þono* for *þone* (A *ðone*); and DEw 31 D *in ealne tid* instead of C's *in ealle tíd* ('at all times'). This last is a poetic formula (Cf. Pnt 17, Phx 77, Sfr 124), and the noun *tid*, 'time', is regularly fem. in gender in OE, not masc., as the form *ealne*, with adjectival acc. sg. masc. inflexion *-ne*, might seem to imply; so simple dittography of the sequence: *ne* seems the best explanation for the mistake. In Gl1 J 55, the grammar requires the acc. sg. *sawle*, as in C, not the nom. sg. *sawul*, as in J:

Gl1 C 55	Gl1 J 55
& him on dydest orð & sawle.	& him on dydest. oruð. & sawul.

'[...] and put breath and soul in him, [...]'

In this case, the faulty J version may owe as much to unconscious assonating as to dittographic repetition. The unusual punctuation in J's version of the line, with a point after *oruð*, 'breath', may reflect confusion about the sense on the part of the scribe responsible for the change. Another example of retrospective dittography is Pra 10 J *þyne* instead of the dat. sg. masc. *þinum*, as in the L text:

Pra 10 L   Pra 10 J

Syle ðine are þinum earminge   sile þyne are þyne earminge.

   'Grant your compassion to your wretched one.'

J has repeated the acc. sg. fem. *þyne* in the a-verse in a context where the dat. sg. masc. is required (the noun *earming* is masc.).

A dittography involving a poetic word probably unfamiliar to the scribe responsible for it is EgC A 2 *corðre micelre* instead of B, C *corðre mycclum*, 'with a mighty troop', where unfamiliarity with the poetic neut. noun *corðor*, 'troop', probably had something to do with the substitution of a false dat. sg. fem. adjectival inflexion *-re* in A.

§2.1.1.5.2 Prospective

Prospective dittography would account for EgD B 17 *welhrær* (not a word) instead of A, C *welhwær*, 'almost everywhere', though confusion of the runic letter *wynn* with *r*, which it often resembles in Anglo-Saxon script, might equally well explain the corruption. Another probable instance is P87.13.1 *þo ðe* instead of *to ðe*, 'to thee', as in F.

Aza 39 *swa waroþa*, which is probably an example of prospective dittography, and Dan 321 *brimfaro.þæs*, which may be another, must be discussed together, for they probably connected:

Aza 37b–39   Dan 320b–322

[...] swa heofonsteorran   [...] swa heofonsteorran.
bugað bradne hwearft oð   bebugað bradne hwyrft. oðþæt
  brimflodas.   brimfaro.þæs
swa waroþa sond ymb sealt wæter   sæfaroða sand. geond sealtne wæg

  Aza: '[...] as the stars of heaven inhabit the broad expanse up to (*or* as far
    as) the sea-floods, as the sand of the beaches around the salt water, [...]'
  Dan: ' [...] as the stars of heaven encompass the broad expanse, up to the
    sand of the seashore, of the sea-coast, throughout the salt water [...]'

Alliteration in Aza 39/Dan 322 must be on *s*, so Aza 39a, with alliteration only on the second of the two nouns in the a-verse (*sond*) is unorthodox and, I assume, corrupt. Dan is regular in this regard, with the double alliteration one would expect in this metrical type if the verse occurred in *Beowulf* (Bliss's type 3E2; see Bliss 1967: 127). However, from another point of view Dan is suspect. If we can accept that a gen. sg. compound *brimfaroþes* underlies Dan 321 *brimfaro.þæs*, it seems probable that a text antecedent to Aza (its exemplar, or an antecedent of its exemplar) contained two compounds in adjacent lines with -*faroð*- as the second element (*brimfaroþes*, *sæfaroða*) — the kind of close repetition that OE poets tended to avoid. Prospective dittography might account for this repetition, with *brimfaroþes* written in anticipation of *sæfaroða* in the following line, perhaps replacing the *brimflodas* that Aza has in the corresponding verse. As for Aza, the simplest explanation of the alliterative anomaly in Aza 39a is perhaps that Aza gets the passage basically right in both *brimflodas* and the element -*waroþa*, but bungles the compound *sæwaroþa*, again, by prospective dittography, in this case of the letter-sequence -*wa*- (*swa wa*- for *sæwa*-). Such an explanation of the alliterative irregularity in Aza 39a, if accepted, would take us back to a somewhat earlier stage in the transmission of the Aza text; but it does not take us as far back as the archetype text that gave rise to both Aza and Dan, because the variation between Aza's use of the element -*waroþa* in 39b and Dan's -*faroða* in the corresponding place remains unexplained.

Other forms which may have arisen by prospective dittography are Gl1 J 45 *þangung* for *þancung*, and three errors in Cæd M, all of which were subsequently corrected: 4 *drintin* for *dryctin*, 7 *mindungeard* for *middungeard*, and 8 *dadæ* for *tiadæ*.[5]

§2.1.2 Substitution of words arising from unfamiliarity with dialectal forms

Sometimes a dialectal (and so perhaps unfamiliar) form seems to lie behind the substitution of one word for another. We have already noticed the Anglian smoothed form *werc*, 'works', which probably underlies the error *wero* in Cæd O 2 (before its alteration to *wera*). Similarly, DEw D 7 *weolan*, 'wealth', with non-W-S *a*-umlaut of *e* to *eo* (*OEG* §210), must surely have something to do with the corruption *weolm* in the corresponding line of this poem in the C manuscript. A reading *weolm*, though formally explicable as a variant of *wielm*, 'boiling', 'stream', 'surge',

---

[5] For the full text of Cæd M, see §1.1 above.

makes no sense in the context in any of its possible senses. A third example is SnS 86, where A's reading *gæst*, 'spirit', suits the context better than B's *gesið*, 'companion':

SnS A 86b–87	SnS B 86b–87
he mæg ðone laðan gæst	he mæg þone laþan gesið
feohtende feond fleonde gebrengan	feohterne feond fleonde gebringan

'[...] he may put the hated spirit (*or* B companion), the fighting fiend, to flight'

Although B's reading does not reduce the passage to nonsense, and might even be defended as ironical, it seems likely on the whole that A has the original reading here and that B's *gesið* owes its origin partly, at least, to a form such as *gæsð* in the text's history, comparable with forms with *sð* for *st* that occur elsewhere in the B text, such as 18 *gesemesð* (for *gesemest*, 'satisfy'; the A text lacks an equivalent form here), 22 *wesðe* (A *weste*), 'barren', and B 36 *eaðusð* (A *eaðost*), 'most easily'. These *sð* spellings, characteristic of the Hatton manuscript of the *Cura Pastoralis* translation, are early W-S (see *OEG* §481.1 and p. 193, note 5).

The corruptions in this category differ somewhat from the varieties of mindless error that we have dealt with so far in this section, for they may be the product of some deliberation on the part of the scribes responsible for them, though it is difficult to judge how much. Most are satisfactorily explained on the assumption that a scribe has mistaken a legitimate but unfamiliar form in his exemplar for an error and has changed it into a word he knows. On the other hand, against the idea that these represent informed editorial decisions on the part of transcribers is the fact that the new readings do not, generally speaking, suit the general context at all well; there seems to have been a concern to produce a recognizable word, but the substitutions show only a very local (i.e. word-bounded) awareness of the sense.

§2.1.3 Problem cases

There are several variants involving the substitution of letters which, though plainly corrupt, do not resemble the form they have supposedly replaced closely enough to suggest merely mechanical copying error. I am unable to offer plausible explanations for any of them, though I add comments to my account of each of them below.

Brb 39 D *hal*, A, B, C *har*: har, 'grey', 'hoary', is clearly the archetypal reading here, but D's *hal* (perhaps 'uninjured') is not palaeographically credible as a simple copying mistake. The adjective applies to Constantine and it is conceivable that the D scribe's form is intended as an oblique comment on his ignominious flight from the battlefield at Brunanburh.

Brb 49 A *culbodgehnades*, B, C, D *cumbolgehnastes*: *l* for *m*, *d* for *l* and *d* for *st* are all palaeographically unlikely. The word itself, the meaning of which is 'clash of banners' (= 'battle'), is unique, but *gehnast*, 'clash', occurs elsewhere as a simplex and as the second element of compound words (e.g. R3.60 *wolcengehnaste*, 'meeting of clouds'; see Campbell 1938: 113).

Brb 55 D *dyflig* (A *difelin*, B *dyflen*, C *dyflin*, 'Dublin'): unfamiliarity with the name might well have contributed to D's corruption here, but it seems unlikely as a simple copying error.

Brb 57 D *ætrunne*, A *ætsamne*, B, C *ætsomne*: it is suggested (Classen & Harmer 1926: 99) that D's form represents ME *ætrinnen*, 'to run away'; but as the subject would have to be the West Saxon royal brothers Æþelstan and Eadward, this seems rather unlikely. D's form is perhaps just credible palaeographically as a simple error.

Cæd 2 Lo *modreþanc*, Ld₁, Hr *modgeþanc*: again, *r* for *g* seems an unlikely mistake.

EgD 8 A *þæt* (abbreviated, B *þær*, C *ðær*): the reading in B and C ('in which', 'when'; the antecedent is *monoð*, 'month') is to be preferred here; but *t* for *r* seems unlikely as a simple copying mistake.

DEw 8 D *he hælo tíd* (with *lo* of *hælo* inserted superscript), C *healfe tíd*: see Plummer 1899: 253.

SB2 65 *ær*, SB1 70 *her* in the line: *secan þa hamas þe ðu me her* (SB2 *ær*) *scrife*, 'to seek the abodes that you ordained for me here (*or* SB2 previously)': SB2's meaning is unexceptionable, but alliteration (on *hamas* in the a-verse) is spoilt by the substitution. Cf. SB2 96 *swylcra yrmþa swa þu unc ær scrife*, where *ær* supplies the alliteration in the b-verse, and the corresponding SB1 102b *swa ðu unc her ær scrife*, in which both adverbs appear but only *ær* alliterates.
SB2 116 *eaxan*, SB1 120 *eagan*, 'eyes'.

SnS 87 B *feohterne*, A *feohtende*; no sense can be made of B's form as it stands; Menner emends it to *feohtenne*, with poetic -*nn*- for -*nd*- by assimilation (Menner 1941: 86; see also *OEG* §484).

§2.2 TRANSPOSITIONS

The unthinking transposition of letters within words is not well exemplified in the poetic texts covered by this study, and most possible instances may be explained in other ways. SnS B 19 *hrigc* ('ridge', 'crest'), with *gc* for *cg*, is explicable as an unusual but attested variant spelling of geminated *g* (an example cited in *OEG* §64 is *garsegc*, 'ocean', in the *OE Orosius*). Brb A 66 *æfer* (for B, C, D *æfre*, 'ever') is called a 'slip' by Campbell in his edition of the poem (Campbell 1938: 120). DEw 25 *lunger* (both texts) for the poetic adverb *lungre* is unlikely to represent genuine phonological metathesis (see *OEG* §459) and is more probably a simple miscopying, perhaps encouraged by unfamiliarity with the poetic word *lungre*, deriving from the archetype of both the surviving texts.[6]

§2.3 OMISSIONS

A much commoner type of mechanical error than either substitution or transposition is simple omission of letters of words or, in a few cases, of whole words. Many of the instances I have noted are classifiable according to the standard types of scribal error recognized by textual criticism (§§2.3.1–2.3.5), but others (§2.3.6) have no obvious cause.

§2.3.1 Haplography

Often haplography (writing once what should be written twice) accounts for omissions. An uncertain example is Brb A 12 *dænede*, a form to which the scribe subsequently added a second *n* superscript to produce *dænnede* (the meaning of the verb is unclear; the readings in the other texts are B, C *dennade*, D *dennode*). Brb contains another somewhat doubtful instance in Brb A 5 *brunanburh*, before correction to *brunnanburh* as in C: but D has *brunanburh*, and Campbell thinks that this was the earlier form of the place-name (Campbell 1938: 60–64). It is therefore possible that the A scribe's original version of the name with single medial *n* repeats the form in his exemplar; but if so, why did he add another *n*?

Relatively clear cases of haplography are EgC C 5 *baþa nemneð* (A

---

[6]   Manuscripts of the North. *eordu* group of Cæd, copied by foreign scribes, show a few clear examples of scribal transposition of letters, notably Cæd Br 7 *middumgaerd* instead of the *middumgeard* of Di and P, and Cæd P 5 *raeirst* for *aerist* (as in Br; Di had *uerst* originally, before an *a* was added above the *u*, no doubt as its replacement), the latter with two transpositions within a single word.

baðan nemnaþ, with *baðan* corrected, perhaps by a later hand, to *baðon*, B *baðan nemnað*), before correction to *baþán nemneð*, '(they) call (it) Bath'; DEw 12 D *ymbclypað*, before correction to *ymbclyppað* (C *ymbclyppað*), '(they) embrace'; and perhaps Cæd M 6 *scepen* (L *sceppend*; see Smith 1968: 39; Anderson 1941: 79; and above, §1.1). A likely fourth example is SB2 109 *hungrum* (which can only be translated as the nonsensical 'for the hungers') in place of SB1 114 *hungregum*, 'for the hungry ones': *hungrum* makes no sense in the context, but *hungregum* is perfectly apt. It would appear that the eye of the scribe responsible for this error jumped from the first *g* to the second in his exemplar form.

Haplography of whole words occurs only rarely. An example is SnS B 11. Although the text of A is badly damaged in this part of the poem, comparison with what is legible in A reveals B's error:

SnS A 11	SnS B 11
[...] oððe æh[.]a oððe eor[...]	elnes oððe æhte eorlscipes

(A) '[...] or of possessions or nobility', (B) '[...] in respect of power or the possession of nobility')

B's omission of the second instance of *oððe* is confirmed by the metrical insufficiency of *eorlscipes* (it has three syllables instead of the minimum four for a verse, as noted by Holthausen 1901: 123–25; Menner 1941: 106).

Other examples of haplography of words may be dealt with briefly. CFB B 6b–7a has *& lindkylne snotingahám* (C has basically the same reading as B) for *& lincylene & snotingahā* ('and Lincoln and Nottingham'), as in A (D has substantially the same reading as A). The metre requires the inclusion of the conjunction here. In Gl1 C 31 *And nu symle* (J *& nu & symble*, 'and now and forever'), the Latin version of the relevant part of the *Gloria Patri, Et nunc & semper*, is included with the OE text and shows reasonably clearly that C has omitted an 'and'.

§2.3.2 Triple consonant groups

In Brb C 3 *ealdorlagne* (A, B, D *ealdorlangne*, 'eternal'), the first of two like consonants in a triple group (*n*) is omitted. DEw D 14, 32 *hodelice*, before correction to *holdelice* ('loyally'), would be closely analogous to Brb C 3 if *holdlice*, the form preserved in DEw C 14, 32, lay behind D's error. In SnS B 81 *earma* for *earmra* (gen. pl., 'wretched'), it is the second of the two like consonants in the triple group which has been omitted. In SnS B 70 *gefæsnað* (before correction) instead of A's correct *gefæstnað*, '(they) fasten', the medial consonant of the three was missed in the original copying. In P 89.15.1 *hwæwiga* instead of F's correct form *hwæthwygu*, 'something', the first two consonants of the group have both been missed out. Finally, in the case of F 58.1.3 *luge* (P *lungre*, 'quickly'), in which the first and third consonants of the group are lost, unfamiliarity with the poetic word *lungre* may have contributed to the mistake.

§2.3.3 Vowels in sequence

When the same vowel occurs at the end of one word and at the beginning of the next, one of them could be omitted by mistake, though this does not seem to have happened very often. Cæd Br 9 *frea llmechtig* for *frea allmechtig*, 'almighty Lord' (as in Di and P) is paralleled, remarkably enough, in a text of Cæd belonging to an entirely different text-family: the Lo text of the W-S *eorðe* group has *frea lmihtyg*. Unfamiliarity with the poetic word *frea*, 'lord', may well have created conditions for error in these two late texts of the poem.

§2.3.4 Dittography

Paradoxically, omissions sometimes occur as a result of dittography, examples being EgC B 20 *On þa on ðam* for *Ond* (MSS &) *þa on ðam*, 'and then on the [...]', as in A and C, with prospective dittography of *on þa-*, and SnS B 77 *wincindra*, before correction to *winciendra* ('blinking'; A's damaged reading *wince[...]a* is presumably *wincendra*) with retrospective dittography of *-in-*.

§2.3.5 Homoeoteleuton

As a term of textual criticism, homoeoteleuton refers to omission provoked by a certain kind of slip of the eye. It assumes that the copyist's normal habit is to look at his exemplar, memorize a certain linguistic sequence (a single word, a phrase, a clause, a sentence) and then write it into his copy. Next his eye returns to his exemplar to find the next sequence which he duly memorizes, writes, and so on. But if his eye returns to the exemplar and catches a form or ending which, though it resembles the ending of the sequence he has just written, is actually lower down on the page of the exemplar, the result is an omission of text from the new copy. The nature of the error would lead us to expect that parts of the text omitted in this way would generally be quite short; but SB2 omits six verses at one point. It is easy to see what provoked the error when we place the text against the corresponding part of SB1:

SB1 19b–26	SB2 19b–23
lyt ðu gemundest	lyt þu geþohtes
to hwan þinre sawle þing siðþan wurde	to won þinre sawle sið siþþan wurde
syððan of lichoman læded wære:	siþþan heo of lichoman læded wære.
Hwæt wite ðu ðu me weriga hwæt ðu	hwæt wite þu me werga hwæt þu
huru wyrma gyfl	huru wyrma gifl.
lyt geþohtest þa ðu lustgryrum	lyt geþohtes
eallū fulgeodest hu ðu on eorðan scealt	
wyrmum to wiste. hwæt ðu on worulde	
ær	
lyt geþohtest hu þis is þus lang hider	hu þis is long hider

Notes on the text: SB2 19b, 23 *geþohtes* shows Anglian *-es* instead of the *-est* inflexion (pres. indic. 2 sg.) which is normal in W-S (*OEG* §752).

'You had little thought for your soul's future circumstances when it would be taken from the body. What do you have to reproach me for, wretch? Lo, food for worms, indeed, (SB1 little did you think, when you fully indulged yourself in all your horrible desires, how you must become the food of worms in the earth. Lo, in the world previously) you little thought how long this lasts [...]'

Although SB2 gives good sense here, it is clear that SB1 23–25 is not an expansion of it but part of the text that SB2 has omitted. If SB1 may be regarded as representative of the original text, the nature of the mistake is clear enough: the scribe who was responsible for the omission in SB2 memorized a piece of the text ending with *lyt geþohtest* (as in SB1 23a) and wrote it down; but when he returned to his exemplar to find where he had left off, his eye found the second instance of *lyt geþohtest* represented by SB1 25a, and continued from there, missing out the intervening passage. The repetitive rhetorical structure of the poem was thus a contributory factor in the faulty transmission, and it is not surprising to find that SB1 has also suffered loss of text through a homoeoteleuton error:

SB2 99b–102	SB1 105b–107
ligeð dust þær hit wæs.	liget dust þær hit wæs.
ne mæg him &sware ænige secgan	ne mæg him &sware ænige gehatan
ne þær edringe ænge gehatan	
gæste geomrum geoce oþþe frofre	geomrum gaste geoce oððe frofre.

'The dust lies where it was; it may not speak (*or* SB1 promise) any answer to it (SB2 nor offer any refuge there), help or consolation, to the sorrowful spirit.'

Here the relative difficulty of the SB1 text's meaning is obvious: the promise (*gehatan*) of an answer (*ondsware*) is puzzling compared with the giving (*secgan*) of one, as in SB2. Again, it is easy to see what must have happened: the eye-slip was from the first *ænige* (represented by SB2 100b) to the second (101b), so that SB1 omits parts of two b-verses and an entire a-verse. In this case, one might have expected the copyist to notice the poor sense that results from his omission; but there is nothing to indicate that he was aware of omitting anything, or that he checked his copy at any stage, though even if he had, an insertion of the missing text might have been found impracticable or unaesthetic.

A third clear instance of homoeoteleuton involving a substantial loss of text occurs in Aza:

Dan 351b–57	Aza 66b–68
wearð se háta líg.	wearð se hata lig
todrifen & todwæsced. þær þa	todrifen & todwæsced þær þa
dædhwatan.	dædhwatan
geond þone ofen eodon. & se engel míd.	
feorh nerigende. se ðær feorða wæs.	
annanias. & azarías.	
& misael. þær þa módhwatan.	
þry on geðancum. ðeoden heredon.	þry mid geþoncum þeoden heredon

'The hot fire was driven away and extinguished where those (Aza three) bold in deeds (Dan walked around the furnace, and with them the angel protecting life who made a fourth there to Hananiah and Azariah and Mishael, where the bold three) praised the Lord with thanksgivings [...]'

Here it is the repetition of the element *-hwatan* (*dædhwatan*, *módhwatan*) that caused the omission.[7]

In all three of the examples of homoeoteleuton we have looked at so far, the omission has resulted from an eye-slip from one instance of a phrase or word to another. An omission clearly caused by the same kind of mistake, but involving a likeness between two words rather than two

---

[7]   Cf. Jones 1966: 101, who prefers the view that Aza's omission resulted from a failure of memory during oral transmission. She thinks that it would have been unlikely that the two compounds in *-hwatan* would have been vertically aligned in the exemplar; but they could easily have been more or less aligned, and in any case vertical alignment is not a *sine qua non* of homoeoteleuton.

instances of the same word, is Brb 35–36, part of which D omits. Here is the context, with text C (which the A and B texts resemble in all essentials here) used for comparison:

Brb C 35–36	Brb D 35–36
cread cnear ón flót cining út géwat.	creat cneár on
on fealone flod feorh génerode.	flod feorh generode

'The ship pressed on to the (C water, the king went forth on to the fallow) sea, saved (his) life.'

Here one assumes that the scribe wrote up to *on* in 35 and then turned back to the exemplar, perhaps already aware that a word such as *flot* was the next word; but he saw *flod* instead (perhaps a more familiar word to him, for simplex *flot* is rare, occurring only here and in Mld; see Campbell 1938: 109), wrote that instead, and carried on, omitting the intervening words. The resulting sense in D is very awkward, giving the impression that it was the ship's life rather than the king's that was saved.

There is one passage in SB1 which appears to show a sequence of error probably caused by a slip of the eye down the exemplar page, followed by a reorganization of the text suggesting a desire to retrieve matters without resorting to anything as drastic as erasure. This is SB1 82–86, with which the corresponding passage SB2 77–80 should be compared:

SB2 77–80	SB1 82–86
ge on westenne wildra deora	oððe on westenne wilddeora
þæt grimmeste þær swa god wolde	*þæt* wyrreste þær swa god wolde.
ge þeah þu wære wyrmcynna þæt wyrreste	Ge þeah ðu wære wyrmcynna
	þæt grimmeste þær swa god wolde.
þōn þu æfre on moldan mon gewurde	Þonne ðu æfre on moldan man gewurde

'[...] or (if you had been) the fiercest (*or* SB1 the worst) of wild beasts, if God has so wished, or even if you were the worst (*or* SB1 the fiercest) of the serpent-kind (SB1 if God has so wished), than you ever had become a man on earth [...]'

SB1 has technical faults: 82b is metrically short (see below, §5.3); 83b has delayed alliteration (the stressed word *god* would normally carry the alliteration in a verse with this form, whereas the a-verse establishes *w* as the alliterating sound; see further, §6.2.1 below); 84 has no b-verse; and 85b repeats 83b (though this time the normal alliterative priorities are observed). SB2 is entirely satisfactory metrically and in all other respects. SB1's irregularities are consistent with the following sequence of events (taking SB2 as representative of the exemplar text):

1. A scribe, intending to copy *þæt grimmeste* as the a-verse of the second line of the passage, instead wrote the similarly-shaped phrase *þæt wyrreste* (nearby on his exemplar page) as 83a.
2. At this point he probably realized his error. He added the b-verse linked to *þæt grimmeste* in his exemplar (against the rules of alliteration), no doubt hoping to find somewhere to include the omitted *þæt grimmeste* later.
3. In 84, the consequences of his original omission become serious: having used *þæt wyrreste* already, he cannot repeat it as the b-verse corresponding to 84a (copied faithfully from his exemplar), so he leaves the a-verse unattached and next brings in the omitted *þæt grimmeste* as the next a-verse. As nothing is available in his exemplar to supply a b-verse, he is forced to repeat the whole line in its exemplar form, even though this involves repeating *þær swa god wolde*.

If this reconstruction is correct, it shows that accidental omissions were occasionally picked up by the scribe responsible for them in the first place, and that attempts to repair the damage were not unheard of. What is most noticeable about SB1, however, is that despite several technical faults, the sense of the original is preserved, albeit in a somewhat repetitive style.

§2.3.6 Difficult cases

There remains a large group of omissions, mostly of individual letters but sometimes of whole words, which are unthinking errors as far as I can see; but I list them below, mostly without any discussion, in the hope that others may notice factors I have missed which might suggest more specific explanations for at least some of them. Omissions of letters are divided up according to whether the omission effects the beginning, the middle or the end of a word, while omissions of words are treated as a single category. Of course, when we are comparing two or more texts, it is sometimes possible that what appears to be an omission in one text is really an addition to another, so I have tried to indicate, in cases where it seems necessary to do so, the kind of evidence which suggests that we are indeed dealing in all these cases with omissions, not additions.

§2.3.6.1 Initial letters

Cæd Ca 5 *orðan* (before correction), beside *eorðan*, 'earth', in all the other W-S *eorðan* texts.

§2.3.6.2 Medial letters

Brb 6 B *heaðolina*, C, D *-linda* (A *-linde*), 'shields' (acc. pl.), in a poetic word.

Brb 10 D *heted*, A, B, C *hettend*, 'enemies' (nom. pl.), in a poetic word.

Cæd 1 Di *hefuricaes* (before correction), P *hefun-*, 'of the heavenly kingdom'.

Cæd 7 L *middingard*, M *-geard*, 'earth' (acc. sg.).

DEw 21 C *brynodan*, D *brytnodon*, 'distributed'.

SB2 48 *acenda* (before correction to *ancenda*, 'only-begotten'), SB1 51 *acenneda*, 'born'.

SnS 73 B *hugor* (before correction), A *hungor*, 'hunger' (acc. sg.).

SnS 86 B *luian*, A *lufian*, 'love' (inf.).

SB2 48 *a^{n}cenda* requires discussion. Here are the two texts' versions of the line in its context:

SB2 47b–48	SB1 50b–51
þōn monna cynn	þonne eall manna cynn
se a^{n}cenda ealle gegædrað.	se acenneda ealle gesamnað

SB2: '[...] when the only-begotten (son) fully assembles the whole of mankind.'

SB1: '[...] when the born one assembles the whole of mankind.'

In an earlier article (Orton 1979b) I suggested that SB1's substitution of *acenneda*, 'born', for SB2's *ancenda*, 'only-begotten (son)', was the result of 'a simple scribal error' (Orton 1979b: 188), by which I meant the omission of the first *n* of *ancenda* (or, perhaps, of the uncontracted form *ancenneda*). My explanation has been justly criticized by Moffat for failing to place sufficient emphasis on the fact that the SB2 scribe's first attempt at the word was *acenda*, a form which might be construed as a (contracted) spelling variant of SB1's corruption *acenneda* (Moffat 1983: 300). We should note first of all that SB2 (after correction) undoubtedly has the better reading here: alliteration in the line is on vowels (*ealle* in the b-verse is the head-stave in both versions); and whereas the prefix *ān-*, as in *ancenda*, regularly bears a metrical stress in OE verse and can carry functional alliteration, the prefix *a-*, as in *acenneda*, is metrically unstressed and never alliterates. On this point, Moffat and I agree.

Moffat, basing his argument on the idea that *acenda* and SB1's *acenneda* are the same word (or the same corruption), concludes that the two texts show 'a coincident error in the initial writing of the same word' (Moffat 1983: 301). Moffat states that the error made initially by the SB2 scribe is 'tachygraphic in nature' (Moffat 1983: 300): a macron indicating a following nasal was, he believes, omitted from the initial *a* of the word in some text antecedent to both SB1 and SB2. This is debatable. First, it seems to me doubtful if it was the omission of a macron that produced the corruption. Both texts use the macron to indicate omitted letters, but in no case in either text is it used to indicate a single *n*. When used on final vowels it indicates *-m* (e.g. SB1 89 *mannū*, SB2 84 *monnū*); over medial vowels it may indicate medial *m*, as in SB1 79 *frȳðe for frymðe*, SB2 10 *sȳle* for *symle*) or, when used over the medial vowel in the form *þōn*, the final *-ne* of *þonne*, 'then' or 'when' (e.g. in SB1, SB2 3; SB2 has *þoññ* in 63). It therefore seems to me unsafe to assume, as Moffat does, that the text of the poem as it stood before the corruption was introduced indicated the *n* of *ancenda* with a macron over the initial *a-* of the word in question. Moffat's interpretation of the corruption is also questionable. His opinion is 'that this coincidence in both versions derives from a common exemplar in which this scribal (or transcriptional) error had already been made.' What this fails to take sufficient account of, it seems to me, is the fact that the SB2 scribe amended the form he originally wrote. If, as Moffat assumes, he was working from an exemplar in which *acenda* (or some similar form) appeared, the SB2 scribe's final version of the word, *ancenda*, must be a conjectural emendation, for SB1 does not confirm it and we have no reason to think that the SB2 scribe had any other authority for it. Moffat believes that *acenneda* (or some similar form) appeared in the archetype, so it is perhaps surprising that he is prepared to trust SB2's *ancenda* as the original reading simply on the evidence of a single text, even though it is, as we have seen, the better of the two readings. The implication of Moffat's argument is thus that the SB2 scribe made a guess at the authorial reading (*ancenda*) and got it right. If, however, SB2's *ancenda* is not a conjectural emendation but simply the exemplar form, originally miswritten but then corrected when the scribe checked his own work, the worries about the authority of *ancenda* raised by Moffat's argument disappear; we may assume that *ancenda* represents the archetype's reading. Moffat does, however, raise one issue which cannot so easily be circumvented: the coincidence that two scribes originally wrote what was essentially the same, wrong form:

acenda or *acenneda* instead of *ancenda*. But perhaps this coincidence is not as remarkable as it might seem. In my article on the relationship between SB1 and SB2 I noted no less than fifty-two lexical variations between the two texts of the poem (Orton 1979b: 179). The two words in question here, *ancenda* and *acenneda*, are quite alike in appearance and it would be easy to confuse them. It seems to me that we cannot be sure that the correspondence between the SB2 scribe's original form (*acenda*) and the SB1 scribe's *acenneda* is significant for the transmission of the poem. Despite Moffat's note, I still prefer my original view that *acenneda* in SB1 represents a copying error, no doubt influenced by the potential for confusion between the two words which is created by the similarity of their appearance, and that SB2's *ancenda* is the archetypal form and appeared in the SB2 scribe's exemplar.

§2.3.6.3 Final letters

Brb 55 D *ofe* (before correction), A, B, C *ofer*, 'over'.

Cæd 4 Bu *astald*, other W-S *ylda* texts *ast(e)alde*, 'established', where the final -*e* is confirmed by the metre.

Cæd 5 Ca *æres* for other texts' *ærest*, 'first'.

Cæd 6 M *scepen*, L *sceppend*, 'creator' (though there is a possibility that *scepen* is a distinct word; see Dobbie 1942: 198).

CFB 4 A *humbra*, B *humbran (C hunbran, D himbran)*: the gen. sg. *humbran* in the phrase *humbran ea*, 'the waters of the Humber', is required here grammatically. The name follows the fem. weak declension (nom. sg. *humbre*; see Bosworth & Toller 1898: s.v. *Humbre*, and Dobbie 1942: 149).

Dan 342 *leoma*, Aza 60 *leoman* (see §6.1.1 below).

DEw 7 C *brytnodo* (before correction to *brytnodon*), D *britnode* (sg.), 'distributed', where the sg. form, as in D, is required grammatically.

DEw 12 C *ceald*, D *cealda*, 'cold' (nom. pl.), where the inflected form is required grammatically and metrically (C 12b *ceald brymmas* has only three syllables, one short of the conventional minimum of four per verse).

DEw 16 C *lang*, D *langa*, where the disyllabic adverb (general OE *lange*) is confirmed by the metre (C *þeah he lang ær*).

DEw 34 C *þearf*, D *ðearfe*: D's -*e* is confirmed by the metre, though the syntax is difficult here and the implications of the difference consequently obscure.

SB2 5 *sawl*, SB1 5 *sawle*, 'soul' (acc. sg.), where the sense requires the inflected acc. sg.

SnS 46 B *egesfullicra*, A *egesfullicran* (nom. pl.), where the nom. pl. is required by the grammar.

§2.3.6.4 Words

Cæd Lo 3 omits the *he* that appears in Ld₁, to the detriment of the sense.

CFB 8 A *deoraby*, B, C, D & *deoraby*, where the & (= *ond* 'and') is necessary for both sense and metre.

Dan 281 *dæda georn*, Aza 3 *dreag dædum georn*, where the verb *dreag* is indispensable metrically (Dan 281 gives a verse of only three syllables).

Dan 292 & *þurh help*, Aza 13 & *þurh hyldo help*, where Dan 292 gives a verse of only three syllables.

Dan 293 *nu þec* (before correction) for Aza 14 *nu we þec*.

EgC 19 A *þis*, B, C *ða þis*, where *ða*, 'when', is necessary for the sense.

Gll 48 J *écan* for C *écan word*, where *word* is necessary for the sense.

SnS 43 B *mid beorhtan*, A *mid ðy be[.]rhtan* (a letter after *e* is detectable but illegible), where the weak form of the adjective suggests that A's *ðy* is original. All other weakly inflected adjectives in both texts of the poem are preceded by a demonstrative or possessive adjective; cf. particularly SnS A 363a *ðone deoran sið* and 444b *wyrd seo swiðe*, both of which would be metrically deficient without the demonstrative.

SnS 62 B *hige heortan*, A *hige heortan neah*, where *neah* is metrically essential (again, as in DEw 12 C, on which see above, the four-syllable rule is violated if *neah* is omitted).

SnS 64 B omits the noun *leaf* which is necessary to the grammar of the sentence (A 64a *hafað sylfren leaf*, 'it has silver leaves').

§2.4 ADDITIONS

Inadvertent additions to the received text are a good deal rarer than omissions. Most involve retrospective dittography, and the instances may be divided according to whether individual letters of words or entire words are added.

§2.4.1 Letters

Simple dittography may explain two forms in the A text of Brb: 25 *heeardes* (B, C, D *heardes*, 'hard'), and 72 *weealles* (B, C, D *wealas*,

'Welshmen'), though of course it does not explain the substitution of *-es* for *-as* in A 72. Campbell, however, suggests that the doubled vowels may originally have been written on purpose to indicate long diphthongs in these words (Campbell 1938: 106). Dittography almost certainly accounts for CFB D 13 *eadweardes eadmundes*, where the gen. sg. *-es* inflexion of the first name has been unconsciously repeated in the second. The A text represents the true reading:

> CFB A 13
>
> afera eadweardes eadmund cyning
>
> '[...] the son of Edward, King Eadmund.'

SnS B 53 *organan* for *organ*, 'song', looks like another example. The A text reads:

> SnS A 53
>
> ac hulic ís se organ ingemyndū
>
> 'But what kind of song is it in the minds [...]'

A fifth instance is SnS 78 B *he his* for A's *he is*, where B's *his* no doubt represents a simple repetition of the initial *h* of the preceding word. In the late Bu text of Cæd, 4 *dridhten* for *drihten*, 'lord', probably resulted from the unconscious repetition of the initial letter *d*. A final example of what was probably an unthinking addition is P118.176.3 *sece* for F's imp. sg. *sec*. Here may also belong PCP 4 T *adihtnode* (H, D *adihtode*), where T seems to have added *n* by mistake, though it is difficult to see why exactly.[8]

§2.4.2 Words

Dittography of entire words is not uncommon, though it would seem that this particular kind of error was more likely to occur when certain contextual conditions obtained. The following is a complete list for the OE poems I am concerned with here:

Gl1 C 36	ealle þe heriað heriað. halige dreamas.
SB1 2	þæt he his sawle sið sið sylfa geþence.
SB1 22	Hwæt wite ðu ðu me weriga hwæt ðu huru wyrma gyfl

---

[8] Two examples of doubling of consonants in Cæd O 8 *teodde* (the manuscript reading is not quite certain here) and Cæd W 3 *metoddes*, with the first *d* underdotted for deletion, are explicable as orthographic variants of a known type; see *OEG* §65.

SB1 151   bygdest ðu þe for hæleðum & ahofe me me*
Cæd W 1   Nu we sculon heria(n) <u>heri</u>** heofonrices we(ard)***
Cæd Ld₁ 1   Nu we sceolan herian <u>herian</u> heofonrices weard.
SnS B 73   huⁿgor <u>hege</u> he gehideð helle gestrudeð

Notes on the text: * First *me* erased. ** The underlinings in this and the next two lines cited are scribal and plainly intended to mark material to be ignored. *** In this line, parts of the text in parentheses are conjectural restorations of letters cut away during trimming by a binder of the folio (81) on which the text of Cæd appears.

In four out of these seven cases, the repeated word is an alliterating element of the line (the three exceptions are SB1 22, 151 and SnS B 73); but an equally significant factor may be the position of the repeated word in the verse of which it is a part: in five of the seven instances, the word repeated is final in the verse (exceptions: SB1 22, SnS B 73), and in all but one of these five the repeated word is the last word of an a-verse and carries alliteration (exception: SB1 151). Although dittography was no doubt automatic in all cases, it would seem that it was provoked in most of them by the expectation of another word beginning with the same sound in the b-verse of the line. In fact, these errors provide an interesting sidelight on the consciousness of OE scribes: perhaps they retained an aural image of the alliteration of each line copied as an aid to memorization and accurate reproduction.

Chapter 3. The Scribe as Editor

§3 *Corruptions corrected, ignored or repaired.*

§3.1 CORRECTED ERRORS

When an OE poem survives in a single copy, it will always be difficult to judge the extent to which faulty transmission has affected the text as we have it. If, of course, the text is full of obvious corruptions, we will draw the obvious conclusion that transmission has been incompetent or careless. In theory, the poor quality of an extant text might be the fault of the original poet; but although there are a few bad versions of poems surviving from the period (the D text of Brb, for example, is a very bad version of that poem), as well as some poems that seem to be weak compositions (the later poems of the *Anglo-Saxon Chronicle*, for example, are little better than collections of poetic clichés used by poets with an erratic sense of appropriateness), it is not generally difficult to distinguish between a poor poem and a poem in a poor state of preservation. What does need to be recognized, however, is that a poem which appears to be in an excellent state of preservation may in fact have been subjected to all manner of modification since it was originally composed. We shall see below that some Anglo-Saxon scribes were sufficiently alert, interested and competent to repair faults (or, in some cases, what they perceived as faults) in their exemplar versions through conjectural emendation, and even, in some cases, to expand on the text as it came down to them. It is important to be aware of capabilities of this sort on the part of transmitters, because it means that when a poem survives in a single copy, it may, for all we can tell, be full of convincing (and therefore undetectable) conjectural emendations imposed at earlier stages in the transmission (mingled, perhaps, with the products of other, unprovoked interventions), so that the surviving work bears a limited resemblance to the work of the original author. *Beowulf* may well be a case in point. It survives only in a single copy. Its subject-matter is continental and such historical basis as it has predates the conversion of the Anglo-Saxons to Christianity (the death of Hygelac, Beowulf's Geatish lord, is recorded independently as taking place in the early sixth century; See Klaeber 1950: xxxix). The story can only have come down to the OE poet in poetic (presumably oral) form from pre-conversion times. Critics have argued strenuously for the view that the Christian references in the poem are integral, part of the conception of 'the poet', whoever he may have been; but if the subject-matter is as old as it seems, there must have been a pre-Christian *Beowulf* (or perhaps several independent compositions out of which the poem as we have it has been woven) without any Christian references. The question of the 'date' of *Beowulf* — a non-question, if one thinks about the implications of the age of its content — is the veil under which these conclusions are most effectively hidden. Other surviving OE poems may have almost as complex histories of transmission behind them. If we are to understand the transmission of OE verse at all, we need as much information as we can acquire about the *general* accuracy and editorial acumen of Anglo-Saxon copyists. The only reliable source of this kind of information is poems surviving in two or more copies; for only when we are in a position to compare different readings from the period do we stand any chance at all of identifying with confidence the uncorrupted version of the text that lies behind the corrupted version, and to see what kind of mistake the corrupted version represents, or even, in some cases, to deduce what provoked it. In this way, a body of conclusions about the transmission of OE poetry can be built up which will enable us, amongst other things, to decide what exactly an OE poem is.

Even when there is a plurality of texts to be compared, of course, it may be difficult to see which of several versions of a line or passage represents the text in its uncorrupted condition; and the difficulty will be especially acute if a transmitter has identified a corruption in his exemplar and managed to produce on his own initiative a variant that is acceptable semantically, syntactically and metrically. The errors I listed above under 'Difficult cases' (§2.3.6) are, for the most part, easy to identify as errors. A collection of errors is, of course, always in danger of creating a one-sided impression of general incompetence or carelessness on the part of scribes; so it is worth emphasising that many of these errors I have identified were corrected by the latest scribes by means of insertions, cancellations or erasures. In fact, of all the varieties of mechanical error exemplified so far, something over a third were spotted and put right by the scribes who were responsible for them in the first place; and if we eliminate cases where ignorance of poetic vocabulary might have confused the issue, the proportion of corrected slips is getting on for half of the total. It seems fair to state that Anglo-Saxon scribes were not, generally speaking, careless or incompetent in their work.

§3.2 IGNORED CORRUPTIONS

When scribes corrected their own mistakes, it is reasonable to conclude (as I do in the case of SB2 48 *ancenda*, considered above, §2.3.6.2) that the restored reading derives from a check of the originally miscopied exemplar; but when scribes found corruptions already present in their exemplars, they sometimes transcribed them faithfully and uncritically. The best evidence of this is to be found in the later W-S versions of Cæd. All the W-S *ylda* texts vary from all the surviving North. texts and the W-S *eorðan* texts in the following readings (using H as representative of the W-S *ylda* group's corruptions and T's forms as representative of the readings of the more authoritative North. and W-S *eorðan* texts):

> H 3 *gehwilc* (acc. sg. neut.), 'every', T *gehwæs*, 'of every';
> H 7 *middangearde* (dat. sg.), 'for the earth', T *þa middangeard* (acc. sg.),
>   'Then [...] the earth';
> H 8 *Æfter tida*, (?) 'after periods of time', T *æfter teode*, 'later made'.

These three variants, which clearly derive from the group archetype, are largely responsible for the relatively unsatisfactory sense of the W-S *ylda* texts (for the OE texts of T and H, see §1.1 above):

T	H
Now ought (we) to praise the guardian of the heavenly kingdom, the might of the creator and his mind, the works of the father of glory; how he, the eternal lord, established the beginning of every wonder. He, the holy creator, first made heaven as a roof for the children of earth. Then the guardian of mankind,	Now ought we to praise the guardian of the heavenly kingdom, the might of the creator and his mind, the works of the father of glory; how he, the eternal lord, established the beginning, every[1] wonder. He, the holy creator, first made heaven as a roof for the children of men, for the earth,[2] the guardian of

---

[1] *gehwilc*

[2] *middangearde*

the eternal lord, the almighty ruler, later arranged the earth, the land for men.	mankind, the eternal lord, the almighty ruler, after periods of time,[3] for men on the lands.

The difference of meaning is fundamental: whereas T, the other W-S *eorðan* texts, and the North. texts all describe the making of both heaven and earth, H and the other W-S *ylda* texts describe only the creation of heaven. The noun *or* (or *ord*) in the phrase: *or(d) onstealde* (or *astealde*), 'established the beginning', invariably takes a dependent gen. elsewhere in OE verse (Bwf 2407, R3.59, XSt 113), as it does here in T; in H, the acc. sg. *gehwilc* involves a relatively awkward parallelism with *ord*. The 'periods of time' in H — for this seems to be the intended meaning of *tida* — after which God is described as having made heaven clashes logically with the 'first' (*ærest*) of line 5; the noun *tida* has replaced T's verb *teode*, 'made', which makes perfect sense. This corruption, coupled with the omission in H 7 of *þa*, 'then', and the adjustment (clearly connected with this omission of *þa*) of the grammar of 7 *middangeard* (acc. sg. to dat. sg.), is what restricts the scope of H's biblical narrative to the creation of heaven.

Later we shall need to consider the possible origins of these corruptions in the archetype of the W-S *ylda* group; I mention them here as obvious corruptions which were slavishly transcribed in all seven of the surviving texts of the W-S *ylda* group of Cæd (W, Bd$_1$, H, Ln, Mg, Tr$_1$, Bu).

There are a few other reasonably clear instances of the faithful transmission of corruptions. One is DEw 25 C, D *lunger* for *lungre*, 'quickly': the fact that both texts preserve the corrupt form indicate that it appeared in the archetypal version of the poem. SB1 and SB2 are both corrupt in line 17 of the poem:

SB1 17	SB2 17
Hwæt druh ðu dreorega to hwan drehtest ðu me	Hwæt drugu þu dreorga to hwon dreahtest þu me,

'What have you done, miserable one? Why do you afflict me [...]'

Both versions bungle what several commentators (e.g. Sisam 1953: 34) and the most recent editor of the poem (Moffat 1990: 67) agree must originally have been *Hwæt druge þu*, with *druge* the pret. 2 sg. of *dreogan* (Sisam compares Gen 888a *Hwæt druge þu, dohtor*). The SB

---

[3]   *Æfter tida*

texts also share a common corruption in 10 *sawle* in the followinig context:

SB1 9–11	SB2 9–11
Sceal se gast cuman geohðum hremig	Sceal se gæst cuman gehþum hremig
symble ymbe seofon niht sawle findan	sȳle ymb seofon niht sawle findan
þone lichoman þe hie ær lange wæg	þone lichoman þe heo ær longe wæg

'The spirit must come lamenting with cares always every seven nights, the soul to find the body which previously it long wore, [...]'

Here the grammar requires a nom. sg. *sawl* or *sawol* in 10b (my translation reflects what must be the original grammar of the sentence), whereas *sawle* looks like the acc., gen. or dat. sg. It is difficult to see how this error arose. One would doubt that even a very inattentive scribe could have taken the sentence to mean that the spirit must come to find itself, especially in view of the fact that the acc. sg. *þone lichoman*, 'the body', plainly the object for *findan*, comes at the beginning of the following line. And yet both texts transcribe the error.

§3.3 TEXTUAL REPAIRS

When a transmitter introduces a corruption into his copy and does not correct it by reference to his exemplar, a subsequent copyist in the chain of transmission will either transcribe his predecessor's corruption unchanged, or try to do something about it. It is, of course, conceivable that a very astute scribe who was sensitive to poetic style would manage to restore the original reading by intelligent guesswork (as Moffat assumes in the case of SB2 48 *ancenda*; see §2.3.6.2 above); much would depend on how radically the exemplar text departs from the original one. If he succeeded, and his exemplar did not survive, we would never realize that the corruption was ever present in the chain of transmission; but if he did not succeed in restoring the original reading, only in compounding the corruption further, the sequence of corruptions should, in theory, be detectable if manuscripts survive showing the three essential stages of the process: the original or archetypal reading; the initial corruption of it; and the compounding of the corruption. There are a few groups of variants in surviving manuscripts of Old English poems that seem to indicate this kind of development during transmission. The best example, which I have discussed in detail elsewhere (Orton 1985), comes in Brb 40b–44a. Here are all four extant versions of the passage:

Brb 40b–44a

A   B

he wæs his mæga sceard.   her wæs his maga sceard.
freonda gefylled. ón folcstede.   freonda gefylled on folcstede.
beslagen æt sæcce. & his sunu forlet.   forslegen æt sace & his sunu forlét.
ón wælstowe. wundun fergrunden.   on wælstowe wundum forgrunden.
giungne æt guðe.   geongne æt guþe

D   C

he wæs his mæga. sceard   her wæs his maga sceard.
freonda gefylled on folcstede   freonda gefylled on his folcstede.
beslægen æt sęcge. & his sunu forlæt.   beslegen æt sæcce. & his sunu forlet
on wælstowe wundum forgrunden.   on wælstowe. wundum forgrunden.
geongne æt guðe   geongne æt guþe.

The substantial variants in this passage are 40 A, D *he*, B, C *her*; 41 C *his*, which A, B and D lack; and 42 A, C, D *beslagen* (*-slægen*, *-slegen*), B 42 *forslegen*. The broad relationships between the four manuscript texts of Brb were established by Campbell in his edition (Campbell 1938: 7–8): none of the four derives, directly or indirectly, from any of the others; A and D, respectively mid-tenth and mid-eleventh century, descend independently from the archetype, whereas B and C, respectively late tenth and mid-eleventh century, both derive from a lost intermediate text B-C*, the evidence for this being the corrupt reading *her* for *he* in B, C 40. I shall explain why 40 B-C* *her* must be regarded as corrupt below.

There is a possibility that this passage was already corrupt in the archetype text from which all four extant texts derive. The main difficulty centres on the words *sceard* (40) and *gefylled* (41) and the nouns in the gen. pl. that depend on them, respectively *mæga* in A and D (on B, C *maga* see below) and *freonda* in all versions. Campbell rejected *gefylled* on semantic grounds: the context seems to demand a word meaning 'deprived', 'bereft', whereas OE *gefyllan* always means 'to kill' in OE (as it does in Brb 67 *folces gefylled*, 'of people slain'). Earlier in the poem we have been told that the Scottish king Constantine, to whom 40 A, D *he* refers, fled the battlefield 'to his homeland in the north' (38 *on his cyþþe norð*); but *gefylled* seems to imply that he died at Brunanburh ('he was [...] killed [...]'). Campbell resolves this inconsistency by emending to *befylled*, 'bereft', though this does not address the whole problem as it presents itself in texts A and D (B and C compound the problem, as we shall see below). A verb meaning 'bereft' would be expected to take the

dat. of whatever the person in question was bereft of. We might compare
Bwf 1590 *ond hine þa heafde becearf*, 'and then cut off his head', in
which *becearf* could be described as meaning 'deprived by cutting' and
heafde, dat. sg., as 'as to the head'. In Brb 41, however, *freonda*,
'friends', is gen., making it uncertain whether the emended phrase
freonda befylled could mean what Campbell thinks it ought to mean in
the context, i.e. 'bereft of friends'. Campbell's emendation addresses
only part of the problem here, the real nature of which Sedgefield seems
to have recognized before him in a note to his edition of the poem
(Sedgefield 1922: 171), without offering any solution to it. Campbell left
he wæs his mæga sceard in the previous line unemended, interpreting it
as 'he was deprived of his kinsmen', meaning that Constantine was be-
reaved at Brunanburh. But *sceard* does not mean 'deprived' elsewhere in
OE; its meanings are 'notched', 'hacked', 'gashed' and 'multilated'; only
here does the context seem to demand the metaphorical 'deprived', and
again, the use of the gen. in the noun for the 'kinsmen' whom
Constantine is supposed to have been deprived of in the battle is not easy
to parallel or explain. Campbell notices the unusual use of *sceard* here
but does not emend it, even though it presents a problem precisely
parallel to the one *gefylled* presents.

   This, then, would have been the state of the passage as the scribe of B-
C* received it. We cannot, of course, assume without argument that he
found it as puzzling as modern editors have done; but the condition of B
and C does suggest that he recognized a problem in the received text. If
he understood *sceard* and *gefylled* in their normal OE meanings —
'mutilated' and 'killed' respectively — he might well have been as
puzzled as we are by the nouns in the gen. pl. that depend on them; but
gefylled in particular might have seemed inconsistent in its implications:
the immediately preceding passage (37–39) makes it clear that
Constantine survived the battle at Brunanburh. How, in that case, could
he wæs his mæga sceard [...] gefylled [...] refer to Constantine's death, as
the passage no doubt appeared to do? If we accept the hypothesis that the
B-C* scribe perceived the problem in this way, his substitution of 40 *her*
for the *he* which appears in A and D becomes intelligible. It gives
acceptable sense if the word *mæga* (B, C *maga*) were interpreted, not as
'of kinsmen', but as the nom. sg. of the poetic word *maga*, 'son', 'descendant'. If, of course, *maga* was the exemplar form, perhaps this was the
way the scribe of B-C* interpreted the word in the first place. If he did,
the centre of difficulty would have been the pronoun *he*, rather than

mæga/maga; but in either case, this misinterpretation of *mæga/maga* would have been encouraged had the scribe read a little further in his exemplar and found that the poem does indeed state, in lines 42b–43, that Constantine's son was killed at Brunanburh. The text is quoted below in B's orthography:

> Brb B 42b–43
>
> [...] & his sunu forlét.
> on wælstowe wundum forgrunden.

'[...] and left his son on the battlefield, destroyed by wounds.'

The alteration of 40b *he* to *her* then gave the meaning: 'here was his son mutilated', making the verse closely parallel in sense to 42b–43.[4]

This substitution of 40 *her* for *he* is the only variant in the passage upon which texts B and C agree, so clearly the B-C* scribe made no further adjustments to the text as he received it. The past part. *gefylled* now made better sense than before as a reference to the death of Constantine's son; but problems still remained in the passage. It now meant (in B-C*) 'here was his son mutilated, killed *freonda* (?) on the battlefield, bereft (C *beslegen*) in the struggle, and left his son in the place of slaughter', etc. The past part. *beslegen*, 'bereft', is now awkward (I assume that it does not involve the introduction of a grandson of Constantine's into the text); and how could a corpse be described as having 'left' (*forlet*) anyone behind on the battlefield? These problems were left untouched in C; but the scribe of B (or possibly the scribe of an intermediate text linking B-C* with B) improved matters by substituting *forslegen* for *beslegen* in 42. No longer is the corpse of Constantine's son 'deprived' of anything; he is now *forslegen æt sace*, 'killed in the struggle', which is consistent with what is said elsewhere in the poem about him.

The only other modification of the text which needs to be explained is C's addition of *his* in 41b *on his folcstede*. Campbell's view, with which I agree, is that *folcstede*, the authorial meaning of which is 'battlefield' here, was misinterpreted as 'dwelling', 'home', and that *his* was therefore

---

[4]   The scribe of B-C* may not have been the only medieval reader of this passage to be confused by it. William of Malmesbury, in his twelfth-century account of the battle in *De gestis regum Anglorum*, says that Constantine fell at Brunanburh (*Cecidit ibi rex Scottorum Constantinus*), though Campbell thinks that William is here drawing on a lost source, not simply on Brb (Campbell 1938: 148).

added to emphasise whose 'home' this was (Campbell 1938: 111). However, Campbell's note does not take account of the effect that B-C* 40 *her* has on the meaning of the whole passage; he concludes that the C scribe 'assumed the passage to imply that Constantine found himself with no kinsmen in his home', whereas any attempt to explain C's *his* must begin with the recognition that it refers (in B-C*), not to Constantine himself but to his son — the *his maga* of B, C 40b. On this assumption, C 41b *on his folcstede* would appear to mean that Constantine's son died 'at home', that is, in Scotland. Part of the problem of uncovering the implications of C's *his* is that we do not know the site of Brunanburh. Its introduction into the text might mean that the transmitter responsible for it thought that Brunanburh was in Scotland. This understanding may be inconsistent with the poem's statement that Constantine fled from the battlefield *on his cyþþe norð* (Brb 38a), 'to his native land in the north', which has been taken as evidence that Brunanburh lay in Anglo-Saxon, not Scottish, territory. We should, however, note that OE *cyþþ* may mean 'fellow-countrymen', 'kinsfolk', or even 'neighbours', so Brb 38a does not necessarily imply that Constantine crossed any important political boundaries on his way home; perhaps his own family and retinue were based in a more northerly part of Scotland.

If Brunanburh lay in Scottish territory, Constantine's son who died in the battle might intelligibly be described as having died 'at home'; but it seems necessary to consider if the transmitter who misinterpreted *folcstede* as 'home' and consequently introduced *his* into the text should have had any independent reason for thinking that this point needed emphasising. Other sources for the battle at Brunaburh confirm the fall of a son of Constantine there. The *Pictish Chronicle*, probably from the tenth century and apparently independent of the OE poem, confirms the death of Constantine's son at Brunanburh (*cecidit filius Constantini*; see Campbell 1938: 157). The seventeenth-century English translation of the Irish *Annals of Clonmacnoise* mentions one 'Ceallagh Prince of Scotland' as being among the casualties in the battle (Campbell 1938: 159); he may be the same son as is mentioned in our poem. More suggestive for present purposes is the mention by Florence of Worcester of an (unnamed) son of Constantine's who was taken hostage by Æþelstan king of Wessex in 934, three years before the battle, no doubt in an attempt to control his father's activities (see Thorpe 1848: 132; Smyth 1979: 65). We are not told of his return to his own people before Brunanburh. The Anglo-Saxon custom was that hostages fought in battles alongside those in whose custody they found themselves.[5] It is conceivable that it is this son whom the C redactor thought was referred to as having died at Brunanburh; and if so, the detail that he died 'at home' might have been added to point up the irony of his death in his own country at the hands of his own kin-group, as he fought on the English side against them. If, of course, the gen. pl. *freonda* in the phrase *freonda gefylled* in 41a was taken as a gen. of agency, meaning 'killed by friends', this might have supported the C redactor in his attempt to improve the text as he received it, though unfortunately this use of the gen. seems to be unattested elsewhere in OE.

The chain of activity that my discussion of the variants in Brb 40b–44a implies is complex enough. I have assumed that the initial difficulty that started the whole sequence of alterations was the grammatical role of the pl. genitives *mæga* (40) and *freonda* (41) in relation to *sceard* and *gefylled*, upon which they respectively depend, and the significance of *gefylled* in the sense of 'killed'. The scribe of B-C* attacked part of the problem in substituting *her* for 40 *he*, though the particular amendment he made might well have been suggested to him by his misinterpretation of 40 *mæga*, actually gen. pl., 'of kinsmen', as *maga*, nom. sg., 'son', and he left the problem of the meaning of *gefylled* unsolved. But once the B-C* scribe had worked on the text, the emphasis of the passage was already beginning to shift away from a description of Constantine's bereavement and towards a description of the death of his son. The substitution, in B, of *forslegen*, 'killed', for *beslegen* (*-slagen*, *-slægen*), 'bereft', confirms this general drift that transmission effected on the text of the passage. The final stage was C's introduction of *his* in line 41, which may possibly reflect some independent knowledge of the historical circumstances under which the battle was fought, though I cannot prove this.

A second, fairly clear example of the constructive modification of an already corrupt text is afforded by the W-S *eorðe* texts of Cæd. A clear view of what happened to the text is best achieved by comparing the first six lines of the text in Ld₁ and Hr:

Cæd Ld₁ 1–6	Cæd Hr 1–6
Nu we sceolan herian <u>herian</u> heofonrices weard	Nu we sceolan herian heofonrices weard

---

[5]   There are several well-known examples of this practice in Anglo-Saxon sources, notably Æscferð son of Ecglaf, a Northumbrian hostage who fought at the battle of Maldon under Byrhtnoð of Essex (Mld 267), and the unnamed Welsh hostage who fought with Cynewulf king of Wessex according to the Anglo-Saxon Chronicle, s.a. 755.

metudes mihte & his modgeþanc.
weorc wulderfæder. swa he wundra
  gehwæs
ece drihten
þa he ærest sceop eorðe bearnū
heofon to hrofe.

metudes mihte & his modgeþanc
weorc wulderfæder swa

he ærest sceop eorðe bearnū
heofon to hrofe.

Corruptions shared by these two texts (as well as by the third member of the same textual family, Lo) are the omission of the second half-line in 4 (represented by *ór onstealde*, 'established the beginning', or its variants in all other textual groups), and the displacement of the b-verse in line 6 to the very end of the text (*halig scyppeod*, with the error *o* for *n*; see §2.1.1.3 above). The scribe of Hr has, however, responded to one of the problems that these omissions produce: noticing that the clause beginning *swa he* in Ld₁ 3b is plainly incomplete, he has omitted the whole clause except the initial *swa he* and run it into the next sentence that begins in Ld₁ in 5a with *þa he*. This is a great improvement on an already much-abused text, though it does not, of course, restore the archetypal readings; on the contrary, it distorts the text still further. An alternative explanation of this variation is that the missing text in Hr was omitted by homoeo-teleuton, the scribe's eye jumping from *swa he* to *þa he*; but the dove-tailing achieved in Hr is impressive, and I am more inclined to think that the scribe responded positively to the corruptions introduced by his predecessors in the transmissional chain.

A third example of the repair of a corrupt text has already been mentioned above in another connection. This is Cæd O 3 *wera*, where other texts of the W-S *eorðan* group have *weorc*, 'works'. As we saw earlier (§1.1), *wera* was originally written *wero* which itself looks like an error for the Anglian form *werc* in an exemplar; but a scribe who encoun-tered *wero* in his exemplar could not to be expected to detect the underlying form without other texts to compare with his exemplar. Con-sequently, having reproduced *wero* from his exemplar, he looked again at it and decided to convert it to *wera*, which gives (as a gen. pl.) good sense in the context: 'Now we should praise the guardian of the heavenly kingdom, the might of the creator and the thoughts of his mind, the glorious father of men', etc. It is difficult to explain the change to *wera* unless we assume that the copyist responsible for it was faced with an already corrupt *wero* in his exemplar. If *werc* stood there, we would expect him to reproduce it.

The three passages discussed so far in this section have provided evidence of the three conditions of the text that I defined earlier in connection with this kind of amendment: the uncorrupted text; the corrupted text; and the repaired text. I also include here two more variations in poems surviving in only two manuscripts: Gl1 and SnS. In both cases, the nature of the corruption in one of the two versions suggests amendment at two distinct stages of transmission, so that these too may be classified as instances of attempts to repair earlier textual damage. The first example is Gl1 43 J *héahþrýnnesse haliges gastes* beside C's *heahþrymnesse halige gastas*. Here are the two versions of the line in its context:

Gl1 C 41–44	Gl1 J 41–44
And on worlda world. wunað & rixað.	& on worulda woruld wúnað. and rixað
cyninc innan wuldre & his þa gecorenan.	cyning innan wúldre. & his þa gecorenan.
heahþrymnesse. halige gastas.	héahþrýnnesse haliges gastes.
wlitige englas. & wuldorgife.	wlítige eńglas. & wuldorgyfe.

C probably means: 'And forever and ever the king dwells and reigns in glory in high majesty along with his chosen ones, holy spirits, beautiful angels and glorious gifts, [...]', whereas J has '[...] along with his chosen ones, the high trinity of the holy spirit, beautiful angels,' etc. I follow Lumby who, translating C, takes *heahþrymnesse* as dat. sg., 'in high majesty, holy spirits', etc. (Lumby 1876: 55). Thomson, who replaces J's version of 43 entirely with C's, translates 'high majesties, holy spirits', taking the compound as nom. pl. (Thomson 1849: 128–29). Ure, editing J, substitutes C's *heahþrymnesse* for J's *héahþrýnnesse*, and like Thomson takes the compound as nom. pl.; but he retains J's *haliges gastes* (gen. sg.), making the whole line mean 'great glories of the holy spirit' (Ure 1957: 84, 139). Dobbie prefers C's version of the whole line, commenting that the apparent meaning in J — 'the high Trinity of the Holy Ghost', as he translates it — has 'little to commend it' (Dobbie 1942: 188).

There is general agreement among editors that J is corrupt in the form of the compound in 43a. This was probably a simple scribal error in origin, involving the omission of a minim (*n* for *m*; see above, §2.1.1.2). It seems doubtful, however, if Ure is right to retain J's version of the b-verse while embracing C's version of the a-verse, for each version of the entire line probably represents an integrated conception of its meaning: it seems likely that J's 'high trinity', once established in the text, led a later transmitter to expect an enumeration of the members of the trinity, and so to turn the nom. pl. *halige gastas*, as in C, actually a reference to the souls of the saints, into the gen. sg., 'of the holy ghost', to form the first item in the list. The list is not continued; nor could it have been without a substantial addition to the text. J's version of 43b is thus probably a secondary corruption representing an unsuccessful attempt to repair the meaning of a text already corrupt in 43a.

The second instance is SnS B 11, mentioned above in a different context (§2.3.1). Here (again) is B's version of the line compared with A's:

SnS A 11	SnS B 11
[...] oððe æh[.]a oððe eor[...]	elnes oððe æhte eorlscipes

Despite the damage suffered by the A text, it is still possible to see that it differs from B both in the presence of an *oððe* in the b-verse as well as the a-verse, and in the inflexion of the noun *æht*, 'possession' (A's form appears to be *æhta*, B has *æhte*). The omission of *oððe* in B spoils both the sense and the metre. The sense in B seems to be 'with respect to power and the possession of nobility', whereas A has '(with respect to power) or possessions or nobility'. If we assume that A shows the original reading here, B has responded to the problem created by the omission of *oððe* in the b-verse (giving the apparent meaning: 'with respect to power or possessions of nobility') by altering the case of *æhta* from gen. pl. to gen. sg., making for a much smoother reading but leaving the metrical problem untouched. The restoration here of reasonable sense in B suggests that there was at least one alert and critical copyist in B's history.

Chapter 4. The Confused Scribe

§4 Unnecessary repairs and modifications

§4.1 MISAPPREHENSIONS OF MORPHOLOGY

Corruptions sometimes arise from misconceptions about the morphology of words, particularly about where one word ends and the next begins; but in several cases there is evidence to suggest that scribal unfamiliarity with dialectal forms in exemplars contributed to mistakes of this kind. A probable example is Brb D 66 *on þisne iglande* beside A's *ón þis eiglande*, 'on this island'. The instr. sg. *þis*, as in A, is required in the context. D's *þisne* is the regular W-S acc. sg. form of the demonstrative, though *igland*, which it governs, is a neuter noun and the form *iglande* must be dat. sg. formally and contextually. I can only suggest that the unfamiliarity of some form such as A's Anglian *eiglande* with the unusual digraph (or diphthong) *ei* resulted in the attachment of the initial *e* to the preceding word, and that *n* was inserted, possibly at a later stage, to make a recognizable form of a known word. If this is the true explanation of *þisne*, the error shows indifference to the meaning and linguistic integrity of the passage: the transmitter produces a known word which is nevertheless quite ungrammatical in the sentence in which it appears.

A second example from the same poem is Brb A 13 *sécgas hwate* ('brave men') for B, C, D *secga swate*, 'with the blood of men', though the origins of this mistake may be more involved. Here is the context, with D representing the reading of the other three texts:

Brb D 12b–13	Brb A 12b–13
feld dennode.	feld dæn^{n}ede
secga swate siþþan sunne úp.	sécgas hwate. siðþan sunne úp.

Notes on the text: A *dænnede* with second *n* added superscript.

B: 'the field resounded (?) with the blood of men, after the sun [...]'

D is preferable metrically and grammatically. The stem-vowel of D's *swate*, dat. sg., 'blood', is long, giving a normal verse of Sievers' type A, whereas A's *sécgas hwate* is metrically inadequate because the stem-vowel in *hwate*, 'brave', is short. The inflexions of A's *secgas hwate* suggest that the phrase is to be taken as either nom. pl. or acc. pl., though neither would suit the context.

As Campbell points out (Campbell 1938: 100), it is likely that A's corruption arose when the initial *s* of *swate* was mistaken for the final letter of the preceding word, turning *secga* into *secgas* and so changing its case and also creating the non-word *wate*, which was built up by the addition of initial *h* into the attested *hwate*, 'brave'. The phrase that results is meaningful as 'brave men', but it cannot be accommodated by the syntax of the sentence in which it occurs — insofar as we understand it. Here we encounter a methodological problem of a kind which we shall meet again in connection with other variants. If we are to understand why a text was intentionally modified (simple mechanical errors do not, of course, require detailed reconstructions of this sort), we need to be able to judge how the transmitter responsible interpreted the passage as it appeared in his exemplar. In the case of Brb 13a, we are somewhat hampered by the fact that we do not understand the meaning of the finite verb of the clause of which *secga swate* is (or, from the perspective of A, was) a part: the verb in A is *dænede* or *dænnede*, in D *dennode*, and in B and C, *dennade* which is no doubt a spelling variant of *dennode*. Campbell has a long note on the various suggestions that had been made by the end of the nineteen-thirties (Campbell 1938: 98–102; see also Dobbie 1942: 147), but convincingly dismisses all of them; none of the variant forms of the verb in 12b, he concludes, 'seem capable of explanation'. There have been conjectural emendations, some of them very attractive (especially Madden's *dunnade*, 'became dark'; an intransitive verb *dunnian* in this sense is attested in the OE version of Boethius in the form *dunniað* (pres. pl.), 'grow dark'; see Campbell 1938: 102); but for present purposes the absence of any consensus about the verb in 12b means that we cannot even guess what the scribe who produced *secgas hwate* made of the sentence in which it appeared. It may be, of course, that his sense of the meaning of the sentence as a whole could accommodate *secgas hwate*.

Confusion over word-division probably lies behind the variant in Gll 26, where the C text has *þu mærsodest* and J, *gemærsodest*:

Gl1 J 26   Gl1 C 26

& gemærsodest hine mánegum to   & þu mærsodest hine manegum to
  hélpe   helpe.

'and you glorified it for the benefit of the many.'

The 2nd person pronoun *þu* in C is not objectionable, though the clause
has no need of it as its subject is the same as the previous clause (25 C
þu). Furthermore, it is much easier to explain C's version as a corruption
of J's than vice-versa: probably J's verbal prefix *ge-* was misinterpreted
as the pl. 2nd person pronoun *gē*, 'ye', in a position where the sg.
pronoun is required, so *þu* was substituted for *ge-*.

Three bad corruptions in the D text of Brb fall in this category, though
they may well betoken an ignorance of poetic vocabulary as much as a
tendency to misinterpret the morphology of individual words. In my text
of these howlers below, C stands for the correct reading to be found in
texts A, B and C in all three places:

Brb C 23   Brb D 23

heowon hereflymon hindan þearle   heowan heora flyman hindan þearle.

'They hewed the fugitive army (*or* D their fugitives) severely from behind
[...]')

Brb C 44b–46   Brb D 44b–46

        gylpan ne þorfte.   gylpan ne þorfte.
beorn blandenfex. billgeslihtes.   beorn blandenfeax billgeslihtes
ealde inwitta. ne ánláf þý ma.   eald in wuda ne anláf þe ma.

'The grey-streaked warrior, the old deceitful one (*or* D the old one in the
wood), had no reason to boast of the clash of swords; no more did Anlaf.'

Brb C 53   Brb D 53

Gewiton hym þa norðmenn.   GEwiton him þa norðmen dæg gled
  negledcnearrum   on garum

'The Norsemen departed in nailed ships (*or* D the day bright (?) on the
spears)'

In all three cases, D's readings involve metrical or alliterative irregularities, as well as problems of grammar and sense. These are some of the
most spectacular corruptions that it is possible to identify in OE poetry.
Campbell's comment on D 53 is worth quoting in full:

D has the astonishing corruption *dæg gled on garum*. It was no doubt caused by the unfamilar second element of the compound. It would be idle to speculate what were the steps by which it arose, but it is instructive to consider how helpless any editor would be in the face of such an error in a work preserved in one MS only: if he did solve it, universal condemnation for audacity would be his only reward. (Campbell 1938: 114)

If, however, Brb D 53 is taken with these other corruptions in the same text of the poem, a few tentative generalizations are possible. The spirit in which these corruptions were imposed remains a mystery. They are more than simple copying mistakes, because recognizable words (albeit in forms and positions quite inappropriate to the context) are put together from the wreckage of the original readings. It is also clear that unfamiliarity with poetic vocabulary contributed to these changes to the text: C 23 *hereflyma*, 'fugitive soldier', C 46 *inwitta*, 'evil one' (the more usual form is A's *inwidda*), and C 53 *negledcnearr*, 'nailed ship', are all words confined to verse.

§4.2 MISAPPREHENSIONS OF SYNTAX OR GRAMMAR

§4.2.1 Clausal relationships

It is sometimes possible to trace the origin of a corruption to a transmitter's failure to grasp the syntax of the passage in which it occurs. Sometimes clausal relationships are misinterpreted, as in the following example, PCP T 8 *forþæm þe* for *Forðæm* (H; D *forðon*), which converts what is properly a principal clause into a subordinate one. Here is the passage, with H representing the better reading that it shares with the D text:

PCP H 5b–10

    ryhtspell monig.
gregorius gleawmod gindwód
ðurh sefan snyttro searoðonca hord.
Forðæm he monncynnes mæst
    gestriende
rodra wearde romwara betest
monna modwelegost mærðum
    gefrægost.

PCP T 5b–10

    rihtspel monig
gregorius. gleawmód geondwód.
þurh sefan snytro. searoþanca hord.
forþæm þe he manncynnes mæst
    gestriende
rodera wearde. romwarena betst
manna modweligost. merþum
    gefrægost.

'The wise Gregorius was steeped in many true doctrines through wisdom of mind, a hoard of skills; therefore (*or* T because) he, best of Romans, most talented of men, most celebrated in glories, won over most of mankind to the guardian of heaven.'

T's *forþæm þe*, 'because', gives inferior sense: Gregory's wisdom and studies were the foundation of his effectiveness as a winner of converts, not a consequence of it.

A second example of confusion over clausal relationships is EgC A 7 *þonne*, 'when', for *þone*, 'which':

EgC B 5b–8a	EgC A 5b–8a
þær wæs blis mycel.	þær wæs blis micel
on þam eadgan dæge eallum	on þā eadgan dæge. eallū geworden.
geworden.	
þone niða bearn nemnað & cegeað.	þonne niða bearn. nemnað & cigað.
pentecostenes dæg	pentecostenes dæg.

'There was great joy for everyone on that blessed day that (*or* A when) the children of men call and name Pentecost.'

It is easy to see how the content of this sentence led to the anticipation of a temporal rather than a relative clause (' [...] on that blessed day when [...]'): the scribe took the 'blessed day' as a self-sufficient reference to the day of Edgar's crowning, not expecting it to be dated so precisely. Even though the mistake makes nonsense of the sentence, it was not corrected.

A third probable example of misapprehension of clausal relationships occurs in the B version of an exceptionally obscure part of SnS. The translation quoted below is Dobbie's, who tries to make sense of the passage in his notes to the ASPR edition:

SnS A 44b–48	SnS B 44b–48
[...] [..]t him dropan stigað	[...] þæt him dropan stigað
swate geswiðed seofan intingum	swate geswiðed sefan intingan
egesfullicran ðōn seo ærene gripu	egesfullicra þane seo ærene gripo
ðōn heo for XII [.]yra tydernessū	þōn for twelf fýra tydernessum
ófer gleda gripe gifrust wealleð	ofer gléda gripe gifrost weallað

'[...] so that drops arise on him, made strong with blood, in the affairs of his mind, more terrible than the brazen cauldron when it wells (*or* B when they well) most eagerly over the grip of coals through the twelve infirmities of men.' (Dobbie 1942: 161–62.)

The essential difference between the two versions here is that whereas A takes the 'when' clause beginning with 47 *ðōn* as descriptive of the boiling of the cauldron (46 *gripu*), B takes it to refer to the drops (44 *dropan*) that arise in the devil — an interpretation that leaves the 'brazen cauldron' unelaborated, as if it were a familiar idea in no need of further explanation. A's version is plainly preferable here. I call this a probable rather than a definite example of the amendment of clausal relationships because the variation in 48b between *wealleð* and *weallað* might be nothing more than a somewhat early manifestation of the merging of front and back vowels in unstressed syllables that Campbell dates to the eleventh century (*OEG* §379); but if the distinction is really one of number (sg. and pl. respectively), B's pl. *weallað* may be interpreted as a deliberate modification of the received text. The reason for the change may have to do with the unusual use here of the verb *weallan*, 'to boil'. This verb usually has a liquid as subject (Bosworth & Toller 1898: s.v. *weallan* V); only here and in Jln 581 *Bæð hate weol* is the containing vessel (here *seo ærene gripu*) the verb's subject (one might compare PE idioms such as 'The kettle is boiling'). If a transmitter had taken *weallan* here in its usual sense, he would have been able to find only the pl. *dropan*, 'drops', in 44 as a possible subject. The gender and number of the pronoun *heo* in A 47 (nom. fem. sg.) clarifies the connection between *gripu* as subject and the verb, so the omission of the pronoun in B is conspicuous: perhaps its omission at an earlier stage of transmission contributed to the confusion. It could, alternatively, be a deliberate modification of the text in line with the interpretation of the passage that seems to have given rise to B's version of it, but this is less likely. The obscurity of the reference to the long-boiling cauldron, for which no close analogue is known (see Menner 1941: 110), may have been a factor in the generation of B's corruption.

A fourth instance of confusion over clausal relationships is betrayed by the A text's version of EgC 13. Below, B represents the more satisfactory and presumably original version of the passage in question:

EgC B 10b–16	EgC A 10b–16
& þa agangen wæs.	& ða agangen wæs
tyn hund wintra geteled rímes	tyn hund wintra geteled rimes.
fram gebýrdtíde bremes cinges.	frā gebyrdtide bremes cyninges
leohta hyrdes butan ðær to láfe þa get.	leohta hyrdes. buton ðær to lafe þa agan
wæs wintergeteles þæs gewritu secgað.	wæs wintergeteles þæs ðe gewritu secgað.
seofon &.xx. swa neah was sigora fréan.	seofon & twentig. swa neah wæs sigora frean.

þusend aúrnen ða þa þis gelamp.   ðusend áurnen. ða þa ðis gelamp.

'And then ten hundred years had passed away, reckoned by number, from the birth-date of the glorious king, the guardian of lights (?), except still there were remaining (*or* A except there had gone (?)) a tally of twenty-seven years, as writers tell, so nearly had passed a thousand of the lord of victories, when this occurred.'

The passage defines the date of Edgar's coronation in relation to the birth of Christ; but its great prolixity stems from the poet's attempt to emphasise how nearly Edgar's crowning coincided with the millennium. The collapse of the sense in A results from the substitution of *agan* in place of B *get*, 'still' (C too has *get*). Plummer took *agan* as the past part. of *āgān*, 'to go', 'to come' (Plummer 1892: I, 303; see *OEG* §768(c) for the paradigm of (-)*gān*). The substitution in A must have been suggested to the transmitter responsible for it by the conspicuous verbal similarities that already existed between the two clauses in 10b–13a and 13b–15a; in fact, A's version of the second clause looks very like a deliberate attempt to mirror the construction and meaning of the first (compare 10b–11 & *ða agangen wæs tyn hund wintra geteled rimes* with 13b–15a [...] *þa agan wæs wintergeteles [...] seofon & twentig*). The result is nonsensical: *agan*, 'gone', conflicts logically with 13 *to lafe*, 'remaining'. It is to be suspected that the scribe who made the change here regarded *þa agan wæs* as the beginning of a clause, parallelling *ða agangen wæs* in 10b, though if so it is impossible to guess what he made of *to lafe*. The variation between A and the other texts of EgC in this passage is difficult to explain with any confidence, but confusion over clausal relationships or boundaries seems to have played a part in generating it.

§4.2.2 Grammatical relationships within the clause

§4.2.2.1 Mistakes about the grammatical functions of words

In Brb 18, A's *guma norþerna*, a phrase in the nom. sg., differs from the other three texts of the poem (B, C, D), all of which have *guman norðerne* (D *norþærne*) which is nom. pl.[1] The implications of the varia-tion are best seen in the context of lines 17b–20a, quoted below in versions A and C:

Brb A 17b–20a   Brb C 17b–20a

þær læg secg mænig.   þær læg secg monig.

---

[1] I have discussed this variant elsewhere (Orton 1994: 3–4).

garū ageted. guma norþerna.   garum ageted. guman norðerne.
ofer scild scoten. swilce scittisc eác.   ofer scyld scoten swilce scyttisc eac.
werig wíges sæd.   werig wigges sæd.

'There lay many a man destroyed with spears, northern men (or A (many a) northern man) shot over the shield, and Scottish too, weary, sated with war.'

The sg. number of A's *guma norþerna* does not translate easily into PE unless we repeat 'many a' from the translation of the phrase *secg monig* (nom. sg.) in the previous line, to which *guma norþerna* is precisely parallel grammatically. There is a fairly close parallel to the kind of construction we have in A in And 1116b–1118a:

> And 1116b–1118
>
>   Þa wæs rinc manig,
> guðfrec guma, ymb þæs geongan feorh
> breostum onbryrded to þam beadulace.

'Then was many a man, (many a) warrior eager for battle, excited in his breast to the battle for the youth's life.'[2]

That the nom. sg. *guma norþerna*, as in A, represents the original poem is suggested by the adherence to sg. number throughout the rest of the sentence in all texts (*scoten, Scittisc, werig, sæd*). Its replacement by the nom. pl. *guman norðerne*, to which B, C and D bear witness, might, as Campbell suggests (Campbell 1938: 103), have arisen by prospective dittography of the initial *n* of *norðerne*;[3] but whatever the cause, the pl. *guman*, once introduced into the text, was found acceptable to at least four subsequent copyists (the scribes of B-C*, B, C and D), presumably because it is semantically (if not grammatically) appropriate as a reference to more than one man.

A second example of a rather similar kind is PCP D 15 *sūme* (H, T *sume*):

PCP H 15b–16   PCP D 15b–16

forðæm hi his sume ðorfton   forðæm hie his sūme ðorfton

---

[2]   *Andreas* is cited here from Brooks 1961: 36. Krapp's ASPR edition of the poem (Krapp 1932) prints 1118b as the beginning of a new sentence, but this arrangement is stylistically suspect and makes for translation difficulties.

[3]   A's *-a* in *norþerna* may, as Campbell thinks, be a slip for the normal *-e* of the nom. sg. masc. adjective, made under the influence of the *-a* of the preceding word *guma*.

Ða ðe læden.spræce læste cuðon.   ða ðe lædenspræce læste cuðon.

   H: '[...] for some of them who knew least Latin had need of it.'
   D: '[...] for those who knew least Latin had need of one of it (?).'

The *his* ('of it') of line 15b refers to the English translation of the *Cura Pastoralis* that King Alfred has commissioned and had duplicated so that his bishops might each receive a copy. Dobbie suspects that a later hand was responsible for the abbreviating macron above *u* in D's *sūme* (Dobbie 1942: 110). Presumably the expanded form implied is *sumne* or *summe*, the acc. sg. masc. (on *summe* for *sumne* see *OEG* §484); but the result is metrical irregularity (the verse, previously a normal Sievers' type C, becomes a type A with polysyllabic anacrusis of a most unusual kind; see Bliss 1967: 40–42 (§§46–48) and 127, Table III) and obscure syntax (my translation of the D version above is offered tentatively). H's *sume* is nom. pl. masc. It seems likely that the grammatical apposition between *hi* and *sume* ('some of them'; see Bosworth & Toller 1898: s.v. *sum*, II.2) was the cause of the difficulty which led to the change.

   There are a few cases in which the internal grammar of clauses has been reorganized slightly without any obvious motive. PCP 9 T *romwarena betst*, 'the best of Romans', with gen. pl. *romwarena*, in place of H, D *romwara bet(e)st*, 'the best Roman', with nom. sg. *romwara*, is a clear case of grammatical modification but the motive behind it is opaque. It involves the substitution of a partitive gen. construction for the simple nom. adjective and noun, possibly under the influence of the grammar of the preceding a-verse, *rod(e)ra wearde*, 'to the guardian of the heavens'. A similarly modest (and equally inexplicable) adjustment of grammatical relations, again with nugatory consequences for the sense, is CFB 10 B *hæþenum*, 'heathen' (adjective, dat. pl. masc.) for A, C, D *hæþenra*, 'of heathens' (noun, gen. pl.):

   CFB 10 C   CFB 10 B

on hæþenra hæfteclommum.   on hæþenum hæfteclammum.

   C: '[...] in the fetters of heathens [...]'
   B: '[...] in heathen fetters [...]'

The word-order of OE verse is more variable than prose, and sometimes unusual arrangements, though transparent enough, could provoke ill-advised modifications of the internal grammar of clauses. An example is SB1 57:

SB2 54–55	SB1 57–58
ne magon þec nu heonan adon hyrste þa readan	Ne mæg þe nu heonon adon hyrsta þy readan.
ne gold ne sylfor ne þinra goda nán	ne gold ne seolfor ne þinra goda nán

SB2: 'Red jewels may not secure your release from here, nor gold nor silver nor any of your goods'

The meaning of SB1 is difficult to render in translation because the modifications it contains have not been properly integrated into the grammar of the clause: the verb *mæg* is left without any obvious subject, and there is a discrepancy between the gender and number of *hyrsta [...] readan* — the noun is historically fem., and the number and case here are supposedly pl., either nom. or acc. — and the instr. sg. masc. or neut. demonstrative *þy*. However, the difference of number in the verb (sg. *mæg* beside SB2's pl. *magon*) and the use of the instr. demonstrative in SB1 presumably imply an intended meaning of the order of 'You may not now escape hence by means of your golden ornament', though this inter-pretation is only partly supported by the SB1 text as it stands. Mitchell accepts the SB1 version as one of a 'hard core of examples in which plural subject is (or appears to be) preceded by a singular verb' (Mitchell 1985: §1522–24, quoted by Moffat 1990: 73–74); but it is difficult to agree, in view of the SB2 variant which effectively removes it. I stand by the comments on this variant that I made in my 1979 article (Orton 1979b: 190): that the transmitter responsible for this modification in SB1 was misled by the late occurrence of the subject of the verb in a clause which has the basic order: V, O, S (*magon, þec* and *hyrste þa readan* respectively in SB2), began to alter the grammar of the first half of the line, but failed to follow through either in the b-verse or in the rest of the clause.

In this last example, a failure on the part of the transmitter to grasp the structure of the whole clause he was copying has led him to introduce a corruption into the text. The same factor undoubtedly contributed to the corruption *me* in PCP T 11 (H, D *min*). Below, H stands for the readings of the H and D versions:

PCP H 11–12a	PCP T 11–12a
Siððan min on englisc ælfred kyning	Seððan me on englesc. ælfræd cynincg
Awende worda gehwelc	awende. worda gehwilc.

'Afterwards King Alfred turned every word of me (*or* T turned me, every word) into English [...]'

The scribe of T, or of one of its antecedents, has anticipated the meaning of the whole clause, but got it wrong: the direct object of the verb *awende* is *gehwilc worda*, 'every word', with *min*, 'of me', dependent on the phrase. Misled by the delay in the appearance of the direct object, our scribe has assumed that the object of Alfred's translation is simply 'me', the *Cura Pastoralis* text that is being made to speak directly to the reader. The punctuation confirms that the scribe thought he knew what he was doing; but the break in the syntax of verse 12a in T is enough to indicate that something has gone wrong with this version of the text.

A curiously similar mistake is revealed in line 3 of the W-S *ylda* texts of Cæd.[4] Here is the line in context, with H representing the W-S *ylda* group as a whole, and T standing for all other surviving versions of the poem (with the exception of text B, on which see below):

Cæd T 3b–4   Cæd H 3b–4

swa he wundra gehwæs   swa he wundra gehwilc
éce drihten ór onstealde.   ece drihten ord astealde.

'[...] how he, the eternal lord, established the beginning of every wonder (*or* H the beginning, every wonder).'

Whereas *wundra gehwæs* in T is a gen. phrase dependent on the direct object *ór* in the following line, *wundra gehwilc* in H is grammatically parallel with *ord* and so introduces a new parallelism into the text. It may be noted that the phrase *or(d) onstellan*, which occurs elsewhere in OE verse, invariably takes a dependent gen. construction (Bwf 2407, R3.59, XSt 113). The sense and the style in H is relatively clumsy. The scribe responsible for introducing *gehwilc* (identifiable with the maker of the archetype text of the W-S *ylda* group) either failed to anticipate *ord* (or *or*) as the direct object of the verb in his exemplar and converted *wundra gehwæs* into its direct object, or simply did not understand the dependence of the gen. noun phrase on *ord* (or *or*). This latter explanation is a likely one in view of the fact that the construction of *gehwa* with dependent gen. that we find in T (and most other texts of Cæd) is almost confined to poetry in OE.[5] It is therefore easy to imagine a transmitter

---

[4]   See above, §3.2 for this variant viewed in the broader context.

[5]   Toller 1921: s.v. *gehwa*, A1(2), identifies a single prose instance in the later manuscripts of the *OE Bede* (Miller 1890: MSS O, B, Ca 194/17 *manna gehwa*, 'every man').

who was unused to poetic language being stumped by *wundra gehwæs*. Nor was the transmitter of the W-S *ylda* group's archetype the only one to be puzzled by the construction. The B text of the W-S *eorðan* group has 3b *wundra fela*, 'many wonders', instead of *wundra gehwæs*, 'every wonder'. This substitution, like the one I have just been discussing, deprives *or* (or *ord*) in the following line of its true grammatical role in the sentence by replacing *wundra gehwæs* with a new and independent object of the verb; but again, the sense that results is poor: in B, the eternal lord 'established the beginning, many wonders'. The beginning of what? one might ask. The scribe who substituted *fela* for *gehwæs* was undoubtedly influenced in his chosen modification by familiarity with *wundra fe(a)la* as a poetic formula (Exo 10, OrW 7, And 564, 584, 699, R21.8, R83.10).

The North. *eordu* texts of Cæd provide another possible example of grammatical confusion on the part of a transmitter, though the evidence is not entirely convincing. The hypothesis was put forward first, as far as I know, by A. H. Smith in his edition of the poem (Smith 1968: 35, §18). The texts of the relevant passage in the two North. versions of the poem are given below, represented by M and Di respectively:

Cæd M 5–6	Cæd Di 5–6
he aerist scop aelda barnū	he aerst scoop eordu bearnum
heben til hrofe haleg scepen.	efen to hrofe halig sceppend

Notes on the text: Di 5 *uerst* with *a* added above *u*.

M: 'He, the holy creator, first made heaven as a roof for the children of men.'

Di: 'He, the holy creator, first made the earth for the children, (and) heaven as a roof.'

Better sense would result if *eordu* were taken as a gen. sg. here ('He, the holy creator, first made heaven as a roof for the children of earth'). In the W-S *eorðan* group, 5 *eorðan* is certainly to be taken as gen. sg.; but there is no other instance of a weak declension fem. noun with gen. sg. -*u* in early North. to support the interpretation of *eordu* as gen. sg.; on the contrary, the normal gen. sg. ending on such nouns in early North. appears to have been -*an*. If, on the other hand, *eordu* is acc., like Cæd L 9 *foldu* (M has *fold⌣*; see above, §1.1), as Smith suggests it may be, the

---

For the normal distinction between poetic and prose usage, compare MB8.6 *anra gehwæm* with *ælcum men* in the corresponding prose passage.

meaning of the whole line would render the order of events in the remainder of the poem confusing, implying that earth was made before heaven, and involving a repetition of the making of the earth in the last three lines of the poem (7–9, 'Then the guardian of mankind, eternal lord, almighty lord, later made middle-earth, the earth for men'). Thus *eordu*, if acc. sg., may well be itself a corrupt form imposed as a result of a misconception of the structure of the clause in which it appears. Subsequent dissatisfaction on the part of a later transmitter with *eordu* as an acc. sg. would, of course, provide a welcome explanation for the substitution of *aelda*, 'of men', as in M, for *eordu*, though the question of the priority of these two basic readings in line 5 of Cæd is a very difficult one (see further Orton 1998). Here we need do no more than recognize *eordu* as a corruption provided that it was intended as an acc. sg. form.

If this last example suggests a possible error over a noun's case, SnS B 75–76 shows the consequences of a misinterpretation of the function of a grammatical case:

SnS A 75–76	SnS B 75–76
he [.]s modigra middangearde	he is modigra middangeardes.
staðole strengra ðōn ealra stana	staðole he is strengra þone ealle stána
gripe	gripe.

> A: 'He is braver than the world, stronger in its foundation than the grip of all stones.'
> B: 'He is braver than the foundation of the world, he is stronger than all stones in grip.'

The difficulties presented by B's version of these lines are best dealt with first. In spite of the scribe's punctuation-point at the end of B 75, this line is difficult to construe as a self-contained clause: the comparative adjective *modigra*, 'braver', indicates comparison with something or someone else; and although comparison might be with 'the earth' (*middangeardes*), its gen. sg. inflexion is difficult to explain on this basis. One fairly obvious solution to this difficulty is to take *staðole*, 'foundation', in the next line as part of the same clause as B 75: it is a noun in the dat. and may therefore denote what the Pater Noster is being compared with here. This enables us to fit in the gen. sg. *middangeardes* as dependent upon *staðole*, as my translation indicates. But this interpretation involves a peculiar arrangement from the stylistic point of view: a clausal division falls in the middle of a verse (B 76a). Such divisions are by no means unheard-of in OE poetry, but one cannot but be suspicious here of the verbal parallelism with the previous verse in the sequence: *he is* + comparative adjective, particularly as the sequence seems so well integrated into the metrical structure in the first instance but so clumsily integrated in the second.

Assuming, therefore, that B's version has undergone amendment, we must examine the quality of A's version of these lines, and the question of how B's version might be derived from it. In A 75, the dat. sg. *middangearde* represents the concept with which the Pater Noster is being compared: the Pater Noster is 'braver than the world'. In A 76, the reader is initially inclined to take *staðole strengra* as the same kind of construction, i.e. comparative adjective with dependent dat., 'stronger than the foundation'; but this interpretation collapses when we come to the b-verse, which consists of a 'than' clause which clearly supplies the point of comparison implied by comparative *strengra* (possibly 'stronger than the grip of all stones'). This means that dat. *staðole* must have some other function and the most obvious alternative is that it is a dat. of respect ('stronger in its foundation'), comparable with Bwf 789 *mægene strengest*, 'strongest in might'. This function, however, is more often performed by the gen. in OE poetry (cf. Bwf 196 *mægenes strengest*, 886 *wiges heard*, etc.) than the dat. It seems likely enough that this unusual use of the dat. in *staðole* is the key to B's corruption: a scribe, assuming that both datives (*middangearde, staðole*) were comparative, and consequently finding the 'than' clause in 76b redundant, made *middangearde* dependent on *staðole* by converting the former word into a gen., and then added *he is* before *strengra* in imitation of the construction in the previous line 75. Here, perhaps, is evidence of the fairly strenuous efforts that transmitters sometimes made to clarify such difficulties as they encountered in the texts that passed through their hands.

A rather simpler case, though one not without its own share of difficulties for the interpreter, is Cæd 9 *on foldu* (North. *eordu* texts; W-S *ylda* texts *on foldum*, W-S *eorðe* texts *on folden*) beside *foldu* (L; M *fold˘*, W-S *eorðan* texts *foldan*). The consequences of this variation emerge from a comparison of the L and Di versions of the closing lines of the poem:

Cæd L 7–9	Cæd Di 7–9
tha middingard moncynnæs uard	da. middumgeard moncinnes peard.
eci dryctin æfter tiadæ	éci drintinc efter tiade
firum foldu frea allmehtig.	firum. on foldu frea allmechtig.

'Then the guardian of mankind, the eternal lord, the almighty ruler, later made the earth (*middingard*), the earth (*foldu*) for men (*or* Di made the earth for men on the earth (*on foldu*)).'

My translation follows Dobbie (Dobbie 1942: 199) in taking *foldu* in L (and in the other manuscripts of the poem which contain this variant) as acc. sg., the object of *tiade*, 'made', and grammatically parallel with acc. sg. *middingard* (M *middungeard*). Some commentators have taken *foldu* as gen. sg. (Wuest 1906: 225; Frampton 1924: 9), though this involves logical difficulties: the earth would be described as created 'for the men of earth' if *foldu* were gen., so the acc. sg. is to be preferred. My translation shows how Di's version involves a similar logical difficulty (the earth is made for men on earth), and there can be no doubt that *on* is a corruption.

Di's phrase *on foldu* presents a difficulty of interpretation which must be considered before we tackle the question of why *on* was added to the text at this point. The context suggests that *foldu* should be dat. sg. after the preposition *on* ('on earth'); but early North. texts offer no supporting instance of a weak declension noun in the dat. sg. with -*u* (Smith 1968: 3, note 3). Perhaps the preposition *on* was added to the text without the subsequent modification of the inflexion of the noun that the new preposition required. The sequence: *on foldu* seems to have misled the redactor of the W-S *ylda* version of the poem: the phrase *on foldum* that we find in all texts of this group has the noun in the dat. pl.; but although the noun *folde* may be pl. in OE in the sense of 'countries', such a specialized meaning is inappropriate here. It seems very likely that the transmitter who wrote the archetypal text of the W-S *ylda* group took *on foldu* in his exemplar as containing an error *foldu* for *foldum* (no doubt he assumed that an abbreviating macron had been omitted by mistake by the scribe of his exemplar) and expanded it to *foldum* without considering the implications of a dat. pl. for the sense. In this case, the preservation during transmission of a dialectal form (*foldu*) has misled a W-S-trained scribe into introducing a corruption into the text.

This substitution of *foldum* for *foldu* was a secondary corruption which must have occurred at a fairly late stage in the transmission of the poem. Underlying it is the addition of 9 *on*, which must have happened relatively early in the textual history of Cæd, for it is present in the North. *eordu* group, the archetype of which could scarcely be younger than the tenth century (Di, the earliest of the three texts, is 11th c.), and may have been a good deal older. Why was *on* added? The misinterpretation and rejection of an exemplar's *foldu* as a gen. sg. rather than an acc. sg. will not account for it, because the addition of *on* would be no improvement: as we saw above, the same logical difficulty (the inhabitants of earth are made to pre-exist its creation) would remain. Perhaps the best available explanation is one based on the potentially confusing *position* of *foldu* in versions of the text that lack *on*, for example L. The grammatical parallelism with *middingard* in line 7 would be more obvious if the order of *firum foldu* were reversed. Furthermore, we should note that when *folde*, or an inflected form of it, occurs as the second fully stressed element of a verse, it is very often governed by a preposition in OE poetry generally,[6] and the most frequently used preposition is *on*.[7] The unthinking introduction of *on* under the influence of the pattern of these common collocations, or others that echo it (e.g. the frequent formula *menn on* (or *ofer*) *moldan*, 'men on (or over) the earth') is not difficult to envisage; but the corruption betrays the scribe as someone whose grasp of the meaning of what he was copying did not extend much beyond the boundaries of the phrase he was working on at that particular moment.

§4.2.2.2 Mistakes about parts of speech

Quite frequently we find evidence suggesting that a transmitter has assigned a word in his exemplar to the wrong class. In the following example it is probable that the noun *æt*, 'food' was omitted from SB1 125 because a scribe mistook it for the preposition *æt*, 'at', which would not make any sense in the context:

SB2 119b–20a	SB1 124b–25a
bið þōn wyrmes giefl	bið þōn wyrma gifel
æt on eorþan	on eorþan

'It will then be the morsel of the worm (*or* SB1 of worms), (SB2 food) in the earth.'

The essential meaning is unaffected, but metrical form breaks down (SB1 125a *on eorðan* is one syllable short of the requisite minimum of four per verse) and the amended version loses an instance of the stylistic device of

---

[6]   I count 51 instances, with 14 exceptions: Ele 973, HbM 38, Gen 1561, 1658, 1752, 2553, XSt 685, Phx 352, FtM 30, R7.9, Bwf 1137, Mld 54, Aza 119, MCh1.35.

[7]   I count 26 instances: Gen 1487, XSt 531, And 1427, SB1 142, DrR 132, Chr 807, Glc 396, 808, Phx 74, 174, GfM 1, Sfr 75, FtM 26, Bwf 2975, P59.6.3, 76.12.2, 77.25.4, 118.98.2, EgD 18, Run 88, SnS 298, Mnl 143, Mx2 33, Crd 56, Gl2 2, SFt 64.

variation (*giefl*, *æt*) which is typical of poetry but practically unknown in prose.

That misapprehensions of this kind could sometimes lead to more elaborate modifications of the received text is shown by the following example from SnS, in which the unsatisfactory meaning of the A text points to a misinterpretation of the word *full* as the adjective 'full' rather than the noun, 'cup':

SnS B 25	SnS A 25
warað windes full worpað hine deofol	worað he windes full worp [.........]ofol

Notes on the text: in A 25, the number of points indicates only the approximate number of letters missing from the manuscript.

'He shall inhabit the cup of the wind (*or* A he shall wander full of wind); the devil will pelt him [...]'

Kemble, in his edition of SnS (Kemble 1848: 176), suggested that *windes full* means literally *poculum venti* and translated B's version as 'He shall inhabit the void expanse' (Kemble 1848: 135). Menner preferred A's reading: *worað* is 'wanders' and *windes full* is translated as 'full of wind', i.e. 'empty', 'devoid of wisdom' (Menner 1941: 108). There is, however, no parallel elsewhere in OE for this phrase or for the image Menner thinks it denotes, whereas Kemble's interpretation is lent some support from the kenning *yða ful*, literally 'cup of the waves', for the sea, in Bwf 1208, which reflects the same kind of imagination that could have produced *windes full* as an image of metaphysical emptiness.[8] If I am right in preferring B's reading here, we must assume that A's substitution of *worað*, 'wanders', for *warað*, 'inhabits', resulted from a transmitter's impression that his exemplar form was the adjective 'full', which would be incompatible with a transitive verb such as *warað*. The image that results, however, carries ludicrous overtones of flatulence.

Both the examples I have considered so far in this category seem to hint at a degree of ignorance of (or indifference to) aspects of poetic style. My next example, however, probably shows little more than the inveterate English difficulty with Irish proper names. Below, B stands for the readings of B, C and D:

---

[8] We may also compare the metaphorical cup of death in Glc 991 *deopan deaðweges* and possibly Mx1 78 *deop deada wæg*; see Brown 1940: 389–99.

Brb B 53–56	Brb A 53–56
Gewitan him þa norðmenn	gewitan him þa norþmen.
nægledcnearrum	nẹgledcnearrū.
dreorig daroða láf on dyngesmere.	dreorig daraða laf. ón dingesmere.
ofer deop wæter dyflen secean.	ofer deop wæter. difelin secan.
eft íra land æwiscmóde.	[&]eft hira land. æwiscmode.

Notes on the text: A 53 *norþmen* with the *þ* added superscript, perhaps by a later hand. A 56 *&* added superscript.

'The northmen, sad leavings of spears, departed, ashamed, in nailed ships on to Dingesmere to seek Dublin, the land of the Irish once more (*or* A and their country once more), across the deep water.'

The words *irland*, 'Ireland', and *iras*, 'the Irish' (the latter possibly a back-formation from *irland*) are not recorded in OE before the tenth century (Campbell 1938: 116), so it is not difficult to see why the A scribe (or a predecessor of his) should have stumbled over the gen. pl. *ira*. But he made reasonably good alternative sense out of the word (it is tempting to assume that he regarded it as an error in his exemplar) by turning it into the gen. pl. 3rd person pronoun *hira*, 'their'. Campbell suggests that *&*, 'and', was added in A because the scribe 'was not pleased with the verse'(Campbell 1938: 117). It is true that the addition of *and* would have made the metrical shape of the verse more conventional: *eft hira land* on its own might have been regarded as passable metrically on the assumption that *eft* bore full metrical stress and carried the alliteration, but the metrical pattern in the verse would still be very unusual (Bliss's type 2B2-; see Bliss 1967: 126). The addition of *and* produces a more regular general type, though the actual sub-type that the verse represents, Bliss's type 2B2a, is also rare in *Beowulf* (three instances; see Bliss 1967: 126). However, it seems to me more likely that the addition of *and* to the text in A was encouraged by a misunderstanding of the adverb *eft*: its meaning in B and the other sound texts is almost certainly 'once more' or 'back': the Norsemen withdrew to their point of origin, and *eft ira land* is simply an elaboration of *Dyflen*, 'Dublin'. The scribe who added *and* may, however, have taken *eft* in the sense of 'afterwards', a meaning which the addition of the conjunction would reinforce. In any case, the introduction of *and* does effectively divide the Norse retreat into two stages, the first extending to Dublin, the second to the tribal hinterland. The poem's historical information is thus somewhat distorted by these changes in A.

We have already identified the D text of Brb as a rich source of fantastic distortions of the received text (above, §4.1). Its handling of the infinitive verb *bryttigan* in Brb 60 is well up to the standard of inventiveness set by some of its other corruptions that we have already looked at. Below, C represents the uncorrupted text as it stands in A, B and C:

Brb C 60–62a	Brb D 60–62a
leton hym behindon hrá brittigan.	læton him behindan hra bryttinga.
salowigpadan þone sweartan hrefn.	salowigpadan þone sweartan hræfn
hyrnednebban.	hyrnetnebban.

C: 'Behind them, they (*sc.* the West-Saxons) let the black raven, dark-coated, horny-beaked, enjoy the corpses, [...]'

D: 'They left behind them the corpses of the (?) British', etc.

It is certainly possible that D's *bryttinga* is nothing more than an accidentally mangled version of the infinitive verb *bryttigan*, 'to enjoy', an Anglian form of the W-S *bryttian* of the A text (*OEG* §757); but there must be at least a suspicion that it is intended to be a noun containing the suffix *-ing*, 'inhabitants of' (as in, for example, *Centingas*, 'inhabitants of Kent'), in the gen. pl., meaning 'of the British'. The finite verb *leton* (*læton*), actually 'allowed' with dependent infinitive here, could alternatively mean 'left' in OE and this is how the D scribe no doubt took it; but problems result later in the sentence, when the beasts of battle — raven, eagle and wolf — become, inappropriately, simply other things 'left behind' on the battlefield by Æþelstan and Eadmund on their triumphant return to Wessex. It seems quite likely that this change in D was provoked by the unfamiliarity of the form *bryttigan* and, perhaps, of its meaning here, 'enjoy', which seems to be confined to verse in OE.

A similar misunderstanding of an Anglian form seems to underlie the corruption *tida*, probably intended as the pl. noun 'times', in line 8 of the W-S *ylda*-text of Cæd. The consequences of this change and its probable cause are revealed when we compare a representative text of the W-S *ylda* group, such as H, with the earliest North. version of the poem, as represented by M. Both of these manuscript texts of the poem have been quoted in full above (§1.1; on H, see further §3.2), where their variants were considered from a different perspective. Here are their versions of line 8:

Cæd M 8	Cæd H 8
eci dryctin æfter tiadæ	éce drihten. Æfter tida

It seems fairly clear that *tida* represents an attempt to make sense of the North. form *tiadæ* (or some similar form), the pret. indic. 3rd person sg. of an infinitive that may be reconstructed as **teogan* (Dobbie 1937: 39; Smith 1968: 33; *OEG* §§238(2c), 761(2)). The W-S *eorðan* and *eorðe* texts, all of which successfully convert this line into standard W-S, have *teode*, the expected W-S form of the verb. This change to *tida* has important implications for the meaning of the text, and is linked with another change in H. Below T stands for the accurately transmitted version, H for the *ylda* texts generally:

Cæd T 5–9   Cæd H 5–9

he ærest sceop eorðan bearnū   He ærest gesceop ylda bearnū
heofon to hrofe halig scyppend.   heofon to hrofe. halig scyppend
þa middangeard moncynnes weard   middangearde mancynnes weard
éce drihten æfter teode   éce drihten. Æfter tida
firum foldan frea ælmihtig.   firum on foldum frea ælmyhtig

'He, the holy creator, first made   'He, the holy creator, first made
heaven a roof for the children of   heaven as a roof for the children of
earth. Then the guardian of   men, for the earth, the guardian of
mankind, the eternal lord, the   mankind, eternal lord, almighty ruler,
almighty ruler, later arranged   after periods of time, for men in
the world, the earth for men.'   the countries.'

In H, the final sentence of the text has been restructured and joined with the previous one (5–6) to accommodate the absence of a verb caused by the conversion of *tiadæ* to the noun *tida*: by changing the acc. sg. *middangeard* in 7 to the dat. sg. *middangearde* and omitting 7 *þa*, 'Then', the roof of heaven becomes a purpose-built structure covering the earth and the people who live on it; but there is no actual description of God's arranging of the earth, as there is in T and its closest textual relatives; the W-S *ylda* version describes only the making of heaven. Despite this narrowing of the meaning of the text as a whole, we can surely see evidence here of editorial intelligence at work. This intelligence was no doubt activated by the failure to see that *tiadæ* is a verb and its consequent replacement with a noun; but it is difficult to judge how many levels of activity these changes to the *ylda* version involved. It may be that *tida* was introduced by one copyist and the related modifications made by one of his successors in response to it; but there can be little doubt about the initial misunderstanding that led to the curious version of Cæd that the *ylda* group presents.

The Ca text of Cæd provides my final example of a corruption arising from a mistake about which part of speech a word represents. Here are T's and Ca's versions of the passage affected:

Cæd T 3–4	Cæd Ca 3–4
[...] swa he wundra gehwæs éce drihten ór onstealde.	[...] swa he wuldres gehwæs ece drihten. ord onstealde

'[...] as he established the beginning of every wonder (*or* Ca of every glory).'

The effect of Ca's substitution of *wuldres* for *wundra* is to convert 3 *gehwæs* from a pronoun into an adjective. Although the sense ('every') is unchanged, and the difference between *wundra*, 'wonders' and *wuldres*, 'glory' is scarcely vital, Ca's version is stylistically inferior in putting alliteration on the same element, *wuldor(-)*, in both halves of the line (3a *wera wuldorfæder*). The word *gehwa* in the sense of 'every' (either as pronoun or adjective) is confined to verse in OE (see above, §4.2.2.1). The scribe responsible for this change appears to have been unfamiliar with the pronominal usage at least.

In most of the passages I have discussed in this section, it seems to me that the evidence for actual misapprehensions on the part of transmitters about which part of speech they were dealing with is reasonably convincing. It might, however, be argued in some of these cases that the amending transmitter knew what his exemplar meant and had no difficulty in interpreting its linguistic forms, but intervened in the transmission of the text simply because he preferred a different arrangement and thought the poem would be improved by imposing it. But here we must distinguish between constructive responses to existing corruptions, as in the case of the final lines of Cæd in the W-S *ylda* version, and the deliberate rejection of valid forms recognized as such. Obviously we must not attribute wanton interference with the received text to transmitters without very good evidence, and I submit that we have seen no such evidence so far in this study. The job of a copyist was to copy. The largely accurate and responsible reproduction of many OE and Latin texts in both prose and verse during the Anglo-Saxon period testifies to the truth of this. Obviously we should remain open to conviction on the possibility of a constructive competence in OE scribes which would enable them to remodel, improve or modernize texts at will in a spirit of active stewardship rather than passive subservience to the text; but again, this kind of attitude must not be assumed without good evidence.

§4.2.3 Other mistakes about the grammar of the received text

This category contains instances of corruptions that seem to have arisen from a variety of misconceptions about the grammar of the exemplar text. Muddles about case and number preponderate, though most of the changes indicated are difficult to account for in any detail.

SB2 108	SB1 113

Bið seo tunge totogen on tyn healfe   Beoð hira tungan totogenne on tyn healfa

> SB2: 'The tongue is torn apart into ten pieces [...]'
> SB1: 'Their tongues are torn apart into ten pieces [...]'

Here number is involved. The general context makes it clear that one (generic) body is the object of the worms' depredations; but the references in the preceding lines to several multiple body-parts — hands (108 *handa*), jaws and gums (109 *geaglas*, *goman*), sinews (110 *sina*), fingers (111 *fingras*) and ribs (112 *rib*) — may have made the SB1 scribe forget that a singular body represents all bodies in the poem. Thinking, therefore, of several (or all) bodies, he changes the generic singular tongue to a plurality of tongues.

Another example of a mistake over number is Dan 296 *dyde* (Aza 17 *dydon*): Dan's sg. verb is clearly wrong; the subject of the verb is 297 *user yldran*, 'our ancestors' (Aza *yldran usse*). I cannot see why the mistake was made.

An equally inexplicable corruption, arising apparently out of a misconception about gender, is Brb 55 D *deopne* (apparently acc. sg. masc., A, B, C *deop*, acc. sg. neut., 'deep'): the adjective modifies the noun *wæter*, 'water', normally neut. in OE, so the masc. gender of *deopne* is puzzling.

Finally, Gll 5 J *worulde* appears to be a corruption of C's *world*. J's form is presumably dat. sg., but this does not suit the context of the clause, which requires the nom. sg. *world*, as in C.

§4.3 MISAPPREHENSIONS OF MEANING

§4.3.1 Polysemes and homonyms

Sometimes a variant will suggest that a word known to transmitters was interpreted in the wrong sense. A probable instance of this is Brb C 41 *folcstede* in a passage which I have already discussed in another connection. Here are the B and C texts of the relevant passage:

Brb B 40b–41	Brb C 40b–41
her wæs his maga sceard.	her wæs his maga sceard.
freonda gefylled on folcstede.	freonda gefylled on his folcstede.

'here was his son mutilated, killed *freonda (?)* on the battlefield (*or* C in his dwelling-place).'

As we saw earlier (§3.3 above), C's addition of *his* might imply that Constantine's son died in Scotland, and even that the site of the battle lay in Scottish territory. We cannot know if this amendment was based on any independent information about the site of the battle or its consequences; what is fairly clear is that the C scribe failed to see that *folcstede* means 'battlefield' here, and added *his* as appropriate to the sense in which he took the word.

A second example of a mistake over the meaning of a word is provided by Aza and Dan:

Aza 61–64	Dan 345–48
ac wæs in þam ofne þa se engel cwom	þa was on þam ofne. þær se engel becwóm
windig & wynsum wedere onlicust	windig & wynsum. wedere gelicost.
þon on sumeres tid sended weorþeð	þon hit on sumeres tíd sended weorðeð.
dropena dreorung mid dæges hwile.	dropena drearung. on dæges hwile.

Notes on the text: 61 *ofne*: MS *hofne* with *h* underdotted for deletion.

Aza: 'But it was windy and pleasant in the oven when the angel came, most like the weather when the falling of drops is sent in summer in the daytime.'

Dan: 'Then it was windy and pleasant where the angel came in the oven, most like the storm when it is sent in summer, the falling of drops in the daytime.'

Only Dan has *hit* in 347a. Its referent is *wedere* in the previous line, which shows that this noun was taken in the sense of 'storm', for the meaning 'weather', as in Aza, is less compatible with *hit* ('like the weather when it is sent in summer [...]'). This affects the grammatical function of *drearung* in Dan 348: in Aza, *dreorung*, 'falling', is the only subject of the passive verb *sended weorþeð* in 63, whereas in Dan *drearung* is an elaboration of *hit* which in turn refers back to *wedere*, 'storm'. Although both versions are quite intelligible, it seems to me probable that Aza has the earlier version of these lines, if only because it is much easier to construct a plausible chain of misunderstandings and responses to explain Dan's version on the basis of Aza's than vice-versa. I suggest, therefore, that Dan's transmitter has misunderstood *wedere*, actually 'weather', as 'storm'. As a consequence, the 'when' clause in the next line seemed to lack a pronoun ('most like the storm when (it) is sent in the summer') so that *hit* was added. This led to no semantic or grammatical problems in the following line: *drearung* became a variation on *wedere* instead of the sole subject of the passive verb as it is in Aza. If we wanted to explain Aza's version as a distortion of Dan's, we would have to explain why *hit* in Dan 347 did not alert the Aza scribe to the fact that *wedere* meant 'storm' rather than 'weather', which would be more difficult. D's corruption was encouraged by two factors: the ambiguity of *wedere* and the relatively late appearance of *dreorung* as the sole subject of the verb, so that the transmitter failed to anticipate it. This is yet another example of the kind of narrow focus on the immediate context which was evidently a common cause of ill-advised adjustments to the text on the part of transmitters. Here, however, it has to be admitted that the results in Dan testify to the editorial skills of the amending transmitter.

A comparison of the two versions of a lengthy passage from SB shows the radical adjustments to the text which were felt to be necessary when a single common word was taken in the wrong sense. This is SB2 39–45, SB1 42–48, quoted below:[9]

SB2 39–45	SB1 42–48
þær þu þōn hogode her on life	Forðan þu ne hogodest her on life
þenden ic þe in worulde wunian sceolde	syððan ic ðe on worulde wunian sceolde
þæt þu wære þurh flæsc & þurh firenlustas	þæt ðu wære þurh flæsc & þurh fyrenlustas
strong gestyred & gestaþelad þurh mec.	strange gestryned. & gestaðolod þurh me
& ic wæs gæst on þe from gode sended	& Ic wæs gast on ðe fram gode sended
næfre þu mec swa heardra helle wita	næfre ðu me mid swa heardū helle witum
ne gearwode þurh þinra neoda lust	ne generedest þurh þinra meda lust.

'If you had then thought (*or* SB1 Because you did not think) here in this life, while (*or* SB1 when) I was compelled to dwell in you in the world,

---

9   For a detailed discussion of these lines, see Moffat 1987; but cf. my remarks below.

that you were powerfully governed by (*or* SB1 strongly begotten through) the flesh and sinful desires, and strengthened by me, and that I was a spirit in you sent from God, never would you have prepared for me (*or* SB1 never did you protect me against) such grim torments of hell, because of the sensuous appetite you had for the things you desired.'

We should first note several minor errors and difficulties in both versions, some of them perhaps connected with the basic reorganization that the passage has undergone, others independent of it. SB1 47 *mid* is accepted by the poem's editors (including the latest: see Moffat 1990: 71) as a corruption of *wið*, 'against', and as we saw earlier (§2.1.1.2), SB1 48 *meda* is an error for *nieda*, a variant form of SB2's gen. pl. *neoda*. In SB2 44, the genitive pl. forms *heardra [...] wita* are not easy to explain on the basis of the grammar of the text as it stands: but a large question-mark hangs over SB2 45 *gearwode*, the verb associated with them, which fails to supply the alliterating *n* which is needed for the line (the head-stave is clearly *neoda*): anyone wishing to emend *gearwode* would do well to look for a verb the stem of which begins with *n* and which takes a gen. object. Moffat hits on the same solution I reached over twenty years ago: that *gearwode* is an error for *genearwode*, from *genearwian*, 'to cramp, press tightly' (my gloss was 'afflicted'), but I retain doubts about this suggestion. For one thing, it takes us no nearer to the archetypal reading (SB1 has the quite different verb *generedest*); and for another, *genearwian* does not take the gen.

In my 1979b discussion of this passage, I was unable to decide the question of priority, finding both versions' arrangement of clauses satisfactory. I now think I can see what might have generated the main syntactical and lexical variants. Originally I translated SB1 42 *Forðan* as 'Wherefore'; but Moffat's more recent discussion of this passage (Moffat 1987) persuades me that *Forðan* is probably the subordinating conjunction 'Because'. A consequence of this understanding of *Forðan*, as Moffat makes clear, is that there is no longer any need to regard SB1 as two sentences rather than one: a subordinate clause opens the sentence and continues down to the end of line 46; the principal clause then begins with *næfre*, 'never'. I continue to regard the whole passage as it appears in SB2 as a single sentence, also one beginning with a subordinate clause, but here a conditional clause (*þær* is, I believe, 'if'). This difference is related to the contrast between subjunctive mood of SB2 39 *hogode* and 45 *ne gearwode*, and the indicative mood of SB1 42 *ne hogodest*, 48 *ne generedest*, as well as the distinction between the positive *hogode* and the negative *ne hogodest*. These things are perhaps self-evident. The structure of the two passages, in broad outline, is therefore 'Because you didn't think [...] you never (did) [...]' (SB1) or 'If you had thought [...] you never would have (done) [...]').

Moffat has studied this passage in considerable depth; an extended version of it, SB1 42–51, SB2 39–48, is the subject of his 1987 article,[10] but he is just as puzzled by the variants as I was in 1979.[11] I now suspect that if SB2 fairly represents an earlier version of the kind that SB1 derives from (on which Moffat and I would probably agree), the changes in SB1 could all derive from an initial misunderstanding of *þær*, 'if', as in SB2 39. If this word were taken in one of its commoner senses, whether as adverb ('There') or conjunction ('Where'), I doubt if any sense could be made of the SB2 version of the passage. However, if this is the explanation for the variants, we must assume that the modifying scribe not only misunderstood his exemplar's *þær*, but also read forwards in his exemplar to see what the consequences of the changes he was contemplating would be, for the integration of SB1's grammatical variants is impressively handled. Again, this is one of those worrying cases of the modification of a text which we would be in no position to detect were it not for the survival of a somewhat more coherent and apposite version with which to compare it.

In this last case, two meanings of a common structure-word have probably been confused. In the case of CFB B 8 *denum* (dat. pl.) in place of *dene* or *dæne* (nom. pl.), we see evidence of a mistake not so much about the meaning of a word as about its application in the context. After describing the extent of King Eadmund's invasion of Mercia, the poem touches on the plight of the *dæne* before Eadmund freed them from pagan oppression:

---

[10]   Moffat 1987. Moffat slightly misrepresents the view I expressed about this passage in Orton 1979b: 188–9, taking remarks I made about the lines quoted above as applying to the extended passage he himself quotes which is three lines longer — three lines, moreoever, in which SB2 preserves alliteration in two places where it fails in SB1 (SB2 46 *gescenta*, SB1 *gesynta*; and SB2 48 *a^ncenda*, SB1 *acenneda*). Even so, whereas I originally found SB1 a somewhat better text than SB2 in the passage I quote above, Moffat has convinced me of SB2's general superiority.

[11]   Moffat 1987: 7: '[...] what reasoning prompted revision at this point in the text of *Soul and Body* remains a mystery to me'.

CFB A 8b–11a	CFB B 8b–11a
dæne wæran ær	denum wæron æror.
under norðmannum nyde gebegde	under norðmannum. nede gebæded.
ón hæþenra hæfteclōmū	on hæþenum hæfteclammum.
lange þraga	lange þrage

A: 'The Danes had previously been subdued by force under the Norsemen, in the bonds of the heathens, for a long time [...]'

B: 'They (i.e. the five boroughs) had previously been oppressed by force by the Danes, under the Norsemen, in heathen bonds for a long time [...]'

In A's version (here representing also the C and D texts), 8 *dæne*, 'the Danes', refers to the naturalized Danes of East Mercia who had long been loyal to the English throne; but the case of B's *denum* indicates that the name parallels 9 *norðmannum* which refers to the Norsemen from Ireland (see Mawer 1923: 551–57; Dobbie 1942: 150). This equation in B of *norðmen* with *dene* has a precedent in the *Anglo-Saxon Chronicle*: the annal for 787 describes the first attack on England by Norsemen who, like the Irish Norse of CFB, were almost certainly from Norway (see Stenton 1971: 239). The force is there called both *iii scipa norðmanna* (the A text omits the last word) and *scipu deniscra manna* in all texts (Plummer 1892: I, 54). The agreement of texts A, C and D on nom. pl. *dæne* (C's form is *dene*) in CFB 8 shows that this was the original reading. The tenth-century copyist who substituted *denum* for *dene* in his exemplar was doubtless misled by the use of *dene* for the Anglicized Danes of the five boroughs and assumed that the poet, like the Chronicler in 787, was content to designate the invaders *dene* in spite of their true origin.

Non-W-S forms in an exemplar could lead to semantic misinterpretations, as in the case of Brb D 39 *hryman* for *hreman* in texts A, B and C:

Brb C 39b–40a	Brb D 39b–40a
hreman ne ðorfte.	hryman ne þorfte.
meca gemanan	mecga gemanan

'He (the Scottish king Constantine) had no need to exult in (*or* D lament) the fellowship of swords (*or* D of warriors).

The verb *hrēman*, 'to exult', is poetic and occurs only once elsewhere in OE (Dan 755 *hremde*; see Campbell 1938: 110). Its stem-vowel is the *i-*

umlaut of *ō* which appears as *ē* in all OE dialects. In D the verb has been mistaken for a non-W-S form (*hrēman*) of *hrīeman* or *hrȳman*, a different word altogether with the opposite meaning of 'to lament', whose stem-vowel is the *i*-umlaut of *ēa*. The difference might appear to have political implications, raising the question of how Constantine, who fled the field where many of his kinsmen lay dead and returned to his home in the north (37–38 *se froda mid fleame com in his cyþþe norð*, 'the old (*or* wise) one came in flight to his native land in the north'), might be expected to feel about the battle. A later passage in the poem confirms what *hreman ne ðorfte* in A, B and C implies: that he 'had no reason to boast of the sword-clash' (44–45 *gelpan ne þorfte [...] bilgeslehtes*), but that need not have prevented the D scribe from seeing 39b–40 as a statement of Constantine's unheroic satisfaction at his own escape. As we have already seen, overall logical consistency was often disregarded by Anglo-Saxon scribes in their modifications of the received text. So far as we can tell, they did not often read on.

This last example is essentially a confusion of homonyms, another instance of which has already been mentioned in another connection (§3.3 above):

Brb D 40b	Brb B 40b
he wæs his mæga. sceard	her wæs his maga sceard.

D: 'He was *sceard* (? = deprived of) his kinsmen'
B: 'Here was his son mutilated'

Here the D text stands for the version of the passage in A and D, and B for B and C. As we saw earlier, what appears to have happened in B and C is that the adjective *sceard*, normally 'mutilated', 'notched' or 'hacked' in OE, has presented difficulties in the context which may have contributed to the mistaken interpretation by the B-C* redactor of what is really the gen. pl. of the noun *mǣg*, 'kinsman' as the nom. sg. of the poetic word *māga*, 'son', 'descendant'. The replacement of the pronoun *he*, 'he', with the adverb *her*, 'here', is obviously closely bound up with this misunderstanding.

§4.3.2 Exclusively poetic meanings of words

It is to be expected that words confined to verse in OE would be likelier to present difficulties for copyists than words of more general use. Some words, though they occur in both prose and verse, have special poetic meanings which might also pose problems, especially, perhaps, for attentive and conscientious scribes who were aware that the texts in their exemplars might already have suffered in transmission. I have been unable to find many unmistakable examples of variants that may plausibly be explained on the basis of this last kind of difficulty, but there are a few likely instances. The first is SB2 13–14, which shows a significant omission when compared with the corresponding text of SB1:

SB1 9–14	SB2 9–14
Sceal se gast cuman geohðum hremig	Sceal se gæst cuman gehþum hremig,
symble ymbe seofon niht sawle findan	sȳle ymb seofon niht sawle findan
þone lichoman þe hie ær lange wæg	þone lichoman þe heo ær longe wæg
þreo hund wintra butan ær þeodcyning	þreo hund wintra
ælmihtig god ende worulde	butan ær wyrce ece dryhten
wyrcan wille weoruda dryhten.	ælmihtig god ende worlde.

> SB1: 'The spirit must come lamenting with cares always every seven nights, the soul to find the body which previously it long wore, for three hundred years, unless before its expiry the king of all nations, almighty God, the lord of hosts, should decide to bring about the end of the world.'
>
> SB2 concludes: '[...] for three hundred years, unless before its expiry the eternal lord, almighty God, should bring about the end of the world.'

Gyger's view that the SB2 version of these lines 'looks generally like an ill-remembered version of' SB1 (Gyger 1969: 241) ignores the special nature of the material which SB2 lacks, chiefly the compound *þeodcyning*, which always has the secular meaning of 'national king' elsewhere in OE. Here it refers to God (my translation adopts Moffat's 'king of nations'; see Moffat 1990: 48). The absence of a b-verse in SB2 12 shows fairly conclusively that the remaining material of the text as it appears in SB1 has been reorganized, with little sacrificed apart from the offending compound itself and SB1 14 *weoruda*. The most conventional of all formulas for God, *ece dryhten*, replaces *weoruda dryhten*, and it is noteworthy that the new verse maintains regular alliteration with the reformed a-verse, *butan ær wyrce*. The new syntax seems, however, to be unconventional: I have been unable to find any parallel elsewhere in OE for the word-order: *butan*, Verb, Subject, Object that occurs in SB2's reformed *butan*-clause. But here is reasonably good evidence of a transmitter's willingness to remove words found meaningless in the context and to adjust the text accordingly to achieve acceptable sense. While acknowledging the failure to maintain the formal requirements of the poetic line in SB2 12, we should also note the success in reforming SB2

13. The transmitter who amended SB2 was probably aware of the structural requirements of the alliterative line.

We have already seem some examples of the havoc wreaked on the text of Brb by the scribe of the D text or one of his predecessors. Words with meanings that were exclusively poetic seem to have caused him particular problems. In line 6 he originally wrote *heaðolinga* before correcting to *heaðolinda*, the same form that we find in C and (with non-W-S inflexion) in A's *heaþolinde*. The compound, here acc. pl., means 'shield' (literally 'battle linden-wood'). It occurs nowhere else and is the only recorded OE compound with *lind* as the final element, though there are several others with *lind* as first element (e.g. Bwf 2603 *lindwiga*, 'shield-warrior'). The B text also misrepresents the word, as *heaðolina*, with the *o* underdotted for deletion, though perhaps by a later reader. So far as D's corruption is concerned, a simple copying error *g* for *d* seems unlikely and it is possible that the scribe responsible for the form thought he was dealing with a term for 'warrior' comparable formally with OE *irþling*, 'ploughman'. D's corruptions, though gross, are seldom completely meaningless, at least at the level of the individual word. Another example of a similar kind is Brb D 5 *heordweal* instead of *bordweal(l)*, 'shield-wall' that appears in the other texts of the poem. The element *bord* in the sense of 'shield' is confined to poetry. D's scribe probably rejected it consciously because it meant nothing to him. His substitute spoils the alliteration of the line which in its correct form runs (in C's orthography) *embe brunnanburh. bordweall clufon*, '(they) clove the shield-wall about Brunanburh'; but one other point about this example is worth noticing: although it could have originated in a simple copying error (*h* for *b*), the new first element has been turned into a real word, the noun *heord* which means 'keeping', 'care' or 'custody', so that the whole compound could conceivably have been intended to mean something like 'protecting wall'. The D scribe is probably here running true to form, producing bizarre distortions of the received text which are, nonetheless, not completely unrecognizable as English (or English-type) words.

§4.4 REJECTION OF UNFAMILIAR WORDS

We saw earlier (§2.1.2) how mechanical error can sometimes account of the replacement of one word by another during transmission. When the replaced word is exclusively or largely poetic in its distribution, we must consider the possibility that it has been rejected deliberately because a scribe, unused to the language of verse, found it meaningless. Two particular texts stand out as rich in substitutions of this sort, but it is possible to see different patterns in each of them and they are therefore discussed separately here. The first is the D text of Brb, the second is SB1.

§4.4.1 The D text of Brb

We have already had cause to notice Brb D 46 *in wuda* as a replacement for the poetic word *inwidda* (as in A; B, C have *inwitta*), 'the evil one' (see above, §4.1); but D's corruption has a certain appropriateness in the context: a description of Constantine as 'the old one in the wood' (*eald in wuda*) recalls Mld 193, where the wood is the place of refuge for the cowardly sons of Odda who fled from the battlefield at Maldon after Byrhtnoth was slain (Mld 192–93 *gupe ne gymdon, ac wendon from pam wige and pone wudu sohton*, 'they had no stomach for the battle but turned away from the fight and sought the wood'). Thus D's version of this line might be read as a hint of the Scottish king's cowardice in leaving his kinsmen dead and unavenged on the battlefield at Brunanburh. However, we must be cautious about attributing to the D scribe purposeful tinkering with the text to make a political point. D 46 *in wuda* must be seen in the context of other corruptions in the same text of a similar nature. The second example is D 64 *cuðheafoc* for *guðhafoc*:

Brb A 64	Brb D 64
grædigne guðhafóc. & þæt græge deor.	grædigne cuðheafóc. & þæt grege deor.

'[…] the greedy battle-hawk and the grey beast.'

This is part of a description of the traditional beasts of battle: raven, eagle and wolf, the last two of which are mentioned in this line. D's corruption, if intended to mean anything in particular, must mean something like 'the usual hawk', in other words the species of raptor usually present on such occasions, that is, the eagle, specified (*earn*) in the previous line. A copying error involving the misreading of *g-* as *c-* seems unlikely, so perhaps unfamiliarity with the poetic element *guð-*, 'battle', decided the transmitter to replace it with something more meaningful to him.

The D scribe of Brb is also responsible for the corruption in Brb 24 *mycelscearp* for A, B, C *mylenscearp*, 'sharpened on a grindstone', describing the West Saxons' swords with which they attacked their fleeing enemies at Brb (see Campbell 1938: 105):

Brb A 24   Brb D 24

| mecum mylenscearpan. myrce ne | mecum mycelscearpum myrce ne |
| wyrndon. | wyrndon. |

A: '[…] with swords sharpened on a grindstone. The Mercians did not refuse […]'

The compound *mylenscearp* occurs nowhere else in OE, and the relationship between the elements might in any case have caused problems for the transmitter of the D text, though his replacement is an oddity, for the adjective *micel* (*mycel*) never occurs elsewhere compounded with an adjective.

In Brb D 7, *eoforan* was originally written for *eaforan* as in B:

Brb B 7   Brb D 7

| eaforan eadweardes swa him geæþele | eoforan eadweardæs swa him geæðele |
| wæs. | wæs. |

'[…] the children of Edward; it was thus inborn in them […]'

A has *afaran*, C *aforan* here. The D scribe put a dot under the first *o* to cancel it, and a later hand ('an Elizabethan corrector', according to Campbell 1938: 97) drew a line through the *o*, perhaps with the intention of making it an *a*. The word *eafora* is a poetic term for 'son', here Edward's sons Æþelstan and Eadmund who led the Wessex army at Brunanburh. There is another instance of the same word in Brb 52, where each text repeats the form already used in 7 except D, which has the same form, *afaran*, as A has in both lines. The form originally written in D 7, *eoforan*, might be interpreted as the work of a scribe who, encountering *eaforan* in his exemplar, thought that he was faced with a North. spelling of W-S *eoforan*, 'boars', 'boar-standards' (see *OEG* §§210.2, 278b) and 'corrected' accordingly, though if this is what happened, we must assume that the scribe responsible did not know the poetic *eafora*, 'son'.

In D 20, *ræd* appears for *sæd*:

Brb A 20   Brb D 20

| werig wíges sæd. wesseaxe fórð. | werig wiges ræd wesseaxe forð. |

A: '[…] weary, exhausted by war. Forward did the West-Saxons […]'

The word *sæd*, 'sated', 'exhausted', is chiefly poetic. The substitute *ræd* might make a kind of sense if taken as 'council' ('the weary battle-council'?), but some forms of *s* in Anglo-Saxon writing resemble *r*, so copying error may well be the explanation here. In 62, D's corruption *hasuwadan* for *hasupadan* (C; B *hasopadan*, A *hasewan padan*), 'the dark-coated one', a kenning for the eagle, is even more likely to reflect a simple misreading of letters, in this case *p* for the letter *wynn*, which it closely resembles in form. A further corruption of a poetic term in the D text is 10 *heted* for A, B, C *hettend*, 'foes', though the form as written in D is meaningless so far as I can see.

In all these examples, a poetic word has been mishandled in transmission. We cannot be certain that ignorance of the word itself precipitated the corruption in every case, particularly the last three (D 20 *ræd*, 62 *hasuwadan*, 10 *heted*), but it is likely to have been a contributory factor in most of them. It is noticeable that in all these places the corrupt reading resembles the original one in general appearance, and in several of them there is a close phonetic resemblance between the two forms. Such resemblances could be explained in various ways. Perhaps the corrupting scribe wanted to disturb the appearance of the text as little as possible. If so, that might mean that the ignorance of poetic words that I have imputed to him led to a false assumption that the text in his exemplar had already been copied inaccurately and that it was up to him to put matters right; but this explanation implies a concern for accuracy and intelligibility that is difficult to reconcile with some of the remarkable distortions of poetic terms that the D text puts before us. It is, of course, also possible that these corruptions, taken as a group, are the results of two separate levels of interference with the text, the first a series of careless copying errors, the second an attempt to put the resulting wreckage into some sort of meaningful order.

§4.4.2 SB1

SB1 contains a number of corruptions that seem to have resulted from ignorance of rare or poetic vocabulary. In the following passage, SB2 112 *genepeð* is matched by SB1 117 *genydde*:

SB2 111–13	SB1 116–18
Gifer hatte se wyrm þam þa geaflas beoð	gifer hatte se wyrm þe þa eaglas beoð
nædle scearpran se genepeð to	nædle scearpran. Se genydde to me
ærest ealra on þā eorðscræfe	ærest eallra on þam eorðscræfe

SB2: 'Gifer is the name of the worm whose jaws are sharper than the needle; he ventures forward before all others into the grave.'

The meaning of SB1 117b is obscure. Editors generally agree that *me* (*to me*, 'to me') is a corruption. In the SB2 version, *to* is plainly an adverb, 'forward', not the preposition that the following *me* in SB1 suggests that it was taken to be there. Krapp is no doubt right to see *me* as the product of 'an unreflecting impulse on the part of the scribe to provide *to* with an object' (Krapp 1932: 128). It is difficult to judge what meaning SB1's *genydde* in 117 was intended to bear. The verb *genydan* normally means 'to compel', 'to press'. Bosworth & Toller tentatively suggest that the verb is here being used in an intransitive sense, 'to force one's way to' (Toller 1921), though there is no support elsewhere for this meaning of *genydan*. The SB2 reading *geneþeð* was no doubt rejected because the verb was unfamiliar: *geneðan* is quite common in verse, but as a prose verb it seems to be more or less confined to translations associated with the revival of learning under Alfred. It might well have been unfamiliar to a scribe working in the later OE period.

The replacement of SB2 46 *gescenta* by SB1 49 *gesynta* presents a rather clearer picture, though there are complications here too:

SB2 46–47a	SB1 49–50a
scealt þu nu hwæþre minra gescenta scome þrowian	scealt ðu minra gesynta sceame þrowian
on þam miclan dæge [...]	on ðam myclan dæge [...]

'You must now (SB2 nevertheless) suffer the dishonour of my confusions (*or* SB1 my health) on that great day [...]'

There is some doubt about the meaning of the gen. pl. *gescenta* in SB2 46, on which see Moffat 1990: 72–73. Moffat defends SB1's *gesynta*, 'health', as 'following ironically ... from the image of passive acquiescence in corruption' (Moffat 1990: 73) that is established in the SB1 version (see also Moffat 1987: 6–7). Only SB2 46 *gescenta*, however, preserves normal alliteration in the line. Presumably it was rejected by a copyist in SB1's background because it meant as little to him as it does to us today. In my 1979 article on the relationship between these two versions of SB (Orton 1979b: 187–88), I argued that *gesynta* produces an inconsistency in the soul's argument: the soul plainly fears that the body's sins will bring them both to damnation. In spite of Moffat's arguments, I still find it difficult to reconcile a reference here to the soul's 'health' with this fear.

A third example is SB2 69 *geahþe* for which SB1 74 has *æhta*:

SB2 69–70

gifre & grædge ne sindon þine geahþe
 with
þa þu her on moldan monnum eawdest.

SB1 74–75

gifre & grædige ne synt þine æhta
 awihte.
þe ðu her on moldan mannū eowdest.

 '[…] eager and greedy. Your follies (*or* SB1 your possessions) that you
 displayed to men here on earth count for nothing.'

Only SB2's *geahþe*, probably meaning 'follies', provides the necessary
alliteration in the b-verse, but it appears not to have been understood by a
copyist in the history of SB1, who replaced it with the non-alliterating
æhta, 'possessions'. Moffat points out that *geahþe* is probably a form of
the nom. pl. of *geað*, a poetic word that occurs elsewhere only in Glc 504,
1233 and Jln 96 (Moffat 1990: 75). If this identification is correct, it is
not surprising that a scribe found such a rare word difficult. In fact, there
is some indication that he failed to grasp the word's morphology: the idea
for *æhta* as its replacement seems to have come from a misapprehension
that *geahþe* contains the prefix *ge-*. When stripped of this, the sequence
ahþe that remains could well have suggested an inflected form of *æht*.
But this similarity of form was evidently not the only factor favouring
æhta, for it makes fair sense in the context and that is unlikely to be the
result of chance.

 Another probable instance of substitution in SB1, in this case leading
to a secondary adjustment to the text, is SB1 73 *slitan* for SB2 68
beslitan:

SB2 67–69a

& þec sculon moldwyrmas monige
 ceowan.
seonowum beslitan swearte wihte
gifre & grædge

SB1 72–74a

& þe sculon her moldwyrmas manige
 ceowan
slitan sarlice swearte wihta
gifre & grædige

 SB2: '[…] and many earthworms must gnaw you, dark creatures tear away
 your sinews, eager and greedy.'

SB2's infinitive *beslitan*, literally 'to deprive by tearing', is a hapax
legomenon and is therefore likely to have been unfamiliar to the transmitter of SB1. His substitute, the simplex verb *slitan*, 'to tear', would
have left *seonowum* grammatically unattached and it is no doubt awareness of this that led to its replacement by the adverb *sarlice*, 'severely'.
These changes involve a new but acceptable metrical pattern for the
verse. There is a loss of precision in the meaning, but the amendment of

the text is neat and would be invisible if we did not have SB2 to compare with it.

In two places, whole verse-lines present in SB2 are missing from SB1:

SB2 93b–96	SB1 100b–102
ac hwæt do wit unc	ac hwæt do wyt unc
þōn he unc hafað geedbyrded oþre siþe	
sculon wit þonne ætsomne siþþan	sculon wit þōn eft ætsomne siððan
brucan	brucan
swylcra yrmþa swa þu unc ær scrife	swylcra yrmða swa ðu unc her ær
	scrife.

'But what shall we do (SB2 when he has regenerated us once more)? We must then afterwards (SB1 again) experience together such miseries as you previously preordained for us (SB1 here).'

SB2 106–08	SB1 112–13
rib reafiað reþe wyrmas	rib reafiað reðe wyrmas
drincað hloþum hrá heolfres þurstge.	
bið seo tunge totogen on tyn healfe	beoð hira tungan totogenne on tyn
	healfa

'Fierce worms will plunder the ribs, (SB2 will drink the corpse in swarms, thirsty for blood,) the tongue (*or* SB1 their tongues) will be torn apart into ten pieces'

Both the lines which only SB2 contains (94, 107) were added to SB1 by Grein in his edition of the latter version (see Krapp 1932: 128). Both are stylistically appropriate, and the first in particular fills out what would otherwise be a rather vague question. Both lines make sense, and both are metrically regular; but both contain rare words: SB2 94 *geedbyrded* and SB2 107 *heolfres*. The first of these is the past part. of a verb that occurs nowhere else in OE, and the second, *heolfor*, 'blood', is exclusively poetic. Omission of both lines from SB1 could be explained on the basis of a transmitter's ignorance of the meaning of these words.

In all these passages from SB, I would maintain that SB2 has the better text and that the SB1 version shows a substitution or omission provoked by ignorance of rare or poetic vocabulary. But although I find it easier in all cases to believe that it is SB1 that has the corrupt version of the lines in question, one cannot feel anything like the same certainty about the direction of change that it is possible to feel about comparable variations between the D text of Brb and the other texts of that poem. This relative uncertainty is, I think, significant and tells us something about the competence of the transmitters who handled the two poems. We have seen the almost irresponsible freedom with which the D text of Brb was handled, controlled, perhaps, by a somewhat puzzling concern to change the appearance of the text as little as possible. The results of the changes I have identified in SB1 are mixed: some preserve reasonably good sense (SB1 74 *æhta*, SB1 73 *slitan*, and the two omissions of lines); some preserve alliteration (SB1 117 *genydde*, SB1 73 *slitan*), and SB1 49 *gesynta* preserves neither sense nor alliteration; but they are, on the whole, better integrated than the emendations represented by the D text of Brb, and in some cases more radical, particularly the omission of entire lines. They suggest a desire for clarity which is only obliquely suggested by the changes to Brb which the D text exemplifies. We shall need to bear these differences in mind in forming a general view of the condition of these texts and the influences to which they have been subject during transmission.

§4.4.3 Other texts

The replacement of poetic words with others of more general distribution and usage is not confined to the D text of Brb and the SB1 version of SB; texts of other poems exemplify the same editorial activity on the part of the transmitters that handled them. This section will deal with the more definite examples that I have collected.

In CFB 2, both the A and the D texts have each substituted different words for the poetic word *mecg*, *mæcg*, 'man', that is used in B and C:

CFB B 1–2	CFB A 1–2
Her eadmund cyning engla þeoden	Her eadmund cing engla þeoden.
mæcgea (C mecga) mundbora myrce	maga mundbora myrce geeode
geeode.	

CFB D 1–2

Her eadmund cyning. engla þeoden
mægþa mundbora myrce geeode.

'In this year King Eadmund, lord of the English, protector of men (*or* A of kinsmen, D of nations) overran Mercia [...]'

The fact that A and D disagree in their replacements for *mæcgea*, *mecga* (on the variation in the vowel of the stem, see *OEG* §193(c)) means that both are probably corruptions, especially in view of the fact that *mecg* (*mæcg*), 'man', is an exclusively poetic word and so likely to have been unfamiliar. D's choice of *mægþa*, 'of nations', as its replacement is perhaps to be preferred to A's *maga*, 'of kinsmen', though the latter might conceivably be meant to recall Eadmund's exploits at Brunanburh alongside his brother Æðelstan. Both replacements, we should notice, maintain regular alliteration; the substitution of any word not beginning with *m-* would have undermined it.

Alliterative requirements are, on the other hand, ignored in the substitution of EgD A 33 *soðboran* for B, C *woðboran*:

EgD B 33	EgD A 33
wíse woðboran wæs geond werþeode.	wise soðboran. wæs geond werðeode.

'[...] wise prophets (*or* A truth-bearers). Throughout the nation was [...]'

The direction of the substitution is indicated by several factors: the status of *woðbora* ('prophet', 'poet', 'singer') as an exclusively poetic word; the fact that the version of the verse in question in B and C is a poetic formula, with two of its five other occurrences consisting of the same collocation as here (OrW 2 *wisne woðboran*, R31.24 *wisum woðboran*); the relative familiarity of the element *soð-*, 'truth', as in A ('truth-bearers'), compared with *woð-* ('noise', 'song', 'voice' etc.) in B and C; and the fact that double alliteration, as in B, C 33a, would be expected in a verse of this metrical type in *Beowulf* (type 1D*1(i); see Bliss 1967: 125) — not, of course, a conclusive argument on its own, though the regularity of B and C in this regard is notable. On the other hand, A's *soðboran*, which makes good sense in the context, is unattested elsewhere in OE. Perhaps it was the A scribe's own invention. If so, it is remarkable to find a transmitter inventing a new compound to replace a traditional one.

SnS A 90–92a	SnS B 90–92a
hafað guðmæcga gierde lange	hafað guðmaga gyrde lange
gyldene gade & a ðone g[...]man feond	gyldene gade & þone grymman feond
swiðmod sweopað	swiðmod swapeð

Notes on the text: the hand that inserted an *o* between the *ð* and the *m* of A's *guðmæcga* looks later than the main hand of the text (Menner 1941: 87, note).

'The battle-warrior has a long rod, a golden goad and (A ever) the stout-hearted one whips (*or* B drives) the grim fiend'

The verb *sweopian* (*swipian*), 'to whip', 'to scourge', as in A, is recorded only here and in Exo 464 (*swipode*). Its status as the original reading is supported by the closely analogous verse SnS A 121a *swiðmode sweopan*, 'sturdy (?) whips', where *sweopan* is the acc. pl. of the weak fem. noun *swipe*, though the sense in which *swiðmode* is being used here is unclear. Its normal meaning in OE is 'stout-hearted', as in SnS 92a, but it seems strange to find it applied to whips. Nevertheless, the collocation in SnS 121a plainly echoes the earlier one in the poem; perhaps the author liked the onomatopoeic ring of this combination of elements. B's *swapeð*, 'sweeps' or 'drives', a common word in OE prose and verse alike, is rather less apt, but preserves the alliterative structure of the a-verse very nicely. It is a good substitute for a copyist who presumably did not know *sweopian*, 'to whip'.

In SnS 73, B's *gehideð* has replaced A's *ahieðeð* in the sentence:

SnS A 73–74   SnS B 73–74

hungor he áhieðeð helle gestrudeð   hu^{n}gor <u>hege</u> he gehideð helle gestrudeð
wylm toweorpeð wuldor getimbreð   wylm toworpeð wuldor getymbreð.

Notes on the text: B 73 *n* of *hungor* added superscript; first *hege* under-lined for deletion.

'It (*sc.* the word of God) destroys (*or* B hides) hunger, it despoils hell, it turns aside the surging flame, builds up glory'

A's *ahieðeð*, 'destroys', represents the rare verb *ahieðan* (*ahyðan*) which occurs only a few times elsewhere in OE and only once outside poetry (in the gloss to the *Vespasian Psalter*). The collocation with *hungor* may have been traditional: cf. FtM 15 *Sumne sceal hungor ahiðan*, 'Hunger shall destroy some', though there the grammatical relationships are reversed: hunger is the destroyer rather than the destroyed, as in SnS. B's *gehideð*, 'hides', a common verb in prose and verse, is somewhat out of step with the imagery of attack in this passage; but it preserves the double alliteration that is usual in a-verses of this metrical type in *Beowulf* (either 1A1b(i) or 1A*1b, depending on whether the parasite vowel in *hungor* is suppressed or not; see Bliss 1967: 124–25). Again, the substitu-tion, though less skilful than SnS B 92 *swapeð* for *sweopað*, preserves the general sense of the passage fairly well.

A probable replacement in SnS B is 62 *hearde* in place of A's *hædre*:

SnS A 61b–62   SnS B 61b–62

hwilum me bryne stigeð   hwylū me bryne stigeð
hige heortan neah hædre wealleð.   hige heortan hearde wealleð.

'Sometimes fervour rises up in me, the mind surges anxiously (*or* B fiercely) (A close) to the heart.'

A's *hædre* is a lexical rarity, recorded elsewhere only in Rsg 63. Its etymology is unclear, there are no recognized cognates and consequently we can only guess at its meaning. B's *hearde*, probably intended as 'fiercely' here, is well-attested, and is presumably the corruption, introduced to replace a word which meant nothing to a transmitter.

In SnS 65, it seems probable that B's reading in the b-verse, *godspellian*, represents the original reading and that B's *godspel secgan* shows the rejection of the compound in favour of a less elliptical expression. The evidence for this view is not conclusive. The compound verb *godspellian* is quite rare in OE verse but common in the prose. A's version which I suggest has replaced it gives a verse of Bliss's type 2A3a(i), which is relatively uncommon as a b-verse on *Beowulf* (see Bliss 1967: 126). B's version follows a well-attested type (1D1).

Two replacements of the variant readings *or* and *ord* in Cæd 4 should be mentioned here, for both probably resulted from transmitters' ignorance of the meanings of these words. The texts which show corruptions at this point, To and W, are members of the W-S *eorðan* and W-S *ylda* groups respectively.[12] Below, T and H stand for the uncorrupted versions of the texts of these groups:

Cæd T 3b–4   Cæd To 3b–4

swa he wundra gehwæs   swa he wundra gehwæs.
éce drihten ór onstealde.   ece drihten ær astealde.

Cæd H 3b–4   Cæd W 3b–4

swa he wundra gehwilc   swa he wu[.]dra gehwilc
ece drihten ord astealde.   ece drih[...] word astealde

Notes on the text: the lacunae in W result from trimming of the folio on which the text is written.

---

[12] For the text of To, see Ker 1957: 457, and Humphreys & Ross 1975: 53. The Tournai MS was destroyed in 1940 but a photograph of the text of Cæd survives and is printed in Faider & van Sint Jan 1950: plate IV.

T: '[...] as he, eternal lord, established the beginning (*or* To previously) of every wonder.'

H: '[...] as he, eternal lord, established the beginning (*or* W the word), every wonder.'

To's *ær*, 'previously', in 4b leaves 3b *wundra gehwæs* detached grammatically. It was no doubt the poetic word *or* which provoked the substitution. The new reading is appropriate to the context in a general way, and preserves the vocalic alliteration in the second half of the line; but the failure to accommodate *ær* grammatically shows a careless attitude to the integrity of the sentence. The substitution of *word* for *ord* in W is obviously inspired, as well as provoked, by the exemplar form; but *word* spoils the alliteration in the line. It has, not surprisingly, been suggested that *word* is a deliberate amendment in imitation of the opening of the gospel of John, *In principio erat verbum* (by Fry 1974: 239, note 38), and certainly the transmitter responsible might well have had this biblical text in mind; but the parallelism it produces between *wundra gehwilc* and *word* raises obvious difficulties of interpretation. It is impossible to attribute much (if any) grasp of the meaning of the text to the transmitter responsible for *word*.

Chapter 5. The Ambitious Scribe

§5 Replacement or modification of understood words or collocations

The last section of the previous chapter was about replacements of words and connected amendments to the text which probably arose from ignorance of words, and consequently their meanings, in the received text. Other modifications are of a nature to suggest that the rejected word was not entirely opaque to the transmitter who altered or replaced it. This may be indicated when the substituted word has the same meaning as the one it seems to have replaced, showing that the transmitter might have been able at least to guess the meaning of the reading in his received text; other cases modify the morphology of exemplar forms without effecting any substantial change of meaning. Examples of the first kind are dealt with first below.

§5.1 COMPLETE REPLACEMENTS

My first example is a double substitution: Brb B 4, 42 has *sake* or *sace* in place of A, C *sæcce* (D 4 *secce*, 42 *sæcge*):

Brb A 3b–4	Brb B 3b–4
ealdorlangne tír.	ealdorlangne tír
geslogon æt sæcce. sweorda écgum.	geslógan æt sake sweorda ecggum.

'[...] (they) obtained by fighting eternal glory in the strife by the edges of swords [...]'

Brb A 42	Brb B 42
beslagen æt sæcce. & his sunu forlet.	forslegen æt sace & his sunu forlét

'[...] deprived (*or* B slain) in the strife, and left his son [...]'

The meaning is unaffected by B's substitutions: *sacu* and *sæcc* are different words but have just the same meaning.[1] Metre, on the other hand, is compromised by B's substitutions because they contain only a single consonant between stem and inflexion, unlike *sæcce* and related forms which contain a geminated consonant, making the syllable long (See Campbell 1938: 19 and 24–25). Clearly *sæcc* was the poet's word in both lines; and the fact that it is a poetic word, unlike *sacu*, explains the substitution. The B scribe could probably see what *sæcc* meant in both lines; but he preferred the more familiar *sacu*.

The B text of Brb 18 has *forgrunden* in place of the *ageted* in all the other texts (A, C, D, represented below by C):

Brb C 17b–18a   Brb B 17b–18a

   þær læg secg monig.   þær læg secg manig.
garum ageted.   garum forgrunden.

'There lay many a man destroyed by spears'

There is no change of meaning or even of metre involved; but the rejection of *ageted* must be related to its status as a purely poetic word (see Campbell 1938: 103) which contains the non-W-S stem vowel *e* (from *ēa* by *i*-mutation; *OEG* §200.5) in all its occurrences (And 1143 *garum agetan*, FtM 16 *sumne sceal gar agetan*, R83.7 *fruman agette*). The collocation with *gar*, 'spear', is clearly traditional and formulaic. The choice of *forgrunden* as its replacement might have been influenced by its use later in the poem (Brb B, C, D 43 *wundum forgrunden*, 'destroyed by wounds'; A has *wundun fergrunden*). At any rate, this is a competent piece of editing on the part of the copyist responsible. If B were our only surviving text of Brb, we should not suspect any corruption of the text at this point.

My fourth and fifth examples may be dealt with in tandem, for they occur in adjacent lines of the same poem and involve the same versions

---

[1]   The difference of form arises from the *i*-umlaut of the stem vowel in *sæcc* only, though analogy with *sacu* has determined the quality of the vowel produced by this process: the *æ* of *sæcc* is the *i*-umlaut of *a* which replaced *æ* (by normal isolative fronting of *a*) before *i*-umlaut by analogy with *sacu*, the *a* of which arose by retraction of *æ* (again, from normal fronting of *a*) before the back vowel *u* in the second syllable. Without this analogical influence, *sæcc* would have developed as *secc*, the form we actually find in D 4, which no doubt illustrates a parallel phonological development in *sæcc* when *sacu* failed to exert any analogical influence on it. On the sound-changes in these and related forms, see *OEG* §§160(3), 193(c).

of it. PCP T 13 *het* seems to have replaced the *heht* of H and D, and PCP
T 14 *bringan* appears for *brengan* in H and D:

PCP H 12b–14a	PCP T 12b–14a
& me his writerum	& me his writerum
sende suð & norð heht him swelcra má	sende. suþ & norþ. het him swylcra ma
brengan bi ðære bisene	bringan. be þære bysene.

> '[...] and sent me to his scribes south and north and ordered more of the
> same agreeing with the exemplar to be produced for him [...]'

T's substitution of *het*, the general OE pret. 3 sg. of *hatan*, 'to command',
calls for little comment: *heht* is a reduplicated pret. form, characteristic of
poetic texts and early or Anglian prose and glosses (see *OEG* §746) and
so always vulnerable to replacement by *het* at the hands of copyists
working late in the period who recognized *heht* for what it was. In line
14, H and D have the weak verb *brengan* and T has the strong verb
bringan, but semantically the two verbs are interchangeable. The distribution of *brengan* is rather unpredictable (*OEG* §753.9.b.5), but it is the
usual word in the *Cura Pastoralis* translation, according to Sweet (Sweet
1871: xxiv), whereas *bringan* is more generally distributed. Again, T's
substitution calls for little comment. Both *het* and *bringan* are cases of
generally distributed OE words being substituted for others which,
though recognizably related to them, are of narrower distribution in OE
generally.

Similar cases occurs sporadically. In Cæd O 4, *oórᵈ* appears for the *or*
which we may assume to have occurred in the archetypal version of the
W-S *eorðan* group of texts (T, and all the North. texts retain *or*):

Cæd T 4	Cæd O 4
éce drihten ór onstealde.	ece dryhten oórᵈ onstealde

> '[...] eternal lord, established the beginning [...]'

Here a word of relatively narrow, chiefly poetic distribution has been
replaced by a more generally distributed one of identical meaning. All the
W-S *eorðan* texts except T (and To, which substitutes *ær*; see §4.4.3
above) have *ord* too; and so do all the W-S *ylda* texts (except W which
substitutes *word*; see §4.4.3 above). It is therefore probable that this
particular substitution occurred independently in more than one line of
transmission. The O text, with its insertion of *d* superscript, provides a

picture of the change actually in progress. The verse in which *or(d)* occurs here is a poetic formula that has either word in its various occurrences (Bwf 2407 *or onstealde*, R3.59 *or anstelle*, but XSt 113 *ord onstealdon*). It is probable that in all contexts *ord* gradually supplanted *or* in the sense of 'beginning' over the OE period (see Frampton 1924: 6–7; Dobbie 1937: 29–30), though insufficient evidence is available to establish its status as a dialectal word (cf. Dobbie 1937: 30).

Two other isolated cases of a similar kind occur in the poems of the *Anglo-Saxon Chronicle*. Brb C 57 has *broðor* in a place where the original version appears to have had *gebroðor*:

Brb B 57–58	Brb C 57–58
Swylce þa gebroðor begen ætsomne.	Swilce þá broðor begen ætsomne.
cing & æþeling cyþþe sohtan.	cing & æþeling cyþþe sohton.

'Likewise the two brothers together, king and prince, sought their native land'

The passage describes the return of Æþelstan and Eadmund to Wessex after their victory over the Irish Norsemen and Scots. The A and D texts both have versions of *gebroðor* here (A *gebroþer*). C has simply substituted the more familar pl. noun for the less familiar collective *gebroðor*; but meaning is essentially unaffected and the new metrical pattern that results is conventional.

The second *Chronicle* example comes in CFB A 8, where the simple adverb *ær* has replaced the rarer comparative *æror*:

CFB D 8	CFB A 8
& deoraby. dæne wæron æror	deoraby dæne wæran ær

'[...] (B C D and) Derby. The Danes had previously been [...]'

The agreement of B, C and D on the double comparative *æror* establishes it as the earlier reading, and *ær* is, as Dobbie points out, 'less satisfactory metrically' (Dobbie 1942: 150). No doubt it was substituted simply because it was more familiar to the transmitter. The meaning is essentially unchanged.

Finally, SB1 114 has *frofor* in place of SB2's *hroþor*:

SB2 108–09	SB1 113–14
bið seo tunge totogen on tyn healfe	beoð hira tungan totogenne on tyn healfa
hungrum to hroþor	hungregū to frofre

'The tongue *(or* SB1 Their tongues) will be torn apart into ten pieces as solace to the hungry ones *(or* SB2 to hungers (?))'

The meaning is unchanged in SB1; but SB2's *hroþor* gives (in spite of the corruption *hungrum* in the same verse) a more regular pattern of (double) alliteration in the a-verse (see Bliss 1967: 37–38, 125). This, combined with the fact that *hroþor* is a poetic word, confirms that SB1's *frofre* has replaced it rather than vice-versa. Again, this is a rejection of a poetic word in favour of a more familiar one with exactly the same meaning.

§5.2 PARTIAL REPLACEMENTS OF COMPOUNDS

There are two cases in which a compound word is rejected in favour of another which contains one of the same elements. One is PCP T 3 *eorðbugendū* which has replaced the H and D texts' *iegbuendum*:

PCP H 1–3a	PCP T 1–3a
ÞIS ærendgewrit Agustinus.	Þis ærentgewryt augustinus.
ofer sealtne sæ suðan brohte.	ofer sealtne sæ. suþan brohte.
iegbuendum	eorðbugendū.

'Augustine brought this written message from the south over the salt sea to the island-dwellers *(or* T earth-dwellers) [...]'

The compound *iegbu(g)end* (*ig-*, *eg-*), 'island-dweller', is clearly the more appropriate word in the context of a description of the activities of the missionary Augustine who arrived in England in 597 A.D. The word is confined to poetry in OE, but *eorðbu(g)end* is more generally distributed. Its substitution for *iegbuendum* does not affect the metrical or alliterative regularity of line 3.

The second example of the partial replacement of a compound word is Cæd B 3 *wuldorgodes* for the *wuldorfæder* which all the other texts of the W-S *eorðan* group exhibit:

Cæd T 3–4	Cæd B 3–4
weorc wuldorfæder swa he wundra gehwæs	weorc wuldorgodes swa he wundra fela
éce drihten ór onstealde.	éce drihten ord astealde

Notes on the text: on 3 B *fela* for *gehwæs*, see above, §4.2.2.1.

'[...] the works of the father of glory *(or* B of the glorious God); how he, the eternal lord, established the beginning of every wonder *(or* B of many wonders).'

This is an unusual case because although it is certain that *wuldorfæder* stood originally in the archetype of this version (as is confirmed by its presence in all the North. texts, as well as in all the W-S *eorðan* texts except B), *wuldorgodes*, which has replaced it in B, is a hapax legomenon, whereas *wuldorfæder*, though rare, is at least known from other poems (Mnl 147, Chr 217). Why *wuldorgodes* should have been substituted by a transmitter in B's history is therefore not immediately apparent. It is not easy to see what difficulties *wuldorfæder* could have presented, even to a scribe who knew little about OE poetic compounds. It seems possible, however, that *wuldorgodes* was preferred because its inflexion *-es* made its grammatical function in the sentence clearer than the uninflected gen. *-fæder*.

§5.3 SPLITTING OR CREATION OF COMPOUNDS

Another kind of change which indicates a reasonable understanding of the received text is the splitting of compounds or the opposite process, the making of compounds out of two distinct words. The A text of Brb has two clear cases of compound-splitting, the first in the following context (where B represents the readings of B, C and D):

Brb B 26–27	Brb A 26–27
þara ðe mid anlafe ofer eargebland.	þæ mid anlafe. ofer æra gebland.
on lides bosme land gesohtan.	on lides bosme. land gesohtun.

> *Notes on the text*: A 26 *þæ* is clearly a corruption, though it is unclear what form of relative pronoun or particle it derives from.

> '[...] of those who with Anlaf sought land in the ship's bosom across the commotion of the sea.'

B's version is confirmed as more authoritative than A's by the agreement of all three other texts against A. A divides the compound *eargebland* into a simplex noun *gebland* (acc. sg.) with dependent gen. pl. (*æra*), though the significance of the *æ* of *æra* is unclear. Dobbie prints A's reading in his edition of the poem (Dobbie 1942: 17), commenting that as *ēar*, 'sea', occurs in OE as a noun in its own right (e.g. in R3.22), 'it is possible to retain A's *æra gebland* as a variant of *eara gebland*' (Dobbie 1942: 148); but why *æra* and not *eara*? The only possibility I can suggest is very speculative: that the A scribe, unfamiliar with *ēar*, 'sea', and ignorant of what word he was in fact faced with, assumed that the vowel of *ear-* in his exemplar was short and was a Mercian spelling of W-S *ær-*

(*OEG* §206), which form he accordingly substituted for *ear-* when he split the compound.

The second example of compound-splitting in Brb is in A 62 (again, B represents B, C and D, which agree substantially here, though D has the copying error *hasuwadan* with *wynn* for *p*):

Brb B 62–63a	Brb A 62–63a
hyrnednebban. & þone hasopadan.	hyrnednebban. & þane hasewan padan.
earn æftan hwít.	earn æftan hwit.

'[...] the horny-beaked one, and the dun-coated one, the eagle white behind, [...]'

The compound *hasupad*, 'dun-coated', occurs nowhere else in OE. Campbell would explain A's splitting of the compound *hasopadan* as a transmitter's attempt to parallel *þone sweartan hræfn* ('the black raven') in 61; and perhaps the transmitter thought that this rare compound would be more transparent if divided into its elements, which he clearly understood. But the resulting verse is technically suspect in its use of anacrusis: three-syllable anacrusis, as in A 62b & *þane*, never occurs in *Beowulf*; two syllables are the limit; and not even one- or two-syllable anacruses ever occur in *Beowulf* in a type A verse with the cæsura in Bliss's position (i) (see Bliss 1967: 40–42, §§46–48) — that is, between two metrical elements of equal weight such as *hasewan* and *padan*. It may be that the A scribe thought he was making the meaning of the text clearer here, though he ignored the metrical consequences and was probably unaware of them.

SnS B 52 *heofonrices* seems, according to metrical considerations, to be a corruption of A's *heofona rices*:

SnS A 51b–52	SnS B 51b–52
stefnū steoreð & h[..] stede healdeð	stefnū stereð & hī stede healdeð
heofona rices heregeatewa wigeð	heofonrices heregeatowe wegeð

'[...] it guides the peoples and keeps a place for them in the kingdom of heaven, it wears armour.'

My translation is essentially the same as Menner's (Menner 1941: 110), but it seems to me possible that *healdeð* does not mean 'keeps' (in the sense of 'reserves') but rather 'protects', 'defends', and that *stede* means 'position' (cf. Mld 19 *and þone stede healdan*), in line with the warlike propensity of the Pater Noster indicated by the final verse of the passage quoted. I mention this possibility because the interpretation of the whole passage might affect the question of the variant readings in 52b. On the face of it, however, A's *heofona rices* is the better reading, for B's *heofonrices* is short of the minimum of four metrical syllables (*heofon-* is resolved because its *eo* is short, and so the whole element is equivalent, for purposes of metrical analysis, to a single syllable).

A similar case is SB1 82 *wilddeora* which is less satisfactory metrically than *wildra deora* in the corresponding line of SB2:

SB2 77–78a	SB1 82–83a
ge on westenne wildra deora	oððe on westenne wilddeora
þæt grimmeste	*þæt* wyrreste

'[...] or the fiercest (*or* SB1 worst) of wild beasts in the wilderness [...]'

Again, it is only the metrical criterion (a verse must contain a minimum of four syllables) that reveals the contraction of *wildra deora* to *wilddeora* in SB1 82b.

These last two cases are rather difficult to interpret. It is perhaps significant that the particular compound words that look as though they were introduced into the text are not confined to verse in OE but also occur in prose. Their introduction might, of course, betray a naive desire to 'poeticize' the text on the part of scribes who thought all OE poetry should contain as many compound words as possible. At any rate, they may reflect tendencies in the scribes who handled these texts that we have not had reason to postulate on the basis of evidence considered so far in this book.

§5.4 REPLACEMENT OF POETIC FORMULAS

Variants involving a single word may sometimes be interpreted as showing a preference for one poetic formula over another. Clear instances are scarce and I have only been able to identify two examples in which the direction of the change is absolutely certain. One is Cæd To 6 *halig drihten* which replaces the *halig scyppend* found in the corresponding place in all the other texts of the W-S *eorðan* group. The change is to be deprecated from the point of view of style, for the poem already contained a repetition of the verse *ece drihten* in lines 4a and 8a. These two instances of the same formula are, admittedly, in different sentences; but a third instance of *drihten* seems excessive for such a short poem. The second example of formulaic substitution is CFB 9 A *nyde gebegde*, 'subdued by force', in place of B, C, D *nyde* (B *nede*) *gebæded*, 'oppressed by force' (the variants are quoted in context above, §4.3.1; see also Dobbie 1942: 150). A's version is a formula represented elsewhere by P72.17.3 *nyde gebiged*, and *nyde gebæded* is echoed in Brb 33 *nede* (C, D *neade*) *gebæded* (A *gebeded*), Jln 343 and HbM 40. The sense is affected only slightly by A's substitution.

§5.5 PUZZLING SUBSTITUTIONS

I include under this heading a number of variations between texts which I am unable to explain. All involve substitutions of one word, case, number etc. for another, and in all cases the direction of the change — which reading has replaced which, in other words — is at least guessable. There is no reason to think that any of them arose out of a misunderstanding of the received text, because the words involved are common enough in OE generally. I feel sure that others will be able to suggest plausible explanations for at least some of these variants. I describe them below, with comments as appropriate.

SnS A 78	SnS B 78
swilce he is deafra duru dumbra tunge	swilce he his deafra duru deadra tunge.

Notes on the text: B *his* is an error (dittography of *h*) for *is* (see §2.4.1 above).

'[...] it is also the door of the deaf, the tongue of the dumb (*or* B dead), [...]'

It seems clear that A's *dumbra* is original. Perhaps the prevalence of assonance, rhyme and double alliteration in the passage immediately following (79–83) encouraged the B scribe to pile on the assonance in this line too (*deafra* [...] *deadra*); but the change to 'of the dead' has puzzling implications.

SnS B 56	SnS A 56
Asceaden of scyldū huru hī sceppend geaf	asceadan of scyldigū huru him scippend geaf

Notes on the text: in B *Asceaden*, *-en* appears for the normal infinitive inflexion *-an* that we see in A.

'[...] separated from crimes (*or* A from the guilty)? Indeed, the creator gave them [...]'

Menner tolerates A's *scyldigum* on the grounds that it gives 'a modicum of sense' (Menner 1941: 110), but favours *scyldum*, as does Dobbie 1942: 33.

PCP H 14b–15	PCP T 14b–15
ðæt he his biscepum	þæt he his bisceopum
sendan meahte forðæm hi his sume	sendan myahte. forþæm hi his sume
ðorfton	beþorftan.

'[...] which he might send to his bishops, for some of them needed it.'

The addition of the prefix *be-* to the verb in T 15 does not affect the sense, but produces an irregular metrical pattern in the b-verse (Sievers' type A with four-syllable anacrusis; see Bliss 1967: 40–42, §§46–48 on the limits on the length of anacrusis in *Beowulf*).

Brb B 27	Brb C 27
on lides bosme land gesohtan.	on liþes bosme land gesohton.

'[...] sought land in the ship's bosom (*or* C in the fleet's bosom), [...]'

Campbell's view that C's *liþes*, construed here as 'fleet's', is in fact 'a mere error' for *lides*, 'ship's' (Campbell 1938: 107) is defensible; but the first undoubted record of this Norse borrowing into English is in 1052; and C is mid-eleventh century. As the word gives quite good sense here, it is certainly possible that it represents a deliberate lexical substitution for *lides*. We should, however, note that in Brb 34, all texts have the native word *lides*.

Brb A 28	Brb D 28
fæge to gefeohte. fife lægun.	fage to feohte fife lagon

Notes on the text: D *fage* for *fæge* is difficult to account for.

'[...] doomed to the battle. Five lay dead [...]'

A, B and C agree on *gefeohte*. D's omission of the prefix alters the metrical pattern, but the type that results is normal.

Brb A 67	Brb B 67
folces gefylled. beforan þissū.	folces afylled beforan þyssum

'[...] of people slain before this [...]'

A, C and D agree on *gefylled*. C's substitution of *afylled* affects neither metre nor sense.

DEw C 28	DEw D 28

soþfæste sawle. innan swegles leoht.   soðfeste sawle inne swegles leoht.

'(carried) the faithful soul within the light of heaven [...]'

D's *inne*, normally an adverb in OE, occasionally functions as a preposition with the dat. (Plummer 1892: Glossary, s.v. *inne*), but there is no support for *inne* with the acc., as here (*leoht*). C's *innan*, on the other hand, may function as an adverb or as a preposition taking the acc., so it probably represents the poet's text here.

§5.6 SUBSTITUTIONS IN CASES OF UNCERTAIN PRIORITY

The last section dealt with apparently motiveless substitutions in cases where the relative priority of the variants in question was reasonably clear. Now we must begin to consider those many substitutions among the texts of our poems where priority is difficult, even impossible, to establish. In such cases, two or more texts of a poem have different readings, both of them meaningful and metrically unexceptionable. Among my first subgroup of examples in this category, rare vocabulary (whether unique to the text, or rare in OE generally, or confined to poetic texts elsewhere) occurs in the text of one or both versions. In cases where only one version has a rare word or combination, we may suspect that this represents the earlier of the two readings, but we cannot be certain.[2]

§5.6.1 Variations involving rare or poetic vocabulary

SnS A 36–38	SnS B 36–38

ac hwa mæg eaðost ealra gesc[..]fta   ac hwa mæg eaðusð eallra gesceafta
ða halgan duru heofona rices   ða haligan duru heofna rices
tórhte ontynan on getælrime   torhte ontynan on getales rime.

> *Notes on the text*: in A 38 the accent is positioned over the *h* of *torhte*, no doubt by mistake.

> 'But who may most easily of all creatures reveal in order the fair holy doors of the heavenly kingdom?'

Neither the compound *getælrime* in A 38 nor the collocation *getales rime*

---

[2]   I continue here to place what I suspect is the earlier version to the left of the page and the supposedly corrupt version to the right, though the distinction becomes tendentious in presenting variants of this kind; each case needs individual consideration.

in B are recorded elsewhere in OE, but both readings seem irreproachable.

SnS B 32   SnS A 32

feðerscette full fyrngestreona   feðersceatū full feohgestreona

'[...] full to its four corners (?) with (B ancient) treasure, [...]'

There are two variants in this line which are relevant to the present discussion: A *feðersceatū*/B *feðerscette*, and A *fyrngestreona*/B *feohgestreona*. A's *feðersceatum* is probably a noun (if so it is unique) meaning 'four corners' (perhaps the compound *fyðerrice*, 'tetrarchy', is morphologically and semantically analogous), so that the dat. pl. here, dependent on *full*, probably means 'to its four corners'. In place of it, B has the adjective *feðerscette*, (*-scitte*, *-scytte*), 'four-cornered', which, though attested elsewhere, is more awkward in the context. It may be that A's noun (if noun it is) is original here. As for the second variant, both the compounds *fyrngestreona*, 'ancient treasure', and *feohgestreona*, 'treasure', suit the context well. Only B's word *fyrngestreon* is unique to this text in OE, though compounds of similar meaning and structure occur, e.g. *ealdgestreon*, 'ancient treasure', in Bwf 1381, 1458 and elsewhere. The trouble is that B's *feohgestreon* is almost as rare, occurring in only four other places in OE poetry (And 301, Jln 42, 102, Ele 910), so the priority is difficult to decide.

SnS B 59   SnS A 59

mod geondmengeð nænig monna wat   mod gemengeð nænig manna wat

'[...] thoroughly disturbs (*or* A disturbs) my heart. No man knows [...]'

B's *geondmengeð* is unique, but its meaning is easily deduced. A involves nugatory semantic variation (see Toller 1921: s.v. *gemengan*, V2) and so again, although B's hapax legomenon is probably original, there are no other grounds for preferring it.

SnS A 90   SnS B 90

hafað guðmæcga gierde lange   hafað guðmaga gyrde lange

Notes on the text: the hand that inserted an *o* between the *ð* and the *m* of A's *guðmæcga* looks later than the main hand of the text (Menner 1941: 87, note).

'the battle-warrior has a long rod [...]'

Neither *guðmæcga* nor *guðmaga* are attested elsewhere in OE, but the meaning in both cases is clearly 'battle-warrior'. The two words are metrically equivalent and there is evidence elsewhere for the interchangeability of the two second elements (both exclusively poetic in simplex or compounded form) in CFB 2 A *maga* beside B *mæcgea*, C *mecga*.

Dan 301	Aza 22
heapum tohworfene. hyldelease.	heapum to^hworfne hylda lease

> *Notes on the text*: Aza 22 *tohworfne* with superscript *h* added.

'[...] crowds of us scattered mercilessly (*or* Aza without protection) [...]'

Aza's *hylda* is the gen. pl. of *hyld*, 'favour', 'protection', whereas Dan's *hylde-* probably derives from *hyldo*, *hyldu*, 'protection', 'favour'. Dan's compound is unique, but neither reading is clearly preferable to the other.

Aza 25–26	Dan 304–05
nu þu usic bewræce in þas wyrrestan	þa us éc bewrǣcon. to þæs wyrrestan.
eorðcyninges æhtgewealda	eorðcyninga. æhta gewealde.

> 'Now you have banished us (*or* Dan [...] who have also banished us) into the power of the worst earthly king (*or* Dan the worst of earthly kings), [...]'

I assume that Aza 25 *þas* is a slip for *þæs*, as in Dan, rather than the fem. sg. acc. or the nom. or acc. pl. of *þes*, 'this', 'these'. The first interpretation seems to be ruled out by the gender of the element (-)*geweald*, 'power', which is normally either masc. or neut. in OE., not fem.; and a pl. 'these' does not fit either because there is no plural noun to which it might refer. This passage has clearly undergone a fairly major reorganization in one of other of the two versions, probably in Dan; but all that concerns us here is the variation between Aza 26 *æhtgewealda* and Dan 305 *æhta gewealde*. The latter collocation occurs again in Dan in 756, but nowhere else in OE verse. Aza's compounded version of the same elements is found elsewhere only once, in And 1110. Again, it is difficult to see why either reading should be preferred.

Two other variants between Aza and Dan may be dealt with in tandem:

Aza 48	Dan 331
wuldres waldend & woruldsceafta	weroda waldend. woruldgesceafta.

> '[...] ruler of glory (*or* Dan of hosts) and worldly creatures [...]'

Aza 74	Dan 363
woruldsceafta wuldor & weorca gehwylc	woruldcræfta wlite. & weorca gehwilc.

Aza: '[...] the glory of worldly creatures and each of your works [...]'
Dan: '[...] the beauty (?) of the world's hosts and each of your works [...]'

Aza's compound *woruldsceaft* in both these lines occurs only in this poem, whereas Dan's corresponding words *woruldgesceaft* and *woruldcræft* occur elsewhere, the latter only once (GfM 22).[3]

Aza 54	Dan 338
Cwom him þa to are & to ealdornere	se him cwóm to frofre. & to feorhnere.

Aza: '(He) then came to them for their benefit and protection of their lives [...]'
Dan: '[...] who came to them for their help and protection of their lives [...]'

Both versions are regular metrically, and there seems little to choose between the different syntax they involve (the clause in Aza is principal, in Dan relative). Aza's *ealdornere* (dat. sg. of **ealdorneru*) is unique, and its first element, *ealdor-*, 'life', is found only in OE verse. The synonymous *feorhnere* in Dan is common in verse (Ele 897, Chr 610, 1596, Glc 917, Pnt 72, P64.10.2), but *feorh*(-) occurs in prose too. If we assume that Aza has the original reading here, the adaptation of the whole line in Dan to meet the new alliterative requirements of *feorh-* is notably skilful: *frofre*, 'help', replaces *are*, 'benefit', in the a-verse, again with little alteration of the sense. The same comment holds, of course, *mutatis mutandis*, if Dan has priority here.

Aza 70	Dan 359
ealle gesceafte ecne dryhten	eall lándgesceaft. écne drihten.

'[...] all creation (*or* Dan all earthly creatures) (to praise) the eternal lord, [...]'

The noun *gesceaft* (and compounds which contain it as a second element) varies considerably in gender in OE. Here, both forms are presumably

---

[3]   Farrell 1974: 131, would translate Dan 363 *woruldcræfta* as 'worldly wisdom'; but cf. Kroesch 1928–9: 433–4, who detects a semantic shift in OE *cræft* from 'power' to 'large number', 'host', and would translate Dan 363 *woruldcræfta* as 'world's hosts' which I have adopted in my translation.

acc., Aza's *gesceafte* probably fem. acc. pl. (*OEG* §603), Dan's *landgesceaft* probably neut. acc. pl. Dan is metrically suspect if judged by Beowulfian standards: we should expect double alliteration in an a-verse with this variety of Sievers' type D in the older poem (Bliss 1967: 55, §61). But Aza's *ealle gesceafte* is also of a metrical type (1A*1a(i)) which would usually have double alliteration in *Beowulf* in the a-verse, though exceptions do occur (Bliss 1967: 125). The priority is thus unclear.

Brb A 71a reads *ofer bradbrimu* (or possibly *brad brimu*, but in either case acc. pl. neut.), 'across the broad seas', beside B, C, D *ofer brade brimu*, with the same meaning, the only difference being in the inflected *brade* which represents a growing tendency in the W-S dialect to use an inflexion for the acc. pl. neut. (*OEG* §641; see also Orton 1994: 4). All three metrical types which these readings would respectively represent (*bradbrimu*, or *brad brimu*, or *brade brimu*) are well-attested ones and there seems to be no way of choosing between them.

The final example I have noted that belongs in this category is Cæd 6 M *til*, L *to*, both prepositions meaning 'to':

Cæd M 6	Cæd L 6
heben til hrofe haleg scepen.	hefen to hrofæ halig sceppend

'[...] heaven as a roof, the holy creator.'

M is the earliest text we have of Cæd, L the second oldest; but we should note that all members of the North. *eordu* group have *to* here. The word *til* is a Northumbrianism and may well have been a feature of the poet's language; but the evidence for this is not really conclusive.

It is significant that SnS and Aza/Dan are particularly well represented in this category (five and six examples respectively). When two texts differ, though in ways which make it difficult or impossible to establish the relative priority of their readings, we are entitled to conclude that one of them, at least, has passed through the hands of a scribe who was willing and able to amend and adapt his received text well enough to cover his tracks. This is not to say, however, that these same texts may not have passed through the hands of incompetent scribes as well; evidence of incompetent transmission will not appear in variants in this category, by definition. However, these two poems have now emerged clearly as belonging to a special category of freely and competently transmitted verse and we shall need to recall this aspect of them when we are in a position to draw some general conclusions about the transmission of OE verse.

§5.6.2 Consistency in linguistic or stylistic preferences

The texts of SB and Aza/Dan show evidence of a general penchant on the part of transmitters who have handled these texts for certain words or constructions in preference to others. Again, like the variants considered in the previous section, it is usually difficult to judge priority. Here is the evidence for these preferences (unless otherwise indicated, meanings in the two texts are indistinguishable and there are no significant metrical implications):

> SB1 7, 33, 43, 90 *on*; SB2 7, 30, 40, 84 *in* (but the texts agree on *on* in fifteen other places).
> SB1 37 *onbád*, 'awaited', 61 *onbidan*, 'remain'; SB2 34 *bád*, 56 *abidan*.
> SB1 65, 74 *synt*, 'are'; SB2 60 *sindan*, 69 *sindon*.
> SB1 65, 74 *awiht(e)*, 'anything'; SB2 60, 69 *wiht*.
> SB1 75, 116 *þe* (relative particle); SB2 70 nom. pl. *þa*, 111 dat. sg. masc. *þam*.
> SB1 109, 116 *(g)eaglas*, 'jaws'; SB2 104, 111 *geaflas*.
>
> Aza 10, 17, 27, 53, 61, 65 *in*, Dan *on* in the corresponding lines. In general Aza prefers *in*, Dan *on*, but the picture is more complicated than in SB. Aza also has *in* in 4, 18, 25 and 69, all places where the corresponding line in Dan has either no preposition at all or a preposition other than *in* or *on*. Dan has further instances of *on* in 326, 343, 344, 348, 357, all places where Aza has no preposition at all or a preposition other than *in* or *on*. There are two overlaps in *on* (Aza 35/Dan 318 and Aza 63/Dan 347) but none in *in*; Aza 8, 33 have *on* beside Dan 286, 316 *in*; Aza has *on* in 36 at a point where Dan has no preposition; and Dan has *in* in 324 where Aza has no corresponding preposition.
> Aza 14 *þreanydum*, 'afflictions', 28 *þreanyd*; Dan 293 *ðeonydum*, 'oppressions', 307 *þeowned*.
> Aza 32 *hleoþorcwidas*, 'words', 'speech', 43 *wordcwidas*; Dan 315 *hleoðorcwyde*, 326 *wordcwyde*.
> Aza 38 *bugað*, 'inhabit', 61 *cwom*, 'came'; Dan 321 *bebugað*, 'surround', 345 *becwóm*, 'came'.
> Aza 48, 74 *woruldsceafta*, 'worldly creatures'; Dan 331 *woruldgesceafta*, 363 *woruldcræfta*, 'world's hosts'.
> Aza 64, 68 *mid*, 'in' (expressing time and manner respectively); Dan 348, 357 *on*.

None of these substitutions can be explained in terms of mechanical error; in each case there is evidence of a preference for one form or construction rather than another. In most cases we cannot tell which text has the original forms, though in the case of SB1 109, 116 (*g*)*eaglas*, 'jaws', matched in SB2 104, 111 by *geaflas* with the same meaning, the fact that SB2's word is confined to verse suggests that *geaflas* is likely to be the authorial word in both places.

§5.6.3 Preferences for certain collocations and whole-verse forms in Aza/Dan

The variants brought together in the last section illustrate marked preferences for some words or constructions over others, irrespective of context. Other variants seem to show preferences for certain verbal collocations or verse-formulas over others. There are not many clear examples of this kind of free formulaic substitution; in fact, the only ones that are reasonably convincing occur in Aza/Dan. We may begin with the following passage which shows a remarkable series of variants within a very short space:

Aza 46–50	Dan 330–334
þæt þú ana eart ece dryhten	& þæt þu ána eart. éce drihten.
sigerof settend & soð meotod	weroda waldend. woruldgesceafta.
wuldres waldend & woruldsceafta	sigora settend. soðfæst metod.
swa se halga wer hergende wæs	swa se halga wer. hergende wæs.
meotudes miltse & his modsefan	metodes miltse. & his mihta sped.

Aza: '"[...] that you alone are the eternal lord, the triumphant maker, and the true creator, ruler of glory, and of worldly creatures." Thus the holy man continued to praise the mercy of the creator and (described) his mind [...]'

Dan: '"[...] and that you alone are the eternal lord, the ruler of hosts, of worldly creatures, maker of victories, the truthful creator." Thus the holy man continued to praise the mercy of the creator and (described) the abundance of his powers [...]'

These variants affect the sense in matters of detail, but the meaning of the passage is overall essentially the same. All the metrical types represented in either passage are normal ones, and the alliterative structure of each line is the same in both versions (allowing for the transposition of the couplet Aza 47–48 and Dan 331–32). The differences boil down to (a) some internal variation in the structure of the verses themselves, mostly minor and not impacting on either the metre or the meaning in any important way, and (b) the transposition of two lines that I have just mentioned. Some of the verbal collocations in this passage are unparalleled elsewhere, but others are common formulas. Aza's *sigerof settend* and Dan's corresponding *sigora settend* are both unparalleled; but Aza's *soð meotod* and Dan's equivalent *soðfæst metod* are well-attested, the former in Gen 1414, 2793, 2807, Exo 479, And 1602, R3.54, Bwf 1611, Pra 27, the latter in Gen 2654, Dan 383, And 386, LP1 8. Aza's *wuldres waldend* and Dan's equivalent *weroda waldend* are also frequent combinations: the former appears in Dan 13, XSt 24, And 193, 539, Bwf 17, 183, 1752, the latter in XSt 187, 251, 563, Ele 751, 1084, Chr 1569, Glc 594, etc. As we saw earlier, Aza's compound *woruldsceaft* occurs only in this poem, whereas Dan's equivalent *woruldgesceaft*(-) is fairly common elsewhere (Gen 101, 110, 863, MB11.2, 19, 84, 101, 20.129, 29.76, Mnl 115). The collocation: *mihta sped*(-), as in Dan, is also common in verse (Gen 1696, Ele 366, Chr 296, 488, 652, 1383, 1401, Phx 640, MB4.9, 32), and may, like Aza's *modsefan*, be linked by alliteration to *me(o)tod* in the same line: cf. Glc 959 *meotud fore miltsum. He his modsefan* and Ele 366a *meotod mihta sped*. Thus in the case of the three pairs Aza 47b & *soð meotod*/Dan 332b *soðfæst metod*; Aza 48a *wuldres waldend*/Dan 331a *weroda waldend*; and Aza 50b & *his modsefan*, Dan 334b & *his mihta sped*, the substitution was of one formula for another and it seems impossible to say in which direction any of these changes took place. The same may be said of the line-transposition which the passage contains. What is clear, however, is that the text has been handled during transmission with a degree of freedom which, though perhaps not unusual historically, is observable only rarely because the evidence for the process does not, generally speaking, survive. Here it does survive; and one might guess too that this passage was a particularly tempting one for transmitters with any poetic ambitions: it praises God in a highly repetitive, formulaic style which is reminiscent of Cæd with its eight terms for God in nine lines of verse. Familiarity with this genre of praise-poetry, coupled with a sense of mastery over its formulas which familiarity with it bestowed on the transmitter, probably had as much to do with his initiative here as the urge to participate actively in the re-creation of the text. It is, from one point of view, a pity that we cannot see which version has been amended more; but it is really the interchangeability of the versions which makes this passage interesting. The fact that we cannot tell which version has been handled by this ambitious and knowledgeable scribe is itself the evidence that points to his possession of these qualities.

Formulaic substitution may account for two more variants in Aza/Dan.

The first is in Aza 4/Dan 282:

Aza 3b–4	Dan 281b–82
dryhten herede	drihten herede.
wis in weorcum & þas word acwæð	wer womma leas. & þa word ácwæð.

'[...] he (sc. Azarias), wise in his works (*or* Dan a man free of sins) praised the lord, speaking these words:'

Aza's version of 4a, *wis in weorcum*, occurs nowhere else in OE verse, but Dan's *wer womma leas* occurs in precisely the same form in Mnl 209, where it refers to a saint (Martin). There are, in addition, five more occurrences in verse of the collocation: *womma leas(-)*, applying variously to Christ (Chr 1451, SFt 170), the Virgin Mary (Chr 188), and the redeemed souls of men (Chr 1464, Jg1 94). Aza's *wis in weorcum* is an altogether less specific expression and looks rather feeble beside Dan's verse. Both verses make sense in the context. Dan's *wer womma leas* accords especially well with one of Nabuchodonosor's criteria for the selection of Jewish boys in the Vulgate Daniel (1.3–4 [...] *pueros in quibus nulla esset macula*); but Aza's version may correspond with other qualities requisite in these youths, such as are mentioned in [...] *et eruditos omni sapientia, cautos scientia*, etc. Thus neither reading is clearly preferable to the other. An important general question raised by this particular variation is how we should interpret two acceptable variants of the same verse when one is a formula and the other is not; and it has to be said that the replacement of an unparalleled verse-form with a formula seems much likelier than replacement the other way round. By this criterion, Aza has the better claim to be original here.

My final example of a variation which may have arisen by formulaic substitution is Aza 11/Dan 290:

Aza 10–11	Dan 289–90
eac þinne willan in woruldspedum	syndon þinne willan. on woruldspedum.
ryhte mid ræde rodera waldend	rihte & gerume. rodora waldend.

'[...] also your wishes (*or* Dan your wishes are) in terms of worldly successes right with reason (*or* Dan right and roomy (?)), ruler of the heavens [...]'

The variation here is hard to account for, and although the broad meaning of the passage is clear, translation is difficult. The collocation of *rihte* with both *ræde* and *-rume* is attested elsewhere in OE verse: cf. LP2 15 *rihte and rume*, Jud 97 *mid ræde and mid rihte geleafan* (though here *rihte* is adjectival). This is, of course, rather slim evidence for the status of either of the verses in our two poems as stock formulas. There is no clear evidence of priority here.

§5.6.4 Problem cases

Here I assemble a large number of variants the nature of which imply the substitution of one word for another during transmission, though no reason for the substitution suggests itself. As the variants are more or less equally acceptable, there is no evidence of relative priority in most cases. SnS and Aza/Dan are both particularly well represented here.

Cæd 5 O *gesceop*, Ca *gescóp*, other texts of the W-S *eorðan* group *sceop*.

Cæd 5 *aelda* (*ylda*), 'of men' (North. *aelda* and W-S *ylda* groups), *eordu* (*eorðan*, *eorðe*, North. *eordu*, W-S *eorðan* and W-S *eorðe* groups): this variant has provoked much discussion; see Orton 1998: 157–58.

SnS 35 A *ungelic*, B *ungesibb*: both words give acceptable sense here, though B's *ungesibb*, 'not at peace', 'at variance', perhaps provides a closer parallel with *fracoð* and *fremde* in the previous line than A's *ungelic*.

SnS 44 A *dream*, B *dry:* both readings appear to be corrupt here. Menner emends to *dreor*, 'blood', providing a parallel to 43 *blod*, but neither form is credible as a simple error for *dreor*.

SnS 57 A *wuldorlicne*, B *wundorlicne*: both words (meaning 'glorious' and 'wonderful' respectively) are acceptable semantically and metrically, though *wuldorlic* is the rarer word.

SnS 82 A & *wyrma* [.]*elm*, B *wyrma wlenco*: both versions present difficulties of interpretation and are probably corrupt. A's reading might be *welm* (with non-W-S *e*) but we cannot be sure, and the A scribe writes *wylm*, with late W-S *y*, three times elsewhere (SnS 74, 423, 467; see *OEG* §§193a, 200). Besides, *welm*, 'flood', would be difficult to make sense of in the context. B's reading *wlenco* (possibly either 'pride' or 'wealth') is, unfortunately, equally obscure.

SnS 85 A *soðlice*, B *smealice*. A's 'truly' suits the context here just as well as B's 'accurately'.

P89.15.2 *eaðbede*, F *eaðbene*: neither word occurs elsewhere in OE. P's scribe originally wrote *eaðmede*, 'humble', which is attested elsewhere though it would be inappropriate in the context here.

P89.18.1 *Beseoh on*, F *Geseoh*: the verb as in P, *beseon*, 'to look', 'to behold', is attested elsewhere in OE with *on* as a phrasal verb (Bosworth & Toller 1898: s.v. *beseon* II).

Pra 9 L *gemilda*, J *gemilsa*: These are both sg. imperatives in the line:

gemilda/gemilsa þin mod me to gode. J's verb is presumably from *gemiltsian*, 'to soften', 'to make merciful', which gives good sense ('Soften your heart for my benefit [...]'); *gemilda* is probably from *gemyldian*, 'to make mild', which fits equally well here.

R30a 3 *fyre gebysgad*, R30b 3 *fyre gemylted*, 'agitated by fire' and 'consumed by fire' respectively. R30, of which two versions written by the same scribe survive in the Exeter Book, has proved difficult to solve (see Krapp & Dobbie 1936: 337–38), with solutions as widely divergent as 'rain water' and 'tree' or 'cross' among the suggestions that have been put forward. Most commentators think the solution is a wooden object of some kind. If so, either of the readings in 3 is defensible.

R30a 6 *cyssað*, R30b 6 *gecyssað*: either variant is metrically acceptable in the context and the meaning is the same (Cæd 5 above is comparable).

Aza 8 *on dæda gehwam*, Dan 286 *in daga gehwam*: Farrell prefers Dan's version here on the grounds that it echoes the Vulgate text of the Bible more closely than Aza (Farrell 1974: 43), but it seems to me uncertain which part of the Biblical version this line is based on.

Aza 14 *þearfum*, Dan 293 *þreaum*: Jones prefers Aza's version ('straits') to Dan's ('troubles'), but her reasons for doing so are not compelling (Jones 1966: 96–97).

Aza 35 *cyneryce*, Dan 318 *cneorissum*: Aza's word means 'realm', Dan's 'posterity', both of which are acceptable in the context.

Aza 38 *bugað*, Dan 321 *bebugað*. Farrell is probably wrong to take Aza's *bugað* here as from *būgan*, 'to bow'; it is surely from *buan (bugan)*, 'to inhabit'. Dan's *bebugað* is from *bebugan*, 'to surround'. Both readings give good sense (Aza: 'as the stars of heaven inhabit the broad ex-panse', Dan: 'as the stars of heaven encompass the broad expanse').

Aza 41 *ymb wintra hwearft*, Dan 324 *in wintra worn*: both readings give good sense (Aza: 'after the course of years', Dan: 'in a great many years'). Cf. Gen 1320 *ymb wintra worn*, which combines elements of both readings here.

Aza 69 *bearn In worulde*, Dan 358 *bearn israela*: Dan's more specific 'the children of the Israelites' compares favourably with Aza's lame 'the children in the world', but either reading is acceptable enough.

Aza 74 *wuldor*, Dan 363 *wlite*: Aza's 'glory' and Dan's 'beauty' are both equally fitting here.

§5.7 TRANSPOSITIONS

In cases of the transposition of words, whole verses or entire lines, relative priority is often difficult to establish. There are not many examples to examine. The first group shows the transposition of individual words, the second of whole lines.

§5.7.1 Words

One of the more interesting examples is SB1 107a *geomrum gaste* compared with SB2 102a *gæste geomrum*:

SB2 102	SB1 107
gæste geomrum geoce oþþe frofre	geomrum gaste geoce oððe frofre.

'[...] either help or consolation to the miserable spirit.'

Moffat does not discuss this variant in his edition (Moffat 1990). As I pointed out in my own consideration of it (Orton 1979b: 192), the nature of the alliterating sound in the line may be the key to the transposition. In the b-verse, alliteration is on *geoce* which has a palatal initial *g* (pronounced like the initial consonant of PE 'young') in both versions. It is clear that in the earliest OE verse we know of, palatal *g* normally alliterated with the velar *g* that remained initially before back vowels, as in SB1 107a *gaste* (SB's *gæste* would have had the same consonant); but by the end of the OE period, velar *g* in initial position had become the velar stop (as in 'ghost', the PE descendant of OE *gast*), with the result that it was no longer felt to alliterate with palatal *g* (on these consonantal developments see *OEG* §§427–30). If the initial *g* of *gæste/gaste* had become the stop by the time that the SB1 text was copied, the word-order as it appears in SB2 102a might have been regarded as showing an irregular alliterative pattern: alliteration fell on the second stressed word of the a-verse *(geomrum)* rather than on the first (because *gæste* had developed a velar stop). Simple transposition of the words in the a-verse to give the order we see in SB1 107a would have solved this problem.[4]

Another place where SB1 has apparently switched the order of words is SB1 98 *anra gehwylcum* compared with SB2 91 *æghwylc anra* in the context:

SB2 91–92a	SB1 98–99a
þæt þu ne scyle for æghwylc anra onsundran	þæt ðu ne scyle for anra gehwylcum onsundrū
ryht agieldan.	ryht agildan.

4   On relevant forms in Brb, see Campbell 1938: 33; but cf. Bliss 1967: 100, §115.

'[...] that you shall not pay just requital for each one of them separately, [...]'

On this variant, see Orton 1979b: 189. The pronoun *gehwylc* is normally preceded in OE poetry by a noun or pronoun in the gen. (as in SB1 98 *anra gehwylcum*); but the two words are usually in the same verse, both bearing metrical stress; here they are in different verses, and if *gehwylcum* is stressed (as its position certainly suggests it should be), the b-verse probably lacks structural alliteration: alliteration in the a-verse is established as vocalic (on *anra* in SB1, *æghwylc* in SB2), but the prefix *on-* of *onsundrū* (or *onsundran*) is not stressed elsewhere in OE verse, so *onsundrū* seems unlikely to carry the alliteration in SB1 98b. Something has gone wrong with SB1 here. SB2's arrangement, using *æghwylc*, presents no difficulties at all.

In the last two cases it is SB1 which seems to have transposed words. There is a third example in SB1 123a, where the verb *bið* seems to have been transferred from the previous b-verse. Here is the affected clause in both versions:

SB2 117b–18	SB1 122b–23
þōn biþ þæt werge.	þonne þæt werie
lic acolad þæt he longe ær	lic acolod bið. þæt lange ær

'When that weary body has cooled, which he long previously [...]'

The SB2 version is unexceptionable in every respect; the only problem with SB1 is metrical: the inclusion of *bið* in SB1 123a means that the verb must bear metrical stress (SB2 puts the verb before the first stressed word of its clause which alliteration confirms is 117b *werge*, 'weary'); but SB1 123a is not to be scanned as a normal verse if *bið* bears stress (see Bliss 1967: 69–70, §§76–77). Perhaps the transposition in SB1 was made in order to achieve normal word-order for a subordinate clause.

The transposition of *lifgendum* and *gode* in SB2 64 is even more difficult to account for:

SB1 69	SB2 64
lifiendum gode lofsang doð	gode lifgendum lofsong doð

'[...] make a song of praise to the living God [...]'

SB2's arrangement lead to irregular alliteration on the second of the two stressed elements of the a-verse rather than on the first as in SB1. No obvious explanation for the transposition suggests itself.

Further examples of single-word transposition within the half-line are to be found in Aza/Dan. Compare Aza 18 *yldran usse* with Dan 297 *user yldran*:

Aza 17b–18	Dan 296b–97
eac þon wom dydon.	eac ðon wóm dyde.
yldran usse in oferhygdū	user yldran. for oferhygdum.

Notes on the text: Dan 296b *dyde* (sg.) is obscure.

'[...] in addition our forebears committed crimes in their (*or* Dan out of) arrogance, [...]'

Transposition has evidently taken place in one version, but which one? When a possessive adjective like Aza's *usse* ('our') follows the noun it qualifies, it usually bears metrical stress, as it clearly does here (Fakundiny 1970: 138). Dan's *user* is almost certainly not a possessive adjective here but a personal pronoun in the gen.; formally, it certainly cannot agree grammatically with the nom. pl. noun *yldran*. One may suspect that this difference, and perhaps different conventions about whether such words were metrically stressed according to whether they were adjectives or pronouns, lies behind the variation here; but the question might bear more detailed investigation.

A third example of transposition of single words within a verse is Aza 45 & *eac fela folca*, Dan 328 & *folca fela*:

Aza 45	Dan 328
& eac fela folca gefregen habban	& folca fela. gefrigen habbað.

Notes on the text: Aza *habban* could possibly represent the pres. subj. pl. (*OEG* §§762, 735.f); but if it is the infinitive it appears to be, it must be a corruption.

'[...] and (Aza also) many peoples have heard, [...]'

Elsewhere in Aza, the word *fela*, 'many', usually follows a dependent gen., as in 23 *londa fela* (where metre confirms the word-order) and 131 *seldlicra fela*. This makes Aza 45 out of step with the rest of the poem. In Dan, on the other hand, the usual order is as here (Dan 302 *landa fela*, 411 *eower fela*, though cf. 15 *fela folca*, as in Aza 45). Both orders make acceptable metre here, and it seems impossible to say which represents the original order.

In SnS 85b–86a, the B version appears to have transposed the words *wile* and *lufian*:

SnS A 85b–86a   SnS B 85b–86a

       & hine siemle wile   & hine symle luian
lufian butan leahtrum   wile butan leahtrū

Notes on the text: B 85 *luian* is probably a simple error of omission for *lufian* (see above, §2.3.6.2)

'[...] and will always sinless love him [...]'

Here Kuhn's law of clause particles tends to condemn B (Kuhn 1933: 8). In both versions the finite verb *wile* is in a position which would normally imply that it bears metrical stress (because it occurs later than the first dip of the clause); but in the B version stressed *wile* precedes the only alliterating word of the verse, *leahtrum*. This is so unusual as to make it fairly certain that A has the original word-order here.

Finally, Cæd B 1 *herigan sculon* reverses the order of words in all the other texts of the W-S *eorðan* group, though no reason for the transposition suggests itself. The result is metrically unexceptionable.

§5.7.2 Lines

The transposition of entire verse-lines is represented by two passages from Aza/Dan and SB. The first of these, Aza 47–48 and Dan 331–32, was quoted and discussed in the previous section (§5.6.3). Priority proved impossible to establish in that case. There are some indications of the likely direction of change in my second example, SB1 120–21 and SB2 115–16, but again the picture is far from clear:

SB2 114–117a   SB1 119–122a

he þa tungan totyhð & þa toþas   þæt he þa tungan totyhð & þa teð
   þurhsmyhð   þurhsmyhð.
& to ætwelan oþrum gerymeð   & þa eagan þurheteð ufan on þæt heafod.
& þa eaxan þurhiteð ufon on þæt   & to ætwelan oðrum gerymeð.
   heafod
wyrmum to wiste   wyrmum to wiste

Notes on the text: SB2 116 *eaxan* is presumably an error for *eagan*; see §2.1.3 above.

'(SB1 [...] so that) he tears the tongue apart and pierces through the teeth and opens up the way for the others to the abundant food (*or* SB1 and eats through the eyes from above into the head) and eats throught the eyes from above into the head (*or* SB1 and opens up the way for the others to the abundant food), for the worms to the feast.'

Moffat thinks the order in SB1 here is 'more straightforward' (Moffat 1990: 80), but refers to the points about the variation that I made in my 1979 article (Orton 1979b: 191). The transposition might have been the result in one version of a scribe's eye-slip from one *ond* to another, followed by a realization of the omission and the adding-on of the line that had been missed out (though in the wrong place). If we reject this explanation, however, and at the same time agree with Moffat that SB1's version is an improvement on SB2's, it seems to follow that SB2 is more likely to have the original order of lines, for it is difficult to see why the order in SB1 should have been rejected in favour of it. However, I cannot agree that SB1's version is necessarily the better of the two. It is true that it divides the worms' assault on the body into two clearly-differentiated stages — the breach in its various defences at the weakest points by their leader Gifer (SB1 119–20), followed by the advance *en masse* of the worm-army to destroy it completely (121–22a); but other descriptions of martial advance in OE poetry depend for their impact, not on an orderly presentation of events in their natural order, but on an accumulation of different perspectives on the progress of battle which pays little heed to the sequence of events in story-time, or to cause-and-effect relations.[5] It seems to me, therefore, that either version of this passage could be the original one. Unless the SB2 text is original (or error was involved) I am unable to explain the transposition.

§5.8 MODIFICATIONS OF GRAMMAR OR SYNTAX IN CASES OF UNCERTAIN
  PRIORITY

The great majority of the variants in this category are in Aza/Dan. They are listed below, mostly with very brief comments on the nature of the problem.

  EgD 16 A *Ða wæs*, B *ða* (C *Þá*) *wearð*: the variation here is comparable with that in Aza 51, Dan 335 below, and perhaps equally inexplicable.

  DEw 25 C *leode*, D *leodan*: here C has the acc. pl. of the masc. pl. noun *leode*, 'people', D the acc. pl. of masc. *leoda*, 'one of a people or country'.

  Gl1 34 C *standað*, J *stándeþ*: if these verbs have different number (the variation in the vowel of the inflexion might be explained as the merging of unstressed vowels under *e*), the subject of J's sg. verb must

---

[5]   See particularly Jud 199–235 and Mld 96–112.

be 35 *handgeweorc*, whereas the subject of C's pl. verb is probably 33 *þine cræftas*, but neither reading has clear advantages over the other.

LdR 7 *scelfath*, R35.7 *scriþeð*, 'shake' and 'move on' respectively. LdR's verb gives a more vigorous reading, but seems to be used here transitively, whereas it is normally intransitive (see Dobbie 1942: 200), and there is also the difference of number (pl. and sg. respectively) which the neut. noun *hrisil* (in which the nom. sg. and nom. pl. were no doubt identical in form) has obviously generated, though in which direction it is impossible to say. The lines in which these verbs occur probably mean, respectively, '[...] nor do resounding shuttles shake me' (LdR), and '[...] nor does the resounding shuttle move on me' (R35). It is not easy to see what has happened to the text here, largely because the relationship between the lexical and the grammatical modifications is opaque.

LdR 8 *ni mec ouana aam sceal cnyssa*, R35.8 *ne mec ohwonan sceal amas cnyssan*. The meaning of the two versions of this line seems to be 'nor must the slay strike me from anywhere' (LdR; the 'slay' is a moveable part of a weaver's loom; Smith 1968: 51, calls it a 'reed'), and 'nor must the slays (? *amas*) strike me from anywhere' (R35), though in the latter version the verb *sceal* remains singular, casting doubt on the interpretation of *amas* as the pl. of *am*, 'slay'. Here the main barrier to any explanation of the variants is the unestablished significance of *amas* in R35. Another uncertainty here is the metrical status — stressed or unstressed — of the finite verb *sceal*.

P102.4.1 *He*, F *Se*: the pronoun renders Latin *qui*, normally *He* in these versions of the Psalms; but there is no clear priority.

R30a 6 *þæt*, R30b 6 *þær*: either conjunction ('so that' or 'where') seems acceptable here.

R30a 8 *monige mid miltse, þær ic monnum sceal* ('[...] in their multitudes with joy, where for men I must [...]'), R30b 8 *modge miltsum swa ic mongum sceal* ('[...] the brave (ones) with joys (?), as to many I must [...]'). A degree of reorganization of the received text has evidently been undertaken here (R30a's *monige* reappears, though with a different case and grammatical function, in R30b *mongum*), but neither version is obviously prior to the other.

SB1 18 *forwisnad*, SB2 18 *forweornast*, respectively 'decayed' (past part.) and 'you decay' (pres. indic. 2 sg.), though the general sense is little affected.

SB1 54 *gesybban*, SB2 51 *gesibbra*, both 'kinsman' (dat. sg. and gen. pl. respectively) in the phrase *ne næn(i)gum gesybban/gesibbra*, meaning 'nor to any kinsman (*or* kinsmen)'.

SB1 124 *wyrma*, SB2 119 *wyrmes*, in the phrase *wyrma/wyrmes gifel* (SB2 *giefl*), 'food of worms' (gen. pl.) or 'food of the worm' (gen. sg.) respectively. SB2's generic sg. is just as acceptable as SB1's pl.

Aza 4 *þas*, Dan 282 *þa*: both demonstratives are acc. pl. neut., governing *word*, 'words'.

Aza 9 *soðe geswiðde*, Dan 287 *soðe & geswiðde*: there is little to choose between Aza's 'truly confirmed' and Dan's 'true and confirmed'.

Aza 19 *þin bibodu bræcon burgsittende*, Dan 298 *bræcon bebodo. burhsittendū*. These variants present considerable difficulties of interpretation in the context; see Farrell 1974: 65, note to Dan 298.

Aza 21 *wurdon we towrecene* 'we were scattered [...]', Dan 300 *siendon we towrecene*, 'we are scattered [...]': the variation in tense is linked to that in Aza 23 *wæs*, Dan 302 *is*. It also affects the appropriateness of the auxiliary verb used: in Aza the dispersal of the Jews is referred to historically, thus throwing emphasis on the event itself and making the use of *weorðan* appropriate according to normal OE usage. The auxiliary *wesan* tends to be used instead of *weorðan* in passive constructions when the consequences of an action are emphasised rather than the action itself; and in Dan, the present consequences of the Jews' dispersal are indeed emphasised, making *wesan* appropriate. These observations, however, do not help us to answer the question of priority here.

Aza 25 *nu þu usic brewræce*, Dan 304 *þa uséc bewræcon*: the sense in Aza seems to be 'now you have banished us', but the meaning of Dan's version is less easy to establish. The syntax of the passage in which the variant occurs is obscure.

Aza 27 *heorogrimmes*, Dan 306 *heorugrimra*: the variation here between Aza's gen. sg. inflexion and Dan's gen. pl. means that in Aza the adjective ('of the fierce one') refers back to Nabochodonossor in particular, and in Dan to the Chaldeans generally. Both readings give acceptable sense.

Aza 27 *sceolon we*, Dan 306 *& we*: the significance of this (and the following) variant is very obscure.

Aza 27 *þær*, Dan 306 *nu*.

Aza 34 *þæt* (abbreviated) *hit*, Dan 317 *þætte* (abbreviated): in Aza, *þæt* seems to parallel 33 *þæt*: both conjunctions introduce a noun clause specifying what was promised (33 *gehete*) to the Jews. In Dan, *þætte* may be relative, 'which', with 314 *frumcyn* as antecedent, though the meaning in both texts of this and the following line is very obscure.

Aza 36 *yced on eorþan þæt swa unrime*, Dan 319 *& seo mænigeo mære wære*. Here Aza is suspect from the point of view of style, because the verb *ycan*, 'to increase', has been used two lines previously in both texts.

Aza 42 *user*, Dan 325 *heora*: see below, §6.1.1, on this variant.

Aza 44 *nu þec*, Dan 327 *þæt þæt* (both instances abbreviated): Dan's repetition of *þæt* may be a scribal error, for no sense can be made of the reading as it stands.

Aza 51 *wearð*, Dan 335 *wæs*: cf. Aza 21 *wurdon*, Dan 300 *siendon* above. Here, by contrast, there is no obvious explanation for the variation.

Aza 52 *ælbeorhta*, Dan 336 *ælbeorht*: the *-a* of Aza's *ælbeorhta* is a weak adjectival inflexion, though there is no preceding demonstrative or possessive and the inflexion might well have been deleted deliberately as inappropriate in Dan.

Aza 55 *þurh lufan & þurh lisse*, Dan 339 *mid lufan & mid lisse*: either *þurh* or *mid* may be used to express accompanying circumstances in OE; see Bosworth & Toller 1898: s.v. *mid*, VII; *þurh*, III(7). Here, the prepositions seem equally appropriate.

Aza 65 *se*, Dan 350 *swylc* (the variants are clearly connected with the presence or absence of the line represented by Dan 349).

Aza 69 *bædon bletsunge*, Dan 358 *bǽdon bletsian*: Dan 358–59 seems straightforward: 'the children of the Israelistes urged (*bǽdon*) all created things to bless (*bletsian*) the eternal lord'. In Aza, the sense seems to be 'the children in the world, all created beings, asked the eternal lord for (his) blessing.' The variation between *bletsunge* and *bletsian* involves taking the verb *bædon* in two different senses ('urged' and 'asked for'; see Krapp & Dobbie 1936: 270, who suspect Aza here).

Aza 73 *Bletsige þec*, Dan 362 *Ðe Gebletsige*.

Chapter 6. The Scribe as Poetaster

§6 Interpolations and extensions

§6.1 INTERPOLATIONS

Above (§2.4) I described a small number of accidental additions to the texts made by scribes who seem to have been paying no attention to the meaning of what they were copying. The present section describes interpolations that appear to have been made deliberately. I deal first with the addition of individual words, then with longer passages.

§6.1.1 Words and phrases

Sometimes transmitters made small additions to the texts they were copying that seem designed to clarify the sense in some way. SB1 has more examples than most texts. In SB1 64 the personal pronoun *þe*, 'you', appears to have been introduced in this constructive spirit:

SB2 57b–59a	SB1 62b–64a
& þec þin sawl sceal	& þe þin sawl sceal
minū únwillan oft gesecan	minum unwillu oft gesecan
wemman mid wordum	wemman þe mid wordū

> *Notes to the text*: SB1 63 *unwillu* is presumably an error for abbreviated *unwillum*.

> '[...] and your soul must often seek you out against my will, reproach you with words [...]'

SB1 64 *þe* offends against Kuhn's law of clause particles (Kuhn 1933: 8) if, as the metre would indicate, it is metrically unstressed; for as an unstressed clause particle, it ought to occupy the very first metrical dip of the clause (occupied in fact by 62b & *þe þin*).[1] No doubt *þe* was added to clarify the grammatical parallel between SB1 62–63 *þe [...] gesecan* and 64 *wemman (þe)*.

A second example in the same text of a pronoun which is probably interpolated is *hit* in SB1 36:

SB2 32b–34a	SB1 35b–37a
þæt me þuhte ful oft	þæt me þuhte ful oft
þæt wære þritig þusend wintra	þæt hit wære .XXX. þusend wintra
to þinum deaðdæge	to þinū deaðdæge

'[...] so that it very often seemed to me that it would be thirty thousand years to the day of your death.'

Comparable impersonal constructions with *þyncan*, 'seem', elsewhere in OE poetry omit the pronoun (a close parallel is SnS 272–73 *ðynceð him ðæt sie ðria XXX ðusend wintra ær he domdæges dynn gehyre*; cf. also XSt 719). It therefore seems likely enough that SB1 36a *hit* is interpolated, but there can be no certainty in this case.

A particularly intriguing pattern of variation occurs in SB1 33, SB2 30, apparently involving a probable interpolation in SB1 and a probable omission in SB2. Although this section covers interpolations, the two cases cannot really be discussed separately:

SB2 30	SB1 33
ic þe In innan no ic þe of meahte	eardode ic þe on innan ne meahte ic ðe of cuman

SB2: 'I (was) within you; I could not (escape) from you,'

In SB2 30b, the ellipsis of the infinitive (*cuman* in SB1) recalls comparable verses from *Beowulf*: Bwf 543b *No ic from him wolde*, 'I did not wish to go from him', and 754b *no þy ær fram meahte*, 'none the sooner for that might he escape'. Assuming, then, that SB2 shows the same idiomatic, poetic omission, the introduction of the verb *cuman* in SB1, with other small adjustments to word order and the negative construction

---

[1] Cf. Lucas 1987: 146, who cites Exo 19 *Heah wæs þæt handlean ond him hold frea* as an instance of an unstressed personal pronoun (*him*) beyond the first metrical dip of the clause, occupied only by *wæs þæt*: the anomaly is justified by the fact that the b-verse is a minor clause (one lacking a finite verb) in which *wæs* is to be understood from the a-verse. SB1 64 is also a minor clause, so perhaps the unstressed *þe* might be justified in the same way; but if so, why should it have been omitted from SB2?

along the lines of OE prose syntax, is not difficult to envisage. In SB2 30a, however, what appears to have happened is that there has been an attempt to imitate this same ellipsis in the a-verse by omitting the verb (*eardode*, 'dwelt', in SB1). Thus one might claim that a scribal attempt to poeticize SB2's version of the line is matched by an attempt to prosify SB1's version.

We have already had occasion (§4.4.2) to discuss SB1 117 *me*, added to the text for obscure reasons connected with the introduction of the corrupt verb *genydde* preceding it in the same verse. The fifth and final case in SB1 of the interpolation of words involves the very last verse (SB1 126b, SB2 121b) of the address of the damned soul in SB:

SB2 120b–21	SB1 125b–26
þæt mæg æghwylcum	þæt mæg æghwylcum
men to gemyndū módsnottera.	men to gemynde modsnotra gehwam.

'That may (act) as a reminder for each man of wise mind.'

Both versions of the final half-line are of normal metrical type. Willard argued that SB1 has the original version of the verse and that *gehwam* has been lost from SB2 because of damage or even deliberate mutilation suffered by SB2's exemplar or one of its antecedents (Willard 1935: 977–78). This hypothesis is closely bound up with Willard's notion that the second part of the SB1 text (lines 127–66) is original to the poem and has been lost or excised in the course of the transmission of SB2. My own views on this variant were put forward in my article of 1979 (Orton 1979a: 457–58). We should begin by noting that the omission of SB1's *gehwam* from the text is not easy to account for (see Moffat 1990: 81). Willard's hypothesis of folio-loss or folio-excision is, of course, a very drastic solution to the problem. Furthermore, SB2's *módsnotterra* as a whole verse is closely paralleled elsewhere in the OE poetic corpus (cf. especially GfM 41b *modsnotterra*, and And 473b *rædsnotterran*, Ele 379b *forþsnottera*). SB1's equivalent form, *modsnotra*, reflects a later phonological development than *modsnotterra*: first, loss of stress in the medial syllable of -*snotterra*, then simplification of the double consonant (giving -*snottera*), and finally syncope of the medial vowel in late OE (*OEG* §§457 and note 2, 392), giving *modsnottra* or *modsnotra*, as in SB1. However, these formal developments have left the word trisyllabic — too short to fill a verse, but long enough with the addition of *gehwam* after it. I therefore much prefer the view that *gehwam* in SB1 is an addition, made to fill out the line metrically in the face of a syllabically reduced form of the original verse *modsnotterra*.

Texts of poems other than SB1 occasionally show reasonably clear evidence (usually prosodic) of similar minor additions. In Dan 341, metrical considerations point to the interpolation of the acc. sg. masc. 3rd person pronoun *hine*, missing from the corresponding line in Aza:

Aza 59–60a	Dan 341–42a
Tosweop & toswengde þurh swiðes meaht	tosweop hine & toswende. þurh þa swiðan miht.
liges leoman	ligges leoma.

Notes on the text: Aza 59 *toswengde* with *g* squeezed in; evidently *toswende*, as in Dan, was the scribe's first form.

'(He) swept (Dan it) away and destroyed (*or* Aza ? struck) the brightness of the flame through that powerful strength, [...]'

Although we are interested here in Dan 341 *hine*, there are several other difficulties in both versions of these lines which we should at least acknowledge first. The variation between Aza 59 *toswengde* (after correction) and Dan 341 *toswende* is generally assumed to have no important consequences for the meaning, though a verb *toswengan* is recorded nowhere else in OE. The significance of the inflexion of Aza 59 *swiðes* is unclear. It looks like a gen. sg. form and as such might qualify either *liges* or *leoman* if these masc. nouns were taken to be in the gen. sg. here by a transmitter, as in '[...] through the strength (*meaht*) of the blaze (*leoman*) of the mighty fire (*swiðes* [...] *liges*)'. In fact it is reasonably clear that these two nouns are gen. sg. and acc. sg. respectively, as my translation indicates. Dan 342 *leoma* is nom. sg. on the face of it but the grammar of the sentence will not accommodate that interpretation of it and it is probably a slip for acc. sg. *leoman*, as in Aza. As for Dan 341 *hine*, it clearly refers back to Dan 399 (Aza 55) *lig*, 'fire'. The omission of object-pronouns is idiomatic in OE when the object may be inferred from the context, as it certainly may be here, so Aza's lack of pronoun need arouse no suspicion. However, the pronoun offends against Kuhn's law of clause particles (Kuhn 1933: 8), which includes the condition that unstressed particles, of which Dan 341 *hine* is an example, cannot occur after the first stressed word of a clause (here *tosweop*) if its first stressed syllable is preceded by unstressed syllables in the same clause (here the verbal prefix *to-* of *tosweop*). Kuhn's first law is not invariably observed in all OE poems, but with Aza 59 to compare it with, it is difficult to avoid the conclusion that *hine* is interpolated — added, no doubt, for motives of clarification.

A second probable minor addition in Dan is 291 *nu*:

Aza 12	Dan 291
geoca us georne gæsta scyppend	geoca user georne. nu gasta scyppend.

'Help us in earnest (Dan now), creator of souls, [...]'

Here the case is rather more involved than the last. Farrell does not comment on it (Farrell 1974). Again, Kuhn's law of clause particles comes into play. The double alliteration in the a-verse here probably indicates that the imperative verb *geoca* bears a full metrical stress, just as the adverb *georne* in the same verse does. If so (I shall consider the alternative view below), the first metrical dip of this clause is occupied by the inflexion *-a* of *geoca* and the personal pronoun *user* (Dan *us*), 'us', a sentence-particle. According to Kuhn's law, clause particles, which are by definition unstressed, should not be divided between two metrical dips in the clause; they must all be in a single sequence in the first dip of the clause. It follows from this that there should be no other clause particles in later dips in this clause in Dan; but *nu*, 'now', is a sentence-particle in a later dip than *user* — unless *nu* bears metrical stress, in which case it ceases to be a sentence-particle and becomes a stress-word. However, it is clear that if *nu* is metrically stressed here, impossible metrical or alliterative patterns are indicated in either the a-verse or the b-verse (the position of *nu* means that it could be assigned to either half of the line). It therefore seems that *nu* is indeed a sentence-particle, but occurring later than its proper position (which would be with *user* in the first dip of the clause) and thus constituting a breach of Kuhn's law. This whole argument, however, depends on the assumption that the imperative verb *geoca*, with which the clause begins, is metrically stressed. According to Bliss, finite verbs like *geoca* may be unstressed even though they carry what he terms 'ornamental' alliteration (Bliss 1967: 12, §15). If this theory stands up, the adverb *georne* could be the first stressed word in Aza 12a/Dan 291a, and *nu* (elevated, according to this arrangement, into a stress-word) the second, giving a normal verse of Sievers' type B. Thus the question of whether *nu* is interpolated in Dan or has been omitted in Aza depends quite heavily on the question of whether *geoca* bears metrical stress or not; but again, the fact that one version of the text does not contain a word which is at least potentially problematic in the other suggests interpolation in Dan rather than omission in Aza.

Suspicion attaches to Dan 283 *hwæt* (missing in Aza 5) on stylistic grounds:

Aza 4b–5   Dan 282b–83

    & þas word acwæð   & þa word ácwæð.

meotud allwihta þu eart meahtum swið   metod alwihta. hwæt þu eart mihtum
                                                swið.

'[...] and spoke these words: "Creator of all creatures, (Dan behold!) you are powerful in strength [...]"'

The interjection *hwæt* is not usually preceded in speeches by any form of address, as it is here; it is normally the first word of any speech in which it occurs. It is, of course, possible that its presence indicates a misapprehension about *metod alwihta*, actually part of the speech but conceivably mistaken as the final phrase of the introduction to it by a scribe who was taking little notice of the context; but whatever the reason was, it is very probable that *hwæt* is interpolated.

Aza has few clear cases of added words, though there is a good chance that the acc. sg. fem. demonstrative *þa* in Aza 42a is an addition:

Dan 325   Aza 42

fyl nu frumspræce. ðeah heora feá   fyl nu þa frumspræce þeah þe user fea
   lifigen.   lifigen

'Fulfil now the promise, though few of us (*or* Dan of them) remain [...]'

Dan's version does not refer to the fewness of the remaining promises but to the fewness of the Jews. In Aza, Azariah speaks as a representative of the race to which the promise was made, but in Dan he refers to the Jews objectively. The sole problem with Aza 42a *þa* is metrical: it creates a verse of Sievers' type D* with two-syllable first thesis (see Bliss 1967: 38, §44); but although these are small grounds for objection, it is probably an introduction nonetheless, for it would be more difficult to explain its deliberate omission. In general, it is always easier to believe that scribes modified their texts without taking any account of metrical factors than it is to believe that they were sensitive to them.[2]

SnS B 25 *he* is a fairly clear case of interpolation:

SnS B 25a   SnS A 25a

warað windes full   worað he windes full

---

[2] Cf., however, my discussion above of SB1 126b *modsnotra gehwam*.

B: 'He inhabits the cup of the wind, [...]'
A: 'He wanders full of wind, [...]'

Here the subject of the verb in both texts (despite the fact that the verb differs in meaning; see above, §4.2.2.2) is the person defined in the previous line as 'unable to praise Christ through the canticle'. Consequently, there is no real need for A's pronoun *he*, and its presence results in a metrical anomaly: the vowel of the verb *worað*, 'wanders', is long. Without the pronoun *he*, A 25a would scan as a straightforward example of Bliss's type 1D*5 with the double alliteration that is normal in this and related types (Bliss 1967: 125); but if the pronoun is included, the verse will not scan as any attested type. Interpolation in A therefore seems fairly certain, as it is also in the case of SnS A 28 *mid* in the same poem:

SnS B 28a   SnS A 28a

írenum aplum ealle beoð áweaxen   mid irenu æpplu [.................]we[.]xene

'with iron apples. All are grown [...]'

The a-verse here refers to the missiles with which the devil pelts (25 *worpað*) those ignorant of the Pater Noster. The preposition *mid* in A marks the instrumental function of the datives it governs, but B's use of the dat. alone is perfectly idiomatic. Furthermore, the presence of *mid* in the verse also leads to a metrical anomaly: B 28a *írenum aplum* is a verse of Bliss's type 2A1a, probably with syncope of the medial syllable of *irenum*; but whether or not syncope is indicated, the anacrusis which the inclusion of *mid* involves is not found in this and related metrical types in *Beowulf* (i.e. when the caesura falls in position (i); see Bliss 1967: 40–42, §§46–48). This seems to indicate that A 28 *mid* is an addition to the text.

Metrical considerations suggest that SnS A 83 *ón westenne weard* is probably a replacement of B's *westenes weard*:

SnS B 83   SnS A 83

westenes weard weorðmynta geard   ón westenne weard weorðmynda geard

'[...] guardian of the wasteland (*or* A in the wasteland), the garden of honours [...]'

The meaning in both versions is acceptable enough, but A has a metrical pattern (Bliss's type 3E1 with anacrusis) unparalleled in *Beowulf* and against the rules of anacrusis as Bliss defines them (Bliss 1967: 43, 52–53, §§50, 59).

In SnS 88, only A has the preposition *on*:

SnS B 88	SnS A 88

Gyf þu him ærest ufan yorn gebringeð.   gif ðu hī ærest ón ufan ierne
                                          gebrengest

Notes on the text: Menner emends B *gebringeð* to *gebringesð* to bring the
form into line grammatically with A's 2nd person sg. indic. *gebrengest*.
On *-sð* for general OE *-st*, see above, §2.1.2.

'[...] if you first bring down on him from above the wrathful [...]'

In A, postpositional *on* governs *him*, 'him'. We should expect *on* to bear
metrical stress in these circumstances, as a displaced proclitic (see
Fakundiny 1970: 141–42), though this would produce a triple alliteration
in the a-verse (on *ærest*, *ón* and *ufan*; no more than two syllables can
alliterate in an a-verse in OE poetry generally). B's version of the verse is
to be preferred on these grounds, though the reason for the introduction of
on in A is unclear to me.

The C text of Brb has added *&*, 'and', in two lines which may conven-
iently be looked at together (here B represents the sounder text of A, B
and D in both places):

Brb B 19b–20	Brb C 19b–20

    swylce scyttisc eac.   swilce scyttisc eac.
werig wigges sæd. westsexe forð.   werig wigges sæd. & wessexe forð

'[...] likewise the Scottish too, weary, sated with war. (C and) Forward did
the West-Saxons [...]'

Brb B 30b–32a	Brb C 30b–32a

    swilce seofone eac.   swilce VII. eac
eorlas anlafes. unrím herges.   eorlas anlafes. & únrím herges.
flotan & scotta   flotan & scotta

'[...] likewise also seven of Anlaf's chieftains, (C and) a countless number
of the army of seamen and Scots.'

In both these cases, the agreement of texts A, B and D against C's & is
sufficient evidence of its interpolation;[3] but the reasons for the
introductions are obscure. In C 19, perhaps the conjunction is meant to
draw a clearer distinction between the retreating army and the victorious
West-Saxons, but it is scarcely a necessary addition. In the case of C 31,
the addition of 'and' has a more obvious motive: to distinguish more

---

[3]   See above, §3.3, on the relationship between the four texts of Brb.

clearly between the 'seven' of Anlaf's chieftains who died in the battle and the 'countless number' of additional casualties: without the 'and', *unrim herges* in 31b is in danger of misinterpretation as a variation on the 'seven' casualties just mentioned, which would, of course, be illogical. It certainly looks as though C's scribe was trying to be helpful here in adding the conjunction.

We have already had reason to mention Brb A 56, which also involves the addition of the conjunction 'and' (§4.2.2.2 above) in a context which suggests that it was part of a transmitter's attempt to accommodate a corruption that he, or one of his predecessors, had already made. The addition in the archetype of the North. *eordu* texts of Cæd of 9 *on* in the phrase *on foldu* has also been explained earlier (§4.2.2.1) as an error based on a failure to appreciate the grammatical function of 9 *foldu* in the text as an acc. sg. We should also consider here the apparent addition of the first person nom. pl. pronoun *we* in Cæd 1 which occurs in all the extant versions except the two earliest (the North. *aelda* texts M and L) and T, the earliest text of the W-S *eorðan* group. T may be compared with H to illustrate the difference:

Cæd T 1   Cæd H 1

nu sculon herigean heofonrices weard   Nu we sculon herian heofonrices
                                             weard.

'Now we must praise the guardian of the heavenly kingdom, [...]'

We saw earlier that in O (like T, a text of the W-S *eorðan* group) the pronoun was added superscript, probably indicating its absence in O's exemplar (above, §1.1). If this is how O's original reading before correction should be interpreted, T and O together point to a group archetype lacking the pronoun and thus linked with the earliest North. tradition of the text as represented by M and L. Technically, the verb *sculon* is ambiguous as to person; but it seems unlikely that any reader or scribe would have taken it as a 2nd- or 3rd-person verb, especially the latter ('Now you must praise [...]' or 'Now they must praise [...]'). The addition of *we* is thus best explained, not as a clarification of the person of the verb, but simply as the adoption of normal OE idiom. The notion that the omission of 1st-person pronouns was normal North. idiom is based on very doubtful evidence (see Orton 1998: 164, note 40). Furthermore, the presence of 1 *we*, not only in the W-S *eorðe* group of texts, but also in the W-S *ylda* group too, which shows no clear sign of being derived from the North. *eordu* group, strongly suggests that *we* was added to the text in more than one branch of transmission.

§6.1.2 Longer interpolations

More substantial additions to texts in the form of phrases, half-lines or entire lines of verse are occasionally detectable, though it is seldom a simple matter to decide between omission in one text and addition in another. One of the smaller but more convincing examples is Gl1 J 23 & *on þone*:

Gl1 22–23 C	Gl1 22–23 J
þu geworhtest. éce god ealle gesceafta	þu gewrohtest éce gód. ealle gesceafta.
on six dagū seofoðan þu gerestest.	on syx dagum. & on þone seofoðan þu gerestest.

'You made, eternal God, the whole of creation in six days, (J and) on the seventh you rested.'

I have recently discussed this variation elsewhere in detail (Orton 1999: 288–90). Lumby, in his edition, translated C as: 'Thou formedst, eternal God, all creatures in six days: on the seventh thou didst rest,' (Lumby 1876: 53); the ordinal *seofoðan* is presumably dat., expressing 'time when' (Mitchell 1985: I, §1421). The only difference that J's more expansive version makes to Lumby's translation is that it adds an additional 'and' in the middle of the sentence; but J's & *on þone* is suspect on grounds of metre and style. Firstly, it creates an unusually heavy anacrusis of four syllables in verse 23b (see Ure 1957: 70, 122); we have already seen in other connections that the normal limit for anacrusis in *Beowulf* is two syllables (see Bliss 1967: 40–42, §§46–48; above, §§4.2.2.1, 5.3 and 5.5). *Beowulf* should not, of course, be regarded as necessarily representing the standard followed by all OE poets, but the Gl1 poet does not use extended anacrusis elsewhere in the text. Secondly, J's version of 23b runs foul of Kuhn's law of clause particles: it involves a division of unstressed particles — *and* and *þu* — between two metrical dips, both before and after the stress-word *seofoðan*, contrary to the general regularity of *Beowulf* in this respect (Kuhn 1933: 8). In spite of these apparent technical shortcomings, J's syntax at this point is acceptable judged by prose standards — appropriate standards here, perhaps, in view of the probable influence on J of an OE prose translation of Genesis II.2 such as the one in the *OE Heptateuch*, which contains the sentence: [...] *and he gereste hine on ðone seofoðan dæg (die septimo) fram eallum ðam weorcum ðe he gefremode* (Crawford 1922: 85). The question of priority is not a simple one here; but C's conventionality in metre and in its obedience to Kuhn's law of clause particles probably indicates its priority. Another consideration here, of course, is that it is much more difficult to envisage the omission of J's extra words than it is to see why they were added. It is hard to believe that J's version of the verse would have been changed to C's simply for the sake of poetic style. Desire for clarity, or at least for a stronger emphasis on the contrast between God's work and rest, coupled, probably, with a memory of some OE translation of the biblical text behind the poem, were no doubt the motives for the expansion of the verse in J.

Gll J 23b shows (I have argued) the amplification of a noun-phrase. We may look next at what I believe are two additions of unattached half-lines to existing texts. The first of these is Dan 288a:

Aza 8–10	Dan 286–89
sindon þine domas on dæda gehwam	syndon þine dómas. in daga gehwam.
soðe geswiðde & gesigefæste.	soðe & geswiðde. & gesigefæste.
	swa þu sylfa eart.
eac þinne willan in woruldspedum	syndon þine willan. on woruldspedum.

'In every deed (*or* Dan Every day) your judgements are truly confirmed (*or* Dan true and confirmed) and victorious (Dan as you yourself are too). (Aza Also) your wishes for worldly successes (Dan are) [...]'

Farrell mentions Dan 288 as one of several unattached verses in the poem (Farrell 1974: 20), but does not draw any conclusions from the fact that it does not appear in Aza (on unattached half-lines generally in OE, see also Bliss 1971: 442–49). There is nothing corresponding to it in the Vulgate Bible, and the verse adds nothing of any substance to the meaning. It contains, however, a palaeographical peculiarity that supports the evidence of its unattached condition in favour of interpolation: the *s* of *swa* is a round *s* which the scribe of Dan uses nowhere else in this part of the Junius manuscript. Elsewhere (I have examined pp. 156–212 of the manuscript to confirm this), the scribe seems to confine himself to the 'low' *s*, somewhat resembling a small *y*, which is usually the favoured form in OE manuscripts. The anomaly here is best explained, I believe, by supposing that the scribe of Dan (or alternatively a scribe who copied the text in an antecedent manuscript), in departing from his exemplar to add this verse, used a form of *s* which was natural to him but was not used in his exemplar, and so left a trace of his initiative.

Another probable instance of the addition of a single half-line to a text is SB1 111:

SB2 103–06	SB1 108–12
biþ þæt heafod tohliden honda tohleoþode	Bið þæt heafod tohliden handa toliðode
geaflas toginene goman toslitene	geaglas toginene góman toslitene
seonwe beoð asogene sweora bicowen	sina beoð ásocene swyra becowen
	fingras tohrorene
rib reafiað reþe wyrmas	rib reafiað reþe wyrmas

'The head is sprung open, the hands disjointed, the jaws split open, the gums torn open, the sinews are sucked away, the neck gnawed through, (SB1 the fingers decayed); fierce worms plunder the ribs, [...]'

Moffat comments: 'Given the similarity of the participial endings in this passage, scribal omission of a verse because of eyeskip would not be surprising' (Moffat 1990: 79); but although that would explain the un-attached condition of the extra verse in SB1, it would not account for the fact that the line in question is missing from SB2, which would, if Moffat's suggestion is correct, be an extraordinary coincidence. I therefore repeat my earlier suggestion (Orton 1979b: 183–84) that SB1 111a represents an amateurish attempt to extend a long series of phrases of similar structure describing the body's destruction by the worm-army.

The addition of an entire line is exemplified by SB1 93:

SB2 86–88a	SB1 92–95a
Ðōn wile dryhten sylf dæda gehyran	Ðōn wyle dryhten sylf dæda gehyran
	hæleða gehwylces heofena scippend
æt ealra monna gehwam muþes reorde	æt ealra manna gehwæs muðes reorde
wunde wiþerlean	wunde wiðerlean.

SB2: 'Then the lord himself will hear from every one of all men about (his) deeds by the mouth's voice, the wound's compensation.'

SB1: 'Then the lord himself, the creator of the heavens, will hear of the deeds of each man, from the voice of the mouth of each of all men,' etc.

Moffat leaves open the question of whether SB1 93 is an interpolation or an omission from SB2, but I repeat the suggestion I put forward in 1979 (Orton 1979b: 184) that we have to deal with an interpolation here. SB1 93 consists of two verse-formulas (cf. MB13.32 *hæleða gehwilcne*; And 192 *heofona scyppend*, MCh11.12 *heofna scyppende*). The second is a variation on SB1 92 *dryhten* and its presence has no significant impact on the meaning or the grammar of the sentence; but the inclusion of *hæleða gehwylces* must surely have something to do with the variation in the following line between SB2 86 *gehwam* (dat. sg.) and SB1 94 *gehwæs* (gen. sg.). The gen. *gehwæs* is, I assume, a modification of original *gehwam*, made to accommodate SB1 93a *hæleða gehwylces*; for if *gehwam* had been retained, the meaning (with SB1 93 included) would be something like 'Then the lord himself, the creator of the heavens, will hear of the deeds of each man, from each man, by the mouth's voice [...]': the construction with the gen. ('of each man') and the construction with *æt* (in essence, 'from each man') would not go easily together. However, as things actually stand in SB1, the result is still unsatisfactory: the preposition *æt* can only govern *reorde*, now involved in the cumbersome construction indicated by my translation above, whereas *reorde* was surely intended originally to be part of an adverbial phrase with *muþes*, something like 'by word of mouth', perhaps in roughly the same sense as the modern idiom 'from the horse's mouth'. Here, a modest show of initiative on a transmitter's part seems to have landed him in trouble. The transmitter who added SB1 93 may, of course, be a different individual from the person who substituted *gehwæs* for *gehwam* in the following line, as Moffat points out; but there is no particular reason to think that the modifications in this sentence took place in two phases rather than one. It would, I submit, be much more difficult to account for the SB2 version here as a modification of the text as it appears in SB1.

In this last case, a single line has been added in SB1. A two-line interpolation seems to be indicated in 59–60:

SB2 54–56	SB1 57–61
Ne magon þec nu heonan adon hyrste þa readan	Ne mæg þe nu heonon adon hyrsta þy readan.
ne gold ne sylfor ne þinra goda nán	ne gold ne seolfor ne þinra goda nán ne þinre bryde beag. ne þin goldwela. ne nan þara goda þe ðu iu ahtest.
ac her sculon abidan ban bireafod	Ac her sceolon onbidan ban bereafod

'Red jewels may not secure your release from here, nor gold nor silver nor any of your goods, (SB1 nor your bride's ring, nor your wealth in gold, nor any of those goods that you previously possessed), but here the plundered bones must remain, [...]'

I have not attempted to translate SB1's version of the first line. In my earlier discussion of it (above, §4.2.2.1) I suggested in general terms what sense it might have been meant to convey. There are several considerations which suggest that SB1 59–60 are interpolated. Firstly, their redundancy in the context is remarkable, for as I pointed out in my 1979 discussion of them (Orton 1979b: 183), SB1 59b adds nothing to the information already provided by SB1 58a, and the whole of SB1 60 is just an expanded version of SB1 58b. Secondly, SB2 55b/SB1 58b seems to sum up the series of useless possessions and so close the list; only in SB1 does it continue — inappropriately. Thirdly, SB1 59b does not alliterate with its a-verse, in which alliteration is plainly on *b* (perhaps, as I suggested in my 1979b article, *goldwela* is a scribal error for the poetic word *boldwela*, 'splendid dwelling', which would have provided the alliterating *b-* the line requires).

Moffat claims that alliteration also fails in SB1 60, but this is doubtful. Alliteration falls on the *g* of *goda* in the a-verse; *iu* in the b-verse is not a diphthong but a well-attested spelling of *geo*, 'formerly' (see *OEG* §58): despite the spelling, the adverb has not lost its initial consonant, and as we have seen above in a different connection (§5.7.1), velar *g*, as in *goda*, alliterated with the palatal spirant *g-*, as in *geo*, *iu*, until the very end of the OE period. These extra lines in SB1 are rather reminiscent of SB1 111a, considered earlier: a list, the individual items of which vary little in their internal grammar, has been extended; but the interpolator, lacking the technical expertise of the poet, is unequal to the task he imposes on himself. He also seems to lack imagination, for his dependence on the words and ideas of his received text is very noticeable.

A second probable case of interpolation of two whole lines is Dan 343–44:

Aza 59–61	Dan 341–45
Tosweop & toswengde þurh swiðes meaht	tosweop hine & toswende. þurh þa swiðan miht.
liges leoman swa hyra lice ne scod.	ligges leoma. þæt hyre líce ne wæs. owiht geegled. ác he on andan sloh. fyr on feondas for fyrendǽdum.
ac wæs in þam ofne þa se engle cwom	þa wæs on þam ofne. þær se engel becwóm.

Notes on the text: Aza 59 *toswengde* with *g* squeezed in; evidently *toswende*, as in Dan, was the scribe's first form. Aza 61 *ofne* originally *hofne* with *h* underdotted twice to indicate that it was an error.

'(He) swept (Dan it) away and destroyed (*or* Aza (?) struck) the brightness of the flame through that powerful strength, so that it did not harm their bodies, (*or* Dan so that their bodies were not at all injured, but in his rage he drove the fire into the enemies because of their evil deeds;) but when (*or* Dan Where) the angel came, in the furnace it was [...]'

There are numerous difficulties of interpretation here, especially in Dan. The noun *lice* (Aza 60/Dan 342) is certainly dat. sg. in Aza, because the verb *sceððan*, 'to injure' (3 sg. pret. indic. *scod*), of which it is the object, regularly takes the dat. in OE. The sense of *lice* must, however, be pl., so that Aza 60 means: 'so that it (*sc.* the fire, referring probably to Aza 60 *liges* rather than to *leoman*, 'brightness') did not harm their bodies'. In this context, *hyra*, 'their', is appropriate; but in Dan, *hyre*, apparently gen. sg. fem., is inappropriate, both in its sg. number and in its gender, for there is no fem. noun (or female person) to which it may refer. Farrell explains *hyre* as showing 'the reduction of the final unstressed vowels which is so often seen in this text' (Farrell 1974: 68), but this seems a soft option; there are eight more instances of *hyra* in Dan.

The only suggestion I can make by way of explanation of the variation between the texts here is that a transmitter in Dan's history has misunderstood 342 *lice* entirely, taking it as the nom. of some noun, though what noun that could be is a puzzle. Evidently he took it as a sg. noun in the context, for he makes it the subject of the verb *wæs* [...] *geegled*. The basis of the misunderstanding could, of course, have been Aza 60b, where the absence of any subject-pronoun for the verb *scod* might have given rise to a misunderstanding of the role of *hyra lice* in the construction with *sceððan*. Two other aspects of the extra lines in Dan should be noted. One is that there is no manuscript point between the two halves of line 344. Metrical pointing is very regularly observed in the Junius 11 manuscript. Only four other lines (279, 292, 314, 319) in Dan 279–364 omit a line-medial point. The other aspect has to do with the biblical source of the missing lines. The incident of the burning of the Chaldeans near the furnace by the spreading fire occurs in the Vulgate Daniel (3.48 *et erupit et incendit quos repperit iuxta fornacem de Chaldeis*), though there it precedes the arrival of God's angel; in Dan, on the other hand, the incident is interposed between the angel's expulsion of the fire and his creation of the fresh breeze in the furnace. Perhaps a scribe in Dan's history, recalling a missing detail of the biblical narrative, saw an opportunity to insert it here, where it is quite appropriate dramatically. Having done so, he appears to have made an adjustment to the context to accommodate his interpolation. In Aza 61, *ac* introduces the actual circumstances in the furnace after a statement in the negative of what did *not* occur there; but the Dan interpolator, having used an *ac*-clause in his interpolation (343), cancelled the *ac* at the beginning of the line represented in what I take to be its original form as Aza 61, and substituted *þa*, 'Then', beginning a new sentence. After a description of what happens outside the furnace, we return, with *þa*, to conditions inside it. Evidently some thought has gone into these amendments in Dan.

Finally in this section I should like to suggest that DrR is an amplification of the RCr inscription. I must begin with some general remarks about these two texts because I have not had reason to mention either of them so far. DrR is an OE poem of 156 lines which, like SB1, survives in the late-tenth-century Vercelli Book. It is often divided by critics into three main parts: an introduction in which a (human) narrator describes the appearance of Christ's cross to him in a dream (1–27); a prosopopoeic speech by the cross to the dreamer in which it tells of its own origins as a tree, describes the crucifixion as the central episode in its life, and explains its consequent significance as a Christian symbol (28–121); and finally a conclusion spoken by the dreamer in which he describes the spiritual impact that his vision of the cross has had on his life (122–56). While it would be rather misleading to say that DrR exists in two versions, the runic inscription on the Ruthwell Cross in Scotland (RCr) consists of four passages from a speech of the cross which closely match passages within the range of lines 39–64 of DrR — so closely that in these passages at least we are plainly dealing with work by the same poet.

The relationship between the two texts, and the historical implications of that relationship, are difficult and complex questions. Here our only concern is the relationship between the two texts in the four passages where they match one another closely. Below the RCr text is given in full with its runic letters transcribed into the roman alphabet and line-references indicating the main correspondences with the DrR text. The text of RCr is incomplete because of damage sustained by the Ruthwell cross in the seventeeth century. The four passages of the inscription are fragments, separated by three lacunae of varying and uncertain size and terminating in a fourth. Dobbie writes (Dobbie 1942: cxx) that 'the runes now missing or illegible on the lower part of the shaft must have accounted for most of the intermediate matter in the poem [*sc.* in DrR]', though there is reason to question this statement, as we shall see below.

As there are so many minor uncertainties about the readings of the RCr inscription, I have decided simply to reproduce Dobbie's text (Dobbie 1942: 115) without altering it in any way except in rearranging it to read in full lines rather than verses. Dobbie's dots, which I reproduce, represent his assessment of the likely number of lost letters. The OE text of the relevant part of the DrR follows,[4] with passages matching those in the Ruthwell text italicized. The two texts are translated separately.

RCr

39–40 [..]geredæ hinæ ḡod alme3ttig, þa he walde on ḡalḡu gistiḡa,
41   [.]od*i*g f[.......] men.
42   [.]ug[............................]

'God almighty stripped himself when he wanted to ascend the cross, brave before men — '

44   ... ic riicnæ k̄yniŋc,
45   hêafunæs h*l*afard, *h*ælda ic ni dorstæ.
48   *Bismæræd*u uŋk̄et men ba ætgad[..]; ic [...] *mi*þ blodæ [.]istemi[.],
49   bi[.................................]

'I (bore) the noble King, the Lord of Heaven, I did not dare bow; men mocked us both together; I was smeared with blood [...]'

56   Krist wæs on rodi.
57   Hweþræ þer fus*æ* fêarran kwomu
58   *æ*þþilæ til anum. Ic þæt al bi[....].
59   S[...] ic w[.]s mi[.] so[.]ḡum gi*dr*œ[..]d, h[.]aḡ [................]

'Christ was on the cross; yet there eager noble men came from afar to him alone; I beheld all that; I was sorely troubled with sorrows [...]'

62   *mi*þ stre*l*um giwundad.
63   Alegdun hiæ *hi*næ limwœrignæ, gistoddu[.] him [......]icæs [..]f[..]m;
64   [...]êa[.]du[..]i[.] þe[.................................]

'[...] wounded with arrows. They laid him out weary in limb; they stood at the head of his body, they beheld there [...]'

DrR 39–64

Ongyrede hine þa geong hæleð, (þæt wæs *god ælmihtig*),
40   strang ond stiðmod. *Gestah he on gealgan heanne*,
    modig on manigra gesyhðe, þa he wolde mancyn lysan.
    Bifode ic þa me se beorn ymbclypte. Ne dorste ic hwæðre bugan to

---

[4]   The text of DrR is from Krapp 1932: 62–3.

eorðan,
    feallan to foldan sceatum, ac ic sceolde fæste standan.
    Rod wæs ic aræred. Ahof *ic ricne cyning,*
45   *heofona hlaford, hyldan me ne dorste.*
    Þurhdrifan hi me mid deorcan næglum. On me syndon þa dolg
        gesiene,
    opene inwidhlemmas. Ne dorste ic hira nænigum sceððan.
    Bysmeredon hie unc butu ætgædere. Eall ic wæs mid blode bestemed,
    *be*goten of þæs guman sidan, siððan he hæfde his gast onsended.
50   Feala ic on þam beorge gebiden hæbbe
    wraðra wyrda. Gescah ic weruda god
    þearle þenian. Þystro hæfdon
    bewrigen mid wolcnum wealdendes hræw,
    scirne sciman, sceadu forðeode,
55   wann under wolcnum. Weop eal gesceaft,
    cwiðdon cyninges fyll. *Crist wæs on rode.*
    Hwæðere þær fuse feorran cwoman
    to þam æðelinge. Ic þæt eall beheold.
    Sare ic wæs mid sorgum gedrefed, hnag ic hwæðre þam secgum to
        handa,
60   eaðmod elne mycle. Genamon hie þær ælmihtigne god,
    ahofon hine of ðam hefian wite. Forleton me þa hilderincas
    standan steame bedrifenne; eall ic wæs *mid strælum forwundod.*
    Aledon hie ðær limwerigne, gestodon him æt his lices heafdum,
    beheoldon hie ðær heofenes dryhten, ond he hine ðær hwile reste,

'The young hero stripped (who was almighty God), strong and resolute; he climbed up on to the high gallows, brave in the sight of many, when he desired to redeem mankind. I trembled when the warrior embraced me; nevertheless I dared not bow to the ground, fall to the surface of the earth, but had to stand firm. As a cross I was raised up. I lifted up the powerful king, the lord of the heavens; I dared not bend. They drove me through with dark nails; the wounds are visible in me, open, malicious wounds. I dared not injure any of them. They mocked us both together. I was made all wet with blood, poured out from the man's side, after he had given up his spirit. On that hill I endured many cruel events. I saw the God of hosts violently stretched out. Darkness had clothed the corpse of the ruler with clouds, the bright radiance; the shadow went forth, dark beneath the clouds. All creation wept, lamented the fall of the king. Christ was on the cross. Yet eager ones came there from afar to the prince. I beheld all that. I was deeply distressed with sorrows and yet, humbled, I bent to the men's hands with great zeal. They took there almighty God, lifted him down from the grim torture. The warriors left me to stand soaked with moisture;

I was badly wounded all over with arrows. They laid down (the man) weary of limb there, they placed themselves at the head of his body; they beheld there the lord of heaven, and he rested there for a while, [...]

The relationship between these two texts is not easy to describe without weighting the argument in favour either of interpolation in DrR or contraction in RCr. The first passage in RCr could be described as a contraction of the whole of DrR 39 into its first a-verse, and a conflation of DrR 40b and 41b in the same line's b-verse. The little that is visible of the next verse in RCr looks as though it corresponded with DrR 41a, but how closely it is now impossible to say. However, metrical considerations tend to point to DrR as having an expanded version of RCr. The first line of the runic text is (we may probably take the *on-* prefix of the initial verb on trust) a perfect hypermetric line with regular alliteration, whereas the a-verses of lines 39 and 40 of DrR are not regarded by Bliss as hypermetric (Bliss 1967: 163).[5] Line 40 of DrR, however, has alliteration falling on a finite verb in the b-verse (*Gestah*) rather than on the noun (*gealgan*), as in RCr. This kind of promotion of finite verbs over nouns and adjectives to stressed and alliterating positions is not unheard of elsewhere in OE verse, even when there are two subsequent stress-words available in the same verse, as there are in DrR 40b (examples I have noted are And 1260b *clang wæteres þrym*, Chr 87b *Cwæð sio eadge mæg*, Jln 623b *wrecað ealdne nið*, Rui 2b *brosnað enta geweorc*, Bwf 2717b *seah on enta geweorc*, SnS 337b *ðonne he demeð eallum gesceaftum*), but the relative conventionality of the inscription's text in this line is conspicuous.

The second passage of RCr matches DrR 44–45 and 48–49 quite closely, but lines corresponding to DrR 46–47 are missing from the inscription and there is nothing to suggest that they were there originally. The second of the additional lines in DrR, 47, is defective in alliteration: the a-verse establishes vocalic alliteration for the line, but the first stressed word in the b-verse is probably *nænigum* with initial *n* and there is no word beginning with the required vowel except *ic*, which cannot bear stress, here or anywhere else in OE verse. Again, we find questionable versification in a line of DrR which is not confirmed as archetypal by the RCr text.

A very close textual correspondence exists between both the third and

---

[5]   Bliss is certainly right about 40a *strang and stiðmod*; in 39a, much depends on whether stress is assigned to the verb *Ongyrede*.

the fourth passages of the RCr inscription and DrR, with only one variation of real substance in RCr *æþþilæ til anum* beside DrR 58a *to þam æðelinge*, but both lines are meaningful and metrically unexceptionable. RCr has the acc. sg. masc. personal pronoun *hinæ* in its line corresponding to DrR 63a, which makes for a slightly smoother reading.

The evidence for priority here is obviously not completely conclusive; but on the whole, appeal to metrical considerations tends to favour RCr as having the best, and so probably the original, text. This need cause no surprise. RCr is, after all, probably nearly three hundred years earlier than the Vercelli Book text of DrR, so it has not had as much time to become corrupted. The preservation of its text on a fixed stone monument also meant that it was always available to Anglo-Saxon readers throughout the period, including any reader with the sort of poetic expertise needed to expand it into a fuller account of the crucifixion from the cross's point of view. Such a reader, I suggest, was the poet of DrR.[6]

Here we must not neglect to mention the two-line poetic part of the inscription on the tenth- or eleventh-century Brussels Cross (text from Dobbie 1942: 115):[7]

BCr 1–2

Rod is min nama. Geo ic ricne cyning
bær byfigynde, blode bestemed.

'Cross is my name. Once, trembling and drenched with blood, I bore the mighty king'.

It is very probable that the text of these lines was influenced, directly or indirectly, by either RCr or DrR; for the first line closely resembles DrR 44 *Rod wæs ic aræred. Ahof ic ricne cyning* (quoted above; compare also RCr 44 [...] *ic riicnæ Kyninc*) in alliterative structure and verbal collocation; the distinctive verb *bifian*, 'to tremble', is used with the same application in DrR 42 (*Bifode ic þa me se beorn ymbclypte*, quoted above); and the poetic formula *blode bestemed*, 'drenched with blood', recurs in DrR 48 (*Eall ic wæs mid blode bestemed*; also Exo 449, Chr 1085, Bwf 486, and RCr 48 *miþ blodæ [.]istemi[.]*).

Such a range of echoes seems too wide to be accounted for simply as a product of conventional links between theme and formula in the poetic tradition, though the brevity of the BCr text makes it difficult to suggest

---

[6] See further below, §6.2.2, on other developments in the textual history of DrR.

[7] For an account of the inscription in its context, see Okasha 1971: 57–8.

more definite conclusions about its relationship to the other two.

§6.1.3 Additions or omissions?

There remains to be considered a large group of variants that could represent either interpolation in one text or omission in another, at least when considered individually; but when we look at the general distribution of these variants, patterns sometimes appear which seem to mark some kind of distinction between texts of the same poem.

§6.1.3.1 SnS

Certain poems are especially rich in variants of this kind. A case in point is SnS, in the A text of which a large number of words occur that are missing from the B text. These are all words of relatively minor importance for the meaning of the text and include adverbs, prepositions, and personal and relative pronouns. The variants are considered in turn below:

SnS B 18	SnS A 18
gesemesð mec mid soðe 7 ic mec gesund fa[..]	me ðōn gesund f[.]r[.]e

Notes on the text: In A, no part of the a-verse is legible. B's form *fa* is inexplicable, though it is often treated as the first part of *fare*, 1 sg. pres. indic. of *faran*, 'to go', 'to travel' etc. (see Dobbie 1942: 161; but cf. Page 1965: 37, who thinks we have to deal with the verb *ferie* here).

'[...] (B (if you) satisfy me with truth, and I) (A then) go safe [...]'

A's *ðōn* (= *ðonne*), 'then', is inessential but unobjectionable here.

SnS B 24	SnS A 24
Se þurh ðone cantic ne can crist geherian	Seðe [..]rh ðone c[..]tic[......][.....] herigan

'He who is unable to praise Christ through the canticle [...]'

The variation between the relative use of the simple demonstrative *Se*, as in B, and the relative *Seðe* in A affects neither sense nor metre and I can see no way of deciding which has replaced which, though we should perhaps note that both texts have *se ðe* in 84.

SnS B 46b–47	SnS A 46b–47
þane seo ærene gripo	ðōn seo ærene gripo

þon for twelf fýra tydernessum   ðōn heo for XII [.]yra tydernessū

> '[...] than the brazen cauldron, when for twelve generations of men (A it) [...]'

A's *heo*, lacking in B, refers back to *gripo*, 'cauldron', in the previous line. It is neither necessary nor objectionable syntactically and metrically.

The current view of the runic letters which in the A text of SnS accompany the roman letters of the Pater Noster (lines 89, 93 and 94 in the part of the poem also represented in B) is that they are scribal additions. As O'Keeffe points out (O'Keeffe 1990: 58) they cannot be pronounced as their names, partly because the alliteration of the lines in which the runes occur will not accommodate them, and partly because if both the roman and the runic letters are spoken, irregular metrical patterns result in all cases. This need not, perhaps, rule out the runes as part of the original poem, for this is certainly a text designed to be seen as well as heard; but on the whole the case for their interpolation in A seems strong.

A has extra words not in B in 91 *a*, the adverb 'ever', and 92 *him*, dat. sg. of the 3rd person pronoun:

SnS B 91–92	SnS A 91–92
gyldene gade & þone grymman feond	gyldene gade & a ðone g[...]man feond
swiðmod swapeð & on swaðe filgið	swiðmod sweopað & him ón swaðe fylgeð

Notes to the text: B 92 *filgið* is a superscript addition above original *læteð*, underdotted for deletion.

> '[...] a golden goad, and (A ever) the stout-hearted one whips (*or* B drives) the grim fiend; and [...] follows in his footsteps [...]'

A 91 *a* suits the context well enough and its presence or absence has no important consequences for meaning or metre. A 92 *him* provides a dat. object for *fylgeð*, 'follows', a verb which may take either acc. or dat. object in OE, though it is difficult to regard it as essential here.

This last passage completes a group of five variants in SnS (six if A's runes are counted) where the A text has words lacking in B. As I have indicated, I can see no compelling grounds in the immediate context for regarding these words as interpolations in A rather than deletions from B; but two facts are conspicuous in this connection. One is that B has no examples of 'extra' words in this category to match A's five examples; and the other is that in a previous section (§6.1.1), where cases of probable interpolation of minor words were identified, SnS A was represented by four examples (A 25 *he*, 28 *mid*, 83 *ón*, 88 *on*) whereas B was not represented at all. An OE scribe who went through a text as he copied it removing words inessential to the sense would have to have been a critical and careful worker. A scribe whose general tendency was to make the text his own by amplifying it in places where a small addition would contribute to the clarity of the meaning (as he understood it), whatever the consequences for the metre, is, in my view, easier to envisage. It is therefore to be suspected that the A text of SnS has been subject to a good deal of conscious modification by such small expansions, and that the B text represents the poem in a relatively unaltered condition.

These five interpolations/omissions in SnS involve 'extra' minor words in A; but B contains an entire line lacking in A in 67:

SnS A 66–69a	SnS B 66–69a
he bið seofan snytro & saule hunig	he bið sefan snytero & sawle hunig
	& modes meolc mærþa gesælgost.
He mæg ða saule óf siennihte	He mæg þa sawle of synnihte
gefeccan under foldan	gefetian under foldan

'It is the wisdom of the heart and honey of the soul (B milk of the mind, most blessed of glories). It may bring forth the soul from perpetual night beneath the earth [...]'

The line is well integrated, though the A text does not suffer for its absence and I can see no evidence for either interpolation in B or omission from A.

§6.1.3.2 SB

The various possible examples of the interpolation or deletion of minor words in SB are dealt with here. Instances are classified according to the part of speech involved. SB1 has by far the larger number of 'extra' words. The relevant lines are quoted in SB1's form, with the word lacking in SB2 italicized:

1. Adverbs:
   SB1 26 lyt geþohtest hu þis is *þus* lang hider
   SB1 38 earfoðlice nis nu *huru* se ende to gód.
   SB1 65 eart ðu *nu* dumb & deaf ne synt þine dreamas awiht.
   SB1 72 & þe sculon *her* moldwyrmas manige ceowan
   SB1 97 þonne ne bið nan *na* to þæs lytel lið on lime aweaxen.
   SB1 101 sculon wit þōn *eft* ætsomne siððan brucan

SB1 102 swylcra yrmða swa ðu unc *her* ær scrife.

2. Prepositions:
   SB1 31 & þu me *mid* þy heardan hungre gebunde
   SB1 80 oððe *on* eorðan neat ætes tilode

3. Demonstratives:
   SB1 16 spreceð grimlice *se* gast to þam duste.
   SB1 96 on *þā* dōdæge dryhtne secgan.
   SB1 100 dryhten æt *þam* dome ac hwæt do wyt unc.

SB2's extra words are as follows:

1. Adverbs:
   SB2 27 & þe *þa* gebohte blode þy halgan
   SB2 46 scealt þu *nu* hwæþre minra gescenta scome þrowian
   SB2 49 Ne eart þu *nu* þon leofre nængū lifgendra
2. Pronouns:
   SB2 21 siþþan *heo* of lichoman læded wære.
   SB2 118 lic acolad þæt *he* longe ær

In none of these cases does the presence or absence of the extra word
affect the sense in any important way, or vitiate the metre. The grammar
is changed only in SB1 80 by the presence of the preposition *on* ('an ox
on the earth' rather than 'an ox of the earth'). Again, the same argument
applies here as it does to the extra words in SnS A: it is easier to envisage
a scribe who interpolated minor words for the sake of greater clarity (or,
perhaps, in some cases, just for the sake of leaving his mark on the text)
than it is to imagine one who deleted such words wherever it was possible
to do so without compromising either meaning or metre. There is no
doubt that SB2 is, overall, the better text than SB1. We may, I think,
conclude tentatively that SB1 has been subject to considerable modification of this kind during transmission, in contrast with SB2 which has
received only very limited attention from scribes with interpolating
tendencies.

§6.1.3.3 Aza/Dan

Aza and Dan both show the occasional extra word in terms of the other,
but the distribution has no obvious significance. Aza's examples are as
follows:

1. Pronouns:
   Aza 1 *Him* þa azarias ingeþoncum
   Aza 34 ycan wolde þæt *hit* æfter him

2. Relative particle:
   Aza 42 fyl nu þa frumspræce þeah *þe* user fea lifgen

3. Adverb:
   Aza 45 & *eac* fela folca gefregen habban

4. Preposition:
   Aza 65 se wæs in þam fire *for* frean meahtum

Dan's instances are:

1. Pronoun:
   Dan 315 þu him *þæt* gehéte. þurh hleoðorcwyde.

2. Prepositions:
   Dan 314 & *to* iacobe gasta scyppend.
   Dan 326 wlitiga þinne wordcwyde. & þín wuldor *on* us.

3. Conjunction:
   Dan 330 & *þæt* þu ána eart. éce drihten.

Aza has a two-line passage which is missing from Dan:

Aza 55b–60a	Dan 339b–342a
se þone lig tosceaf	se ðone lig tosceaf.
halig & heofonbeorht hatan fyres	halig & heofonbeorht. hátan fyres.
þæt se bittra bryne beorgan sceolde	
for þæs engles ege æfæstum þrim.	
Tosweop & toswengde þurh swiðes meaht	tosweop hine & toswende. þurh þa swiðan miht
liges leoman	ligges leoma

'[...] who, holy and bright as the heavens, scattered the flame of the hot fire (Aza so that the bitter burning had to spare, through awe of the angel, the three law-abiding ones). He swept (Dan it) away and destroyed (*or* Aza ? struck) the brightness of the flame through that powerful strength, [...]'

The extra lines in Aza are metrically regular and not to be distinguished linguistically from the surrounding text. There is no reason that I can see to suspect either interpolation in Aza or omission from Dan.

Dan has two single extra lines which do not appear in Aza. This is the first:

Aza 44b–46	Dan 327b–330
nu þec caldeas	þæt þæt caldeas.
& eac fela folca gefregen habban	& folca fela. gefrigen habbað.

ða þe under heofenum. hæðene
lifigeað.

þæt þú ana eart ece dryhten   & þæt þu ána eart. éce drihten.

'[...] now that (*or* Dan which) the Chaldeans and (Aza also) many peoples
have heard tell who live as heathens beneath the heavens, (Dan and) that
only you are the eternal lord [...]'

The only reason to suspect interpolation in Dan here is the form
heofenum, with *e* in the medial unstressed syllable which is not characteristic of the scribe in this part of the manuscript,[8] though this is plainly not
enough to prove interpolation in Dan rather than omission from Aza. The
second example is Dan 349:

Aza 62b–65	Dan 346b–350
wedere onlicust	wedere gelicost.
þon on sumeres tid sended weorþeð	þon hit on sumeres tíd sended weorðeð.
dropena dreorung mid dæges hwile.	dropena drearung. on dæges hwile.
	wearmlic wolcna scúr. swylc bið
	wedera cyst.
se wæs in þam fire for frean meahtum	swylc wæs on þam fyre. fréan mihtum

Aza: '[...] most like the weather when the falling of drops is sent in
summer in the daytime. Throught the powers of the lord, in the fire that
was [...]'

Dan: '[...] most like the storm when it is sent in summer, the falling of
drops in the daytime, a warm shower from the clouds. As is the
choicest weather, so it was in that fire through the powers of the lord
[...]'

There is nothing suspicious about this 'extra' line in Dan, nor is there a
sense of anything missing in Aza.

§6.1.3.4 Other poems

Examples in other poems are very rare. The only one I have noticed is
EgD 29, where the A text has &, 'and', but the B and C texts lack the
conjunction; conversely, the B and C texts have *eac* but A lacks the
adverb:

---

[8]   Cf. Dan 426, 441, 625 *heofona*, 364 *heofonas*, 533, 563, 619 *heofonum*; three forms
with *e* occur near the beginning of the manuscript in Gen 33 *heofena*, 97, 240 *heofenum*.

EgD 29 A	EgD 29 B
& þa wearð atywed. uppe on roderum.	þa wearð eac ætywed uppe on roderum.

'(A And) then was (B also) displayed up in the skies [...]'

Here we should compare the same texts' versions of EgD 24:

EgD 24 A	EgD 24 B
& þa wearð eac ádræfed deormod hæleð.	Ða wearð eac adræfed deormód hæleþ.

'(A And) then the brave-hearted man was also driven [...]'

Both lines introduce a new section within the annal, dealing with Oslac's banishment and the comet's appearance respectively. The A text distinguishes both by the combination: & *þa*, the B and C texts by the sequence: *þa wearð eac* [...]; but it seems impossible to say which of these sets of variants is the more authoritative.

§6.2 EXTENSIONS IN POEMS IN THE VERCELLI BOOK

I distinguish expansions — relatively minor interpolations in the body of existing texts, dealt with in the previous section — from extensions, which involve substantial additions of new material at the end of an existing poem. Here there are only two poems to discuss, SB and DrR.

§6.2.1 SB

The transmission of SB presents us with two main questions: the relationship between SB2 and the first part of SB1 (SB1 1–126) which matches it (the subject of Orton 1979b); and the relationship between SB1 1–126, the address of the condemned soul, and 127–66, the address of the blessed soul, unmatched by SB2 (the subject of Orton 1979a). It is with the second question that this section is concerned.

In Orton 1979a I argued that the address of the blessed soul was an addition to the original poem represented by the first part of the poem which occurs in both the Vercelli and Exeter Books.[9] I began by analysing the structure of SB1 1–126 and concluded, on the basis of a

---

[9] My argument that the two halves of the poem are the work of different poets has recently been supported and extended by Moffat in the introduction to his edition (Moffat 1990: 41–4).

'circular or symmetrical ordering of material' in this part of the poem, that there was a 'sense of completeness' by the time we reach 126. We should also note that no distinction between the address of a condemned soul and another of the blessed soul is implied in the first half of the SB1, so that the reference to the blessed soul at the beginning of the second part of the poem (127 *sio halige sawl*) comes as something of a surprise. The blessed soul's address suffers from what I called 'emotional flatness, a negative and retrospective bias, and lack of explicitness' when compared with the startlingly grisly exploration of the destruction of the human corpse by worms in the grave which makes the first part of the poem so memorable.

Evidence is available of a relatively inept employment, in the address of the blessed soul, of phrases and verses drawn from the first part of the poem. One example is the verse *wyrmum to wiste* (SB1 25a, 122a) and the sequence *god wolde* (SB1 83b, 85b), which appear combined in a single line in the address of the blessed soul:

SB1 154

wyrmū to wiste ac þæt wolde god.

'[...] as food for worms, but God willed it, [...]'

Here the alliteration in the b-verse is irregular, falling on the verb *wolde* rather than on the noun *god*, though the first half of SB1 also contains a breakdown of alliteration in a line employing some of the same materials as in SB1 83:

SB1 83

þæt wyrreste þær swa god wolde.

Here the metrical irregularity is twofold: alliteration in the b-verse falls on the verb *wolde*, which here not only alliterates in preference to the noun *god* (as in 154), but also occupies the second stressed position in the b-verse: the standard arrangement in OE poetry is for alliteration to fall on the first stressed element of the b-verse. Even so, it is not impossible that the irregular alliteration on the verb here gave the poet of 127–66 the idea for his own version of this collocation in 154.

Two other instances of dependence by the poet of 127–66 on material from the first part of SB1 may be identified. SB1 70b *þe ðu me her scrife* (in which *her* carries the alliteration) and 102b *swa ðu unc her ær scrife* (where *ær* alliterates) are combined and recycled in SB1 141b *swylc swa ðu me ær her scrife*, this time with *her* carrying the alliteration; but the imperfection of the adaptation emerges when we compare lines 102 and 141 in more detail:

SB1 102	SB1 141
swylcra yrmða swa ðu unc her ær scrife.	heofona wuldor swylc swa ðu me ær her scrife

SB1 102: '[...] such torments as you previously ordained here for the two of us.'

SB1 141: '[...] the glory of heaven such as you previously ordained here for me.'

The idea for 141 *swylc* in association with the repeated b-verse no doubt came from 102 *swylcra*; but the use of this word involves a problem of verse-grammar in 141. Indefinite adjectives such as *swylc* are normally unstressed in OE verse only when they immediately precede the noun they qualify (as in 102a *swylcra yrmða*, where the noun carries the alliteration). When displaced from that position, as in 141 (*swylc* qualifying *wuldor*), they normally bear stress (Slay 1952: 1–14). However, *swylc* here cannot bear stress because of the alliteration rule just stated: if *swylc* were stressed in the b-verse, alliteration, which can only be on *h* in this line (141a *heofona*), would fall on the second stressed word of the verse (*her*), not on the first (*swylc*). The problem cannot be solved by regarding *swylc* as the final word of the a-verse, for that would produce an a-verse of Bliss's type D*4 with single alliteration, whereas double alliteration is invariable in this type (and others resembling it) in *Beowulf* (see Bliss 1967: 73–74, §81). It would appear likely that the poet of the address of the blessed soul drew inspiration from SB1 102 for his own line 141, but was not competent to integrate the material properly into his own work.

Another probable example of the limited technique of the poet of the blessed soul's address is SB1 158. Below is the sentence in which this line occurs, beside the lines from the first part of SB1 that seem to have inspired it:

SB1 101–02	SB1 158–59
sculon wit þōn eft ætsomne siððan brucan	moton wyt þonne ætsomne syþan brucan
swylcra yrmða swa ðu unc her ær scrife.	& unc on heofonū heahþungene beon.

SB1 101–02: 'We must then later together experience such torments as
   you previously ordained here for the two of us.'
SB1 158–59: 'We must then later experience together [...] and be exalted
   in the heavens.'

In 158–59, *brucan* lacks an object; Grein invented an entire line based on
SB1 102, *swylcra arna swa þu unc her ær scrife*, to make good the defi-
ciency, inserting it between 158 and 159 (Grein 1857: I, 203). It seems
clear that the poet of 158 has been influenced by 101, as Grein's
attempted restoration seems to imply; but if Grein was wrong in identifying an omission here, this seems like another example of how the pirating
of the first part of the poem led to unfortunate results.

   The case for SB1 127–66 as the work of a poet different from the one
who composed the first part of SB may be backed up by a piece of
phonological-metrical evidence. It has to do with the form of the noun
sawol, 'soul' in the original composition of SB. The relevant lines in
which this noun is used are as follows:

   SB1 10–11a

symble ymbe seofon niht sawle findan
þone lichoman

'[...] always every seven nights, the soul (must come) to find the body
[...]'

   SB1 62

besliten synum. & þe þin sawl sceal

'[...] torn away from the sinews, and your soul shall (often seek) you [...]'

   SB1 127

Ðonne bið hyhtlicre þæt sio halige sawl

'Then will it be more joyous when the holy soul (will go [...])'

In all three of these passages, the word 'soul' (*sawle, sawl*) is nom. sg.
The form written in SB1 10b, *sawle*, shows an inflexion which suggests
that the word was taken as acc. or gen. or dat. sg., but the context forbids
any of these cases; only the nom. sg. will do. The fact that SB2 10b also
has *sawle* shows that there was a corruption in the common archetype
which neither version corrected (see above, §3.2). However, the contexts
in which these three instances of *sawl* occur have interesting implications
for the form of the word in the original composition. In SB1 10 and 62, a

two-syllable word (such as would be indicated by the spelling *sawol*, a common form of the word in OE generally) is metrically required; for if the noun were monosyllabic (as reflected by a form such as *sawl*) in 10b, the verse would be short of the required minimum of four syllables per verse. In 62, a disyllabic form is also required to make a regular verse of Sievers' type B; if it were monosyllabic, a verse closing with two full stresses would result, an arrangement that OE poets avoided. In SB1 127, on the other hand, the word *sawl* must be monosyllabic; for if it were disyllabic, the verse in which it occurs would be a balanced type A verse with anacrusis, a combination never found in *Beowulf* (see Bliss 1967: 127). What this evidence indicates is a different pronunciation of the nom. sg. of the word *sawl* (*sawol*) in the two parts of SB1, disyllabic in the first, monosyllabic in the second, suggesting that they are the work of two different poets.

§6.2.2 DrR

One of the most striking aspects of DrR is the large and mostly solid blocks of hypermetric lines in DrR 8–10, 20–23, 30–34, 39–43 (except 39a and 40a), 46–49, 59–69, 75. We may note that all of these fully hypermetric lines occur in the first two sections of the poem as defined earlier (above, §6.1.2). The late Professor Bliss used to point to several individual a-verses in the second and third sections of the poem that look as though they were meant to be hypermetric (98a *se ðe ælmihtig god*, 102a *mid his miclan mihte*, 125a *afysed on forðwege*, 133a *gewiton of worulde dreamum*, 153a *Anwealda ælmihtig*), though all are linked to normal b-verses. These are not as impressive as the earlier blocks of full hypermetric lines I have listed, and might even be interpreted as a rather feeble attempt to introduce a hypermetric element into a text by a poet lacking the expertise to make a proper job of it.[10]

This raises the possibility that DrR has undergone extension by an inferior poet whose work we see in the second half of the poem, perhaps from as early as line 78. Line 77 represents an important division in the narrative: it is not the end of the speech of the cross, but it terminates the cross's account of its former life up to its exhumation by St Helena, and its adornment with jewels, marking the beginning of its new life as a

---

[10] I would add to this list 2b *to midre nihte* (type a1a[2A1a] in Bliss's notation), which would pass muster as a normal type A verse were it not for the anacrusis represented by *to*; 'balanced' type A verses such as this never have anacrusis in *Beowulf*; see Bliss 1967: 127.

Christian symbol. The case for extension of an existing poem may be supported with two kinds of evidence. One is the distribution of metrical types between the two halves of the poem. In lines 1–78, there are thirteen normal a-verses of types 1A or 1A*, all with the double alliteration that is usual in a-verses of these types in *Beowulf* (lines 7, 12, 13, 14, 15, 16, 36, 38, 44, 53, 55, 71, 74; see Bliss 1967: 127); but from 78 to the end of the poem there are nineteen such a-verses (82, 85, 89, 101, 108, 114, 125, 130, 131, 132, 135, 136, 140, 141, 143, 149, 150, 151, 155), and five of them have single alliteration (101, 108, 136, 140, 151). In *Beowulf*, only 6% of such a-verses show single alliteration; in DrR 78–156 the percentage is 26%, compared with 0% in the first 77 lines. This difference seems to me significantly large.

The other kind of evidence for extension is the kind of 'pirating' of existing material that I identified earlier in my discussion of the address of the blessed soul in SB1. The first example of this is the repetition of line 12 as line 82:

DrR 12 men ofer moldan, ond eall þeos mære gesceaft.
DrR 82 menn ofer moldan, ond eall þeos mære gesceaft,

'men over the earth, and all this glorious creation'

Also conspicuous in the second half of the poem is the use of certain phrases and words which have already been worked fairly hard in the earlier part of the poem, particularly the very distinctive phrase *elne mycle* in line 123, which has been used before in both lines 34 and 60, and *mæte werede* in the following line 124, a phrase which has already been used in line 69. It is instructive to compare the later passage in which these two phrases occur with line 69 in its context:

DrR 67b–69

Ongunnon him þa sorhleoð galan
earme on þa æfentide, þa hie woldon eft siðian
meðe from þam mæran þeodne. Reste he ðær mæte weorode

'Then they began to sing a lament for him, wretched in the evening, when they wished later to depart, exhausted, from the glorious prince. He rested there with a small company.'

DrR 122–24a

Gebæd ic me þa to þan beame bliðe mode,
elne mycle, þær ic ana wæs
mæte werede.

'I prayed then to the tree with a joyful heart, with great zeal, where I stood alone with a small company.'

In the first of these passages, the phrase *mæte weorode* may refer literally to a company of faithful watchers over the body of Christ — the three Marys, possibly, who attend Christ's body in the Bible, or perhaps even the other two crosses the presence of which is implied (for the first time in the poem) by the pl. 1st person pronoun in the following line (70 *Hwæðere we ðær greotende* [...], 'yet we weeping there [...]'); the alternative interpretation of *mæte weorode* is as an example of litotes, implying that Christ is quite alone. But whichever interpretation of 69 we may prefer, one can see how the poet of 124a understood this phrase: by using it as a variation on *ana*, a quite unambiguous word meaning 'alone', in the previous line, he shows that he regards it at least as open to interpretation as a figure of speech meaning 'alone'. What is interesting here is not that the poet of 124b has misinterpreted the phrase as it was used earlier in the poem in 69b, for I doubt if we can be certain of whether its meaning there is literal or figurative; it is rather his mixing of the literal *ana* with what the context would indicate is the figurative sense of *mæte werede*. The effect of this is very odd, rather as if something were described as 'not too good' and 'dreadful' in the same breath. Here, too, I suspect that we have to deal with an inadequate poet's adaptation of received material in ready-made, textual form.

Part 2:

Faithful Transmission

Chapter 7. The Fixity of Linguistic Forms

§7 The faithful transmission of linguistic forms

If an OE copyist chooses the spellings he uses, these may reflect either his own preferences (perhaps representing the dialect he himself speaks), or a tradition of spelling to which he has been trained to conform, irrespective of the forms he finds in his exemplar. Alternatively, he may make no choices but instead aim simply to reproduce the forms of his exemplar as accurately as possible. In practice, of course, the forms a scribe writes may be a mixture of chosen and copied forms. The question arises of the extent to which it is possible to trace the spellings of an extant OE text back to earlier texts which underlie it in the history of its transmission. There are two points of reference which may help us in looking for evidence of the linguistic character of lost versions underlying extant texts. One is the consistency of the scribe's usage — whether or not his spelling of words is constant, or consistently reflects the sounds of a certain dialect or period. If, of course, he varies from text to text in the spellings he uses, we may suspect that he is reproducing the spellings of his exemplar or, at least, not consistently imposing forms he himself prefers to use. Preliminary deductions based on this simple methodology can sometimes, and to some extent, be checked when we are dealing with texts that survive in more than one version; for forms that are unusual in the context of one scribe's work, or forms which mark out a particular text from others that he copied, may be found repeated in other versions; and if these forms in other versions are similarly unusual against the background of the normal usages of the scribes who copied them, we may be in a position to identify forms deriving from earlier, lost versions of the text with a fair degree of confidence. The present chapter pursues the practical implications of these remarks in comparing and contrasting texts of the same poem, and poems written by one scribe with other texts or parts of texts written by the same scribe in the same manuscript.

§7.1 THE PRESERVATION OF EXEMPLAR FORMS

Sometimes it is possible to trace a certain form in a certain place in a text back to the text's exemplar but no further. In such cases, it is always possible that the exemplar spellings derive, in their turn, from even earlier, lost versions, though it is seldom possible to make any kind of case for this without the support of other, independent witnesses to the archetype. An example of this kind of evidence is provided by certain Kt. forms in the latter part of the H text of PCE. The text of the *Cura Pastoralis* translation in this manuscript is written by two hands, a main one which does most of the copying,[1] and continues as far as f. 98r, ending his contribution by writing the first ten lines of PCE (to 10 *gode*, f. 98ʳ/26); and a minor hand which takes over from the main hand at thirteen points in the manuscript and includes among his contributions to the work the second part (10–30) of PCE, where he makes each line he writes shorter than the last, so that the penultimate written line of the text consists of nothing more than the final -ðe of *weorðe*, the last word of the poem, and the very last line has only a final mark of punctuation. It is in the part of the poem copied by this minor hand that we find two Kenticisms, 21 *werð* (*OEG* §§201.1, 288) and 24 *welle* (*OEG* §200.1), with 10 *herdon* as a possible third (*OEG* §200.5). None of these spellings occur anywhere else in the minor scribe's work in the MS, nor are they characteristic of the main scribe's work. The minor scribe seems to have been a meticulous worker (see Ker 1956: 23), for correspondences with the D text of PCE, and comparison with the work of the main hand in H, indicates that he reproduced the punctuation, and possibly even some of the letter-forms, of his exemplar with unusual fidelity.[2] The distribution of the Kt. forms in his work suggests that such spellings may have been characteristic only of the PCE text in his exemplar, not of the entire *Cura Pastoralis* translation. A linguistic distinction between PCE and the remainder of the text in this exemplar is most simply explained as

---

[1] The the text of PCP on f. 2ᵛ/10–19 is the work of the main scribe, according to Ker 1956: 22, though cf. Sisam 1953: 143, who says that the hand of PCP shows 'distinguishing characteristics'. Ker 1957 is silent on the matter.

[2] A rare, *f*-shaped form of *y* appears in PCE 22 *dryhten* and 27 *ðyrelne*, which the scribe uses nowhere else in his contribution to the H manuscript; it probably comes from the exemplar. See further below, §8.1.

deriving from the stage of transmission at which PCE was added to the main text; but it may be that what we see in H is rather the result of different spelling systems used by two or more scribes who copied H's exemplar (or an antecedent of it). This second possibility has to be admitted because D, the other surviving text of PCE, provides no evidence to support the view that PCE was from the first distinct linguistically from the main *Cura Pastoralis* text.

Similar reasoning seems to apply in the case of forms of the word for 'king' in the D text of DEw. The part of the D manuscript in which the text of DEw occurs is characterized by a series of sudden changes in the appearance of the writing which probably indicate discontinuous work by one scribe rather than contributions by several different ones.[3] In DEw D, the scribe's forms are 1 *cing*, 13 *kinge*, 15 *king*, 23 *kinigc* and 34 *-kyngces*; but elsewhere in the same section of his work he writes only the forms *cyng*, *cynge*, *cyning* and *cyninge*. Spellings of this word with initial *k* are not uncommon in other parts of the scribe's work; but *i* in the first syllable is rare, so it is likely that *i*, and perhaps the sequence: *ki-*, derive from the scribe's exemplar. However, the C text of the poem provides nothing to support the idea that these forms go back as far as the common archetype from which both texts of the poem derive (though that does not, of course, prove that they do not).

§7.2 THE PRESERVATION OF PRE-EXEMPLAR FORMS

The previous section drew on the evidence of the H text of PCE. Horgan mentions no evidence for other, intermediate texts between the exemplar of H and the primary copy of Alfred's work (Horgan 1973), so there is a possibility that H's exemplar was the archetype from which the D text of PCE also descends. Certainly H and D are very close; they exhibit no differences of substance (no substitutions, omissions, or additions), and the high level of overlap in the distribution of punctuation is probably another sign of the close relationship between them.[4] Roughly the same is

---

[3]   The contribution to the D manuscript of the scribe responsible for DEw is not easy to define. Ker distinguishes seven sections (Ker 1957: 254), all of them possibly by this one scribe, the sixth of which (1065 & *ofslogon his hiredmen* to the end of 1065, ff. 78^r/19–79^r/14) includes DEw.

[4]   Correspondences in punctuation are especially frequent in the latter part of the text (10–30) — in H, the work of the minor scribe of the MS who, as we saw earlier, seems to have been an unusually accurate copyist. In the first nine lines of the text there are only two correspondences, at the ends of 2 and 3, with extra points at the ends of D 1, 5, 6 and

true of the two surviving texts of DEw: there is no evidence against the view that the exemplar of the D text of DEw was also the archetype from which C too descends.[5] I mention these considerations only to make the point that the linguistic forms identified in the last section as deriving from the exemplar of one of the texts of PCE and DEw may in fact derive from the archetype of each poem, though we cannot be certain of it.

There are, however, cases where it is possible to trace specific forms back to an earlier, lost text of a poem which was intermediate between the archetype and the extant texts of the poem, but not necessarily the actual exemplar of any of them. Thus in the case of Brb B, C 40 *maga*, we have seen that this word was probably misinterpreted in an antecedent text (B-C*) from which both B and C derive as the poetic word *māga*, 'son' (see above, §3.3). It therefore seems quite likely that the exemplar of B-C* itself contained this form, which was actually the gen. pl. of *mæg*, 'kinsman', showing W-S retraction of *æ*) to *ā* under the influence of the back vowel *-a* in the next syllable (*OEG* §162); for any other form of the word, *mæga* for example, would have been unlikely to trigger the confusion of the two words. We cannot, however, trace this form any further back in the transmission of the poem than the exemplar of B-C*, for A and D have *mæga* and there is no particular reason to think that this form has been substituted for *maga* at any stage in the transmission of the A or D text.

Also in Brb, 46 B, C *inwitta* (A *inwidda*), 'evil one', is a sufficiently unusual form of the word (see Campbell 1938: 112) to be traced back to B-C*. In Brb 12, B and C both have *dennade*, in which the form of the inflexion *-ade* is not the form which the scribe of either manuscript usually writes for the pret. of Class 2 weak verbs; in both, *-ode* is the usual form (e.g. in Brb 12 D *dennode*).

Certain spellings of the B-C* version of EgC can similarly be reconstructed on the basis of correspondences between the B and C texts of the poem residing in forms for which neither scribe shows any preference in

---

9 and mid-line in D 8; but from 10 to the end there are ten such agreements, at the ends of lines 10, 11, 15, 17, 19, 21, 23, 24, 26 and 28, with extra points in H only at the end of 20 and mid-line in 30, and in D at the end of 12.

[5]   The two texts are roughly contemporary with each other palaeographically: Ker 1957: 251–5, dates both the C and D texts to the second half of the eleventh century. But it is clear that neither derives from the other, for C has independent corruptions in 7 *weolm* for *weolan*, 12 *ceald* for *cealda*, 16 *lang* for *langa*, as does D in 28 *inne* for *innan*, 31 *ealne* for *ealle*, 34 *ðearfe* for *þearf*.

this part of his copy of the *Anglo-Saxon Chronicle*. Examples are EgC B, C 2 *kinge* with initial *k* (A *cyninge*),[6] and 4 *egbuend*, 7 *cegeað* (by *i*-umlaut of *ea*; *OEG* §120.3) and 13 *get* (by failure of W-S palatal diphthongization of *ē*; *OEG* §185),[7] all with non-W-S *e* beside A's forms with *i* (*igbuend, cigað*; in place of 13 *get, agan* appears in A; see above, §4.2.1).[8]

The B and C texts of EgD also show a correspondence which may be similarly interpreted: EgD B, C 12 *aldor*, with early or Anglian *a* (the retraction of *æ*) before *l* plus consonant (*OEG* §143). In the corresponding lines in A we find the normal W-S form *ealdor*, with fracture of *æ*. The B and C scribes both normally write *ea* in conditions where *æ* is vulnerable to fracture before *l* plus consonant.

The scribe of the O manuscript of Cæd writes the form *oór*,*[d]*, with doubled *o*; no other text of the W-S *eorðan* group doubles the vowel in this word; all have *ord* except T with *ór* and To with the corruption *ær* (see above, §4.4.3). O's scribe writes doubled vowels very seldom elsewhere in his work on the O manuscript of the *OE Bede*; but in the T manuscript of this work, vowel-doubling is much more frequent, and there is a significant degree of overlap with O.[9] It seems very likely that the doubled vowel appeared in a text of Cæd from which both T and O derive, but the absence of support in the other texts for this feature means that we cannot trace it back to the archetype of the whole group. Similarly, the distinction observed in texts T and Ca between *a* in 2 *modgeþanc* and *o* in 7 *moncynnes* may derive from a common source in some antecedent text, but the evidence is not by any means conclusive.[10]

---

[6] In the B MS of the *Chronicle*, the word 'king' is normally spelt with initial *k* up to annal 654; thereafter, *k* is used sporadically beside commoner *c*. The same may be said of the C MS, except that there, spellings with initial *k* are even rarer after annal 654; one example is 685 *king*.

[7] Elsewhere in the B and C scribe's work, this and related words are spelt with W-S *y* (918 *gyt*, Brb 66 *gyta*).

[8] The *e* forms from *i*-umlaut are more unusual in the C scribe's work on the *Chronicle* than in the B scribe's: C has only EgD 37 *egbuend*(-) in addition to the two instances quoted here; but B has *e* in all three words, plus 716 *beardan ege*, 832 *sceapege*, 873 *turkesege*, 895 *mereseg* (first instance), in all four of which words C has W-S *i*.

[9] The instances of overlap I have noted are Miller 1890: 82/32 *wiif*, 84/9 *wiifu̅*, 332/29 *wiic*; the remaining seven instances of doubled vowels in O are 278/26 *clofeshooh*, 320/28 *saa run*, 336/17 *boosle*, 336/19 *taatfrið*, 372/14 *þaa*, 404/11 *deera*, 406/13 *tííd*.

[10] T's scribe invariably writes *o* in the element (-)*mon(n)* in compounds, and Ca's scribe usually does too, so it is impossible to prove that Cæd 7 *mon-* in both texts has a common

In the W-S *ylda* group of texts of Cæd, most of the texts have 2 *metudes* (Bu *mecudes* with the error *c* for *t*, W *metoddes*, corrected to *metodes*; see above, §2.4.1) with distinctive medial unstressed *u*, an early feature in all dialects (*OEG* §373; cf. *me(o)todes* in all the W-S *eorðan* texts) which probably derives from the group prototype. The same form also occurs in all three of the W-S *eorðe* texts and also, no doubt, derives from their group original.

§7.3 THE PRESERVATION OF ARCHETYPAL FORMS

When texts of the same poem agree on a form and it is an unusual one in the work of at least one or (ideally) more of the scribes involved, it may be judged to derive from the archetype text, provided that there are enough independent witnesses to the form in question. Such forms are discussed here.

> PCP H, D, T 8 *gestriende* with early W-S *ie* (*i*-umlaut of *ī̆o*; *OEG* §202.3). This form is normal in the context of the work of the H and D scribes, but the scribe of T writes *y* elsewhere in the stem of this element (Sweet 1871: 43/14 *gestryne*, 55/10 *strynþ*; the third scribe of the MS normally has *y* too, as in Sweet 1871: 333/17, 333/18, 335/3, 397/10, beside non-W-S *eo* in 343/23, 399/4). In view of the likelihood that the archetype of PCP contained a substantial early W-S phonological stratum, it is reasonable to supposed that this form was a component of it.

> Brb A, C 47 *þorftun* with early or Anglian *-un* (general OE *-on*) for the pret. pl. indic. inflexion (see *OEG* §735(e)). The A text of Brb has five

---

textual source; both scribes might have imposed it as their favourite form. As for the element (-)*þanc*(-), T's scribe writes *a* rather rarely (Miller 1890: 188/1, 320/13 *þanc*, as well as Cæd 2 *modgeþanc*) beside commoner *o* (I count ten instances), whereas Ca shows great variation, with *a* preponderating (twelve times, *o* five times, in Miller 1890: 122/28, 128/3, 278/8, 278/21, 290/15). Ca's distribution therefore does not support the view that the form 2 *modgeþanc* derives from an earlier, lost text of Cæd, though its distribution of forms of (-)*þanc*(-) or (-)*þonc*(-) shows an almost exact overlap with that of the O text of the *OE Bede*, adding to ample evidence of a very close connection between these two texts of the Bede translation. It is conceivable that Ca is a copy of O, though this possibility seems never to have been thoroughly investigated; see Orton 1998: 163, note 13. A close connection between the O and Ca texts of Cæd is also probably behind their agreement in the late W-S or late Kt. final *-an* of O 1 *sculan*, Ca *sceolan* (see *OEG* §§373, 377), for neither scribe favours this late form of the inflexion: O's scribe usually writes *-un*, Ca's scribe *-on*. Examples of *-an* in O are Miller 1890: 64/7, 68/9, and in Ca, Miller 1890: 72/15, 84/10; no doubt there are others. For details of these distributions, see Deutschbein 1901: 211; Eger 1910: 26).

further instances of this form of the inflexion, beside three forms with
-*on* but no less than twelve with -*an*.[11] Elsewhere in his work on the
MS, the scribe of A writes -*an* invariably. The C text of Brb has -*on*
usually, -*an* once (12 *feollan*) and -*un* only in 47 *þorftun*. Elsewhere in
his work on the Chronicle MS, the C scribe most often writes -*an*
before annal 628, -*on* very occasionally; thereafter, the pattern is
reversed, with -*on* usual, -*an* rare, -*un* even rarer.[12] If *þorftun* is the
archetypal form in 47, it follows that the form in B and D, *þorftan*, with
Kt. or late W-S -*an*, is a later substitution.

Brb 7, 52 A *afaran*, C *aforan*, D 52 *afaran* (cf. B 7, 52 *eaforan*) suggests
the presence of a form with initial *a*- rather than *ea*-, as in B's *eaforan*,
in the archetype of Brb in both places in the text. In the A scribe's
work, the only comparable form is CFB 13 *afera*. The B scribe writes *a*
usually, but *ea* in CFB 13 and EgC 17 *eafora*. The C scribe writes *ea*
only once, in EgC 17 *eafora*. In this word, *ea* is proper only to the
Merc. dialect of the *Vespasian Psalter* gloss, but is frequent in West-
Saxonised verse-texts (*OEG* §§205–07; Campbell 1938: 10, 14 and
note 1). The *a*- in several of the texts is probably sufficiently distinctive
in the context of the scribes' work generally to signal its derivation
from the archetype, in which case B's forms with *ea* are substitutions.

Brb 31 A *heriges*, B, C, D *herges*: In the work of the scribes of B, C and
D, forms with *herge*(-) are less common overall than spellings such as
here(-) and *herig*(-); but there are several correspondences between
these manuscripts in the rarer *herge*(-) forms, notably 918 B, C, D
herges, 894 B, C, D *herge* (twice), 896 C, D *herge*. It therefore seems
very likely that the archetype of Brb had 31 *herges*. The form has no
particular dialectal significance, unlike A's *heriges*, which shows
typical W-S parasiting before *g* (*OEG* §§365, 577).

Brb 60 B, C *bryttig(e)an* with Anglian -*ig*- (A *bryttian*; on these forms, see
OEG §757). The scribes of B, C and D all write only -*i*- elsewhere in
the infinitive ending of Class II weak verbs. D's corruption *bryttinga*
seems to have been modelled on the -*ig*- form (see above, §4.2.2.2),
suggesting that it was archetypal.

CFB 6 A *ligoraceaster*, B *ligeraceaster*, C *ligeracester*, D *ligereceaster*:
here the essential common ground between the texts is uncontracted
ligora- (B, C *ligera*-, D *ligere*-) in the place-name 'Leicester'. The
form as in B and C is atypical of the scribes: the B scribe writes 917

---

[11] The rarer forms are as follows: with -*un*, Brb A 10 *crungun*, 22 *legdun*, 27 *gesohtun*,
28 *lægun*, 48 *wurdun*; and with -*on*, 4 *geslogon*, 24 *wyrndon*, 58 *sohton*.

[12] Examples of -*un* I have noticed are 755 *gemettun*, 774 *gefuhtun*, 856 *sætun*, 886
gewitun, 894 *genamun*, 897 *begeatun*.

ligraceastre, 918 *legraceastre*, the C scribe 917 *ligreceastre*, 918 *ligraceastre*, all contracted forms; so it is likely that the archetype featured an uncontracted form of the element.

CFB 6 A *lincylene*, B *lindkylne*, C *lindcylne*, D *lincolne*: the only comparable form in any of these scribes' work is D 1016 *lincolnescire*; but the erased form *lind-* in the A text of CFB suggests that the archetypal text exhibited *lind-* rather than *lin-*.

EgC 1 A, B, C *waldend*, EgD A, B, C 17, 22, 34 *waldend(es)*, with Anglian or early W-S or early Kt. *a* by retraction of *æ* before *l* plus consonant (*OEG* §143). In the A scribe's work, *ea* in these phonological circumstances is invariable except here, and usual also in the B and C scribes' contributions to their respective texts of the *Chronicle*. We may safely assign *waldend(-)* in all four lines to the archetypes of these two poems.

DEw 7, 21 D *weolan*, where C has the corruption *weolm* in 7 (see §2.1.2 above) and *welan* in 21. D's form shows Anglian or Kt. *a*-umlaut of *e* (*OEG* §210), and C's corruption seems to be based on the same form. C's scribe writes no other instances of *eo* the *a*-umlaut of *e*; D's scribe writes *e* frequently in such positions, *feola* once in 1065 (beside frequent *fela*). It seems probable that *weolan* occurred at least in line 2 of the archetypal text of DEw, and perhaps in 21 too.

SnS 77 A *lamena*, B *lamana*: the ending *-ena*, *-ana* in the gen. pl. of weak adjectives is characteristic of early W-S (*OEG* §656); such an ending is therefore likely to have occurred in the archetype of SnS.

§7.4 METRICAL EVIDENCE FOR THE LANGUAGE OF THE ORIGINAL POEM

Metrical criteria sometimes enable us to deduce at least certain aspects of the form of individual words in the poem as it was originally composed. Examples are given below.

Brb 59 all texts *hremige* (originally written *hramige* in A, then corrected). Campbell 1938: 18, argues for a disyllabic *hremge* in the original poem on metrical grounds (the verse in question is 59b *wig(g)es hremige*).

CFB 13 A, B *eadmund cyning* (B *cining*), C *eadmund cing*. Here C's version is short of the four-syllable minimum for a half-line; the original work presumably had a disyllabic form of the word, such as we see in A and B. C's monosyllabic form is evidently a late Merc. or late W-S substitution (*OEG* §391).

SnS A 77 *wince[...]a* (for *wincendra*), B *winciendra*: a trisyllabic form, as in A, is required metrically (see Menner 1941: 20). We may compare

SnS A 105 *hangiende*, where again the metre requires *hangende* (Menner 1941: 113) and SnS A 250 *geomrende*, where a trisyllabic form is also confirmed by metrical considerations. Thus B's *winciendra* seems to represent a later substitution. Medial *i* in the pres. part. of Class II weak verbs is characteristic of W-S; its absence after long syllables, as in these examples from SnS A, is Anglian (*OEG* §757).

Gl1 J 30a *on drihtnes namon*, C *on drihtenes naman*: C's unsyncopated *drihtenes* produces a suspect variety of type B verse with a two-syllable second dip (see Bliss 1967: 126); J's disyllabic *drihtnes* no doubt reflects the language of the original composition more faithfully than C's form. J's scribe writes no further inflected forms of *drihten*; but C's scribe writes *drihtenes* again in LP2 98; it appears to have been the form he himself preferred.

Aza 6a *niþas to nerganne*, Dan 284 *niðas to nergenne.*; Aza 37a *had to hebban*, Dan 320 *hat to hebbanne*. The scribe of Aza writes inflected infinitives as *-anne* or *-enne* in about equal proportions. In the position in which one expects to find the inflected infinitive, i.e. after *to*, uninflected forms are occasionally written, as in Aza 37 (Chr 1555, Glc 531, Phx 275, Jln 54, 408, 557, Pre 25). Dan's scribe usually writes *-anne*; *-enne* is very rare in his work (e.g. Exo 438 *gesecgenne*), and he writes no uninflected forms after *to*. In both these lines of Aza/Dan, the uninflected form *(-an)* of the infinitive is required metrically, though it is only written as uninflected in Aza 37 *hebban*. If we were to accept the inflected infinitives, both verses here would resemble somewhat metrical type *D; but in normal *D verses the caesura falls immediately before the second full stress of the verse; here the rule is violated (the caesura comes before the proclitic *to*). The substitution of uninflected forms in both places produces verses of normal type (Sievers' type A; on the metrical difficulties of verses in *Beowulf* with inflected infinitives, see Bliss 1967: 38, §44). All the instances of uninflected infinitives after *to* in the Exeter Book (listed above) are confirmed by the metre, though many of the inflected forms require shortening for regular types to emerge (Phx 226, Jln 569, GfM 76, R28.12, 31.23, 39.22, 88.26). We may assume that in this respect, Aza reflects the language of the original composition better than Dan in 37, but not in 6.

Aza 15b *arena biddaþ*, Dan 294b *arna biddað*. The metrical pattern represented by Aza's version here, with trisyllabic first stressed word, is rare in *Beowulf* (four instances in b-verses; see Bliss 1967: 31–32, §38). Aza's scribe usually writes *arna* (Chr 255, 1231, 1352, Jln 715, Rsg 49, 67); this is his only instance of *arena*. Dan's scribe always writes *arna*. It thus seems probable that Dan's form reflects the language of the original poem more closely than Aza here.

Aza 22 *heapum tohworfne* (*h* inserted superscript), Dan 301 *heapum tohworfene*: here a syncopated form of past part., as in Aza, is indicated by the metre (see Bliss 1967: 45–46, §52).

§7.5 THE FORMS OF POETIC WORDS AS EVIDENCE OF TRANSMISSION

The existence in the OE period of a 'general Old English poetic dialect' which transcended regional dialect boundaries was posited by Kenneth Sisam in a much-quoted passage.[13] After arguing that OE poetry was composed (as long as 'verse was the medium of vernacular literature') in all the Anglo-Saxon kingdoms, not just in some of them, he suggests that there existed a common stock of OE poems 'for the entertainment or instruction of the English peoples':

> A poem, wherever composed, might win its way into the common stock. The native metre, based primarily on the alliteration of stressed syllables, carried well because in this essential the usage of seventh-century Northumbria and tenth-century Wessex was the same; but any local dialect forms that affected the verse-structure were a handicap to circulation. A poet might prefer to take his models from the common stock rather than from the less-known work of his own district. In this way poems could be produced that do not belong to any local dialect, but to a general Old English poetic dialect, artificial, archaic, and perhaps mixed in its vocabulary, conservative in inflexions that affect the verse-structure, and indifferent to non-structural irregularities, which were perhaps tolerated as part of the colouring of the langage of verse (Sisam 1953: 138).

If such a dialect did develop, attention to the forms of words of purely or largely poetic distribution is unlikely to be very productive in illuminating the processes of OE verse-transmission; for if a dialectally mixed verse-language existed, doubtless the sort of spellings that we might confidently take as evidence of regional dialectal influence on the text when they occur in common, widely distributed words should be classed as merely 'poetic' in items of poetic vocabulary. When a poet wrote down his own composition, or a scribe transcribed an oral performance of a poem by somebody else, the text thus produced might exhibit apparently dialectal forms of poetic words indicating, not the regional dialect of either poet or scribe, but simply the assimilation of a word in an

---

[13]   For a recent reassessment of Sisam's idea, see Megginson 1995.

originally dialectal form into this 'general Old English poetic dialect', with its tolerance of 'non-structural irregularities'. One of Sisam's examples is the word *mēce*, 'sword', invariably written with non-W-S *e* in OE poetic texts (Sisam 1953: 126–28; see also *OEG* §128, note 2). The only possible exception in OE is Brb A 40 *mæcan*, apparently with W-S *æ*. As Sisam points out (Sisam 1953: 127, note 1), the final *n* shows that the reading is corrupt, and in his view this disqualifies the form as an example of the word in W-S form. It is difficult to argue with Sisam's main conclusion, which is that in *mece* the *e* spelling, though originally a reflection of a pronunciation used only in non-W-S dialects, came to be widely accepted as the proper spelling of the word. In a poem composed and subsequently transmitted in an Anglian dialect or in Kt., the word would be faithfully transcribed in this form; but even when such a text passed into late W-S, *mece* would remain unchanged. A question that arises here, however, is whether such a word would have remained un-West-Saxonised simply because scribes were most familiar with it in non-W-S form, or because scribes working in the late W-S spelling tradition did not know the word in any form other than its non-W-S form, perhaps because the word itself had disappeared from W-S regional dialect, or even had never been part of it. At any rate, it would seem that poetic words with non-W-S forms, even when distributed over a number of manuscript texts, cannot be taken with confidence as reflections of the language of the archetype or the original composition, because we can never be certain that they are not themselves the product of transmitters' poeticization of W-S forms in their exemplars as they brought the text into the 'common stock' of standardized verse-texts. Although phonological evidence from the period enables us to identify a word like *mece* as showing the results of sound-changes which took place in some regional dialects of OE but not in others, the fact that the word is confined to verse makes it difficult to judge how widely the word itself was known in the poetic traditions of different regional dialect areas — particularly, in this case, the W-S dialect area. These considerations tend to make us look more critically at Sisam's dismissal of Brb A 40 *mæcan* as evidence of the existence of *mece* in W-S form. Certainly the form is part of 'a bungling of the difficult phrase *mec(e)a gemanan*' (Sisam 1953: 127, note 1); but we cannot be certain that the phrase did not include, in its earlier, unbungled condition, the W-S form *mæce*. There is, as we shall see below, some evidence which might support the idea that 'poetic' (i.e. non-W-S) and W-S spellings of poetic lexical items sometimes replaced each other during transmission.

The great majority of the data relevant to the treatment of dialectal forms of poetic words during transmission derives from the poems of the *Anglo-Saxon Chronicle*. The forms are listed below, with discussions.

Brb 6 A, B, C, D *heapo-*, 48 *beado* (A *beadu-*), both with Merc. *ea* by *u*-umlaut. These are poetic elements exhibiting the same stem vowel that they exhibit in all their instances in OE. Evidently they entered the poetic dialect in Mercian form and were never West-Saxonised (see *OEG* §§206–07).

Brb 61 B, C, D *salowig-* (A *saluwig-*), with early or non-W-S *a* (*OEG* §143; cf. EgD 25 A *gewealc*, B, C *gewalc*, discussed below).

Brb 18 A, C, D *ageted* with non-W-S *e*. This poetic verb contains the non-W-S stem vowel *e* (from *ēa* by *i*-mutation; *OEG* §200.5) in all its occurrences (see Campbell 1938: 103, and above, §5.1; B has replaced *ageted* with *forgrunden*).

CFB 10 A, C, D *hæfteclommum* with *o* before a nasal consonant, beside 9 *norðmannum* and 11 *lange*, both with *a* in all texts. B 10 has *-clammum*. Of these three words, only the element *-clomm* is poetic, and the imposition or survival of *o* in it, in contrast with the general tendency of all the scribes involved to write *a* in stressed syllables before nasals, is probably connected with this distribution. If so, B's *a* in this element is to be interpreted as a scribal substitution, for the evidence for *-clommum* in the archetype is relatively strong (though see my cautionary remarks earlier in this section).

EgC 9 A *gefrege* with non-W-S *e* beside *gefrœge* in B and C, and EgD 34 A *gefrege*, B, C *gefrœge*, whereas all texts have *gefrœge* in 16. All the scribes involved here usually write *œ* for Prim. Gmc. *ǣ* (*OEG* §128), though the A scribe varies between W-S *œ* and non-W-S *e* in this poetic word. We may tentatively interpret the variety of forms and variants here as a manifestation of the tendency, postulated above, for 'poetic' and W-S forms of such words to replace each other freely during transmission.

EgC 17 all texts *eafora* with *ea*, in conjunction with other evidence, may also illustrate the same phenomenon; only in the B MS is *ea*, proper to the Merc. dialect of the *Vespasian Psalter* gloss, invariable in this word (Brb 7, 52, CFB 13 and here; cf. Brb 6 *heapo-* etc. above). On the other hand, we have already noted that some form such as C's *aforan*, with initial *a*, probably appeared in the archetype of Brb (above, §7.3). It may be, therefore, that the whole range of forms of this word in the various manuscripts of the *Chronicle* poems illustrates the contrary tendencies I posited earlier: on the one hand, to West-Saxonize the spellings of poetic vocabulary; and on the other, to restore or impose what were felt to be the proper 'poetic' (originally dialectal) forms.

EgD 25 A *gewealc*, B, C *gewalc* with early or Anglian *a* before *l* plus consonant. A's scribe normally writes *ea* in this position, the only exceptions being in the word *waldend* in EgC 1, EgD 17, 22 and 34. The B and C scribes also write *ea* normally, but *a* in these same instances of *waldend*, in EgD 12 *aldor*, and here in *gewalc*. It seems likely that this identical distribution in B and C is a reflection of their common original; but again, there is no good evidence that the archetypal form of *gewalc* in 25 was necessarily the same, for it lacks the vital support of A. Here, too, there may have been an interchange of forms operating in either direction.

EgD 26 A *gamolfeax*, B, C *gomolfeax*: *a* is usual in all the scribes' work for Gmc. *a* before a nasal consonant in stressed syllables (see my discussion of CFB 10 -*clommum* above); *gomol*- is a poetic element. This case is thus similar to that of *gewalc* in the same poem: we cannot be certain that *gomol*- with *o* reflects the archetype, for A has *gamol*-. Again, there may have been an interchange of forms during transmission.

Few other poems show evidence of the treatment of special forms of poetic words, but we should mention here the late manuscripts of Cæd. No doubt because the transmission of two of the later W-S versions of this poem (the W-S *ylda* and *eorðe* groups) was slavish and uncritical, there is a tendency for the spellings of poetic words in particular to become fixed, probably because their meanings were no longer understood. An example is, perhaps, 2 *metudes* with medial *u* (late OE *o*): in all three of the W-S *eorðe* texts, and in all but the very earliest (W) of the W-S *ylda* texts (W, which has *metoddes*, corrected to *metodes*), this spelling is constant. We may compare the situation in the W-S *eorðan* texts, all of which have *me(o)todes* with late OE *o*. Perhaps only W of the W-S *ylda* group represents a period (W is mid-eleventh century) when poetic words were sufficiently familiar to transmitters for them to modernize or standardize their forms.

§7.6 LINGUISTIC DISTINCTIONS BETWEEN POEMS AND OTHER TEXTS WRITTEN BY THE SAME SCRIBE

The distribution of linguistic forms in OE manuscripts will sometimes provide evidence of the separate transmission, at some earlier stage, of the texts they contain. The two texts which shows the clearest evidence of this kind are SB1 and both versions of SnS. The evidence is given below for each poem.

§7.6.1 SB1

The following late W-S forms are atypical of the scribe in the part of the Vercelli Book in which SB1 appears:

> SB1 62 *synum*, 110 *swyra*, 92 *wyle*, 95 *wylt* all have late W-S *y* for earlier *i* (*OEG* §§317–18).
>
> SB1 69 *lifiendum* (*OEG* §762), 115 *werian*, 122 *werie*, 161 *cearie* (*OEG* §341), all have unstressed *i* for earlier *-ig-* of various origins.
>
> SB1 114 *huxlicum* with metathesis of *sc* to *x* (*OEG* §440).
>
> SB1 135 *gyt* with *y* for earlier *ie* by palatal diphthongization of *ē* (*OEG* §§185, 299, 300, 301)
>
> SB1 153 *hige* with *i* for *y* (the *i*-umlaut of earlier *u*; *OEG* §316)
>
> SB1 153 *hynðum* with *y* for earlier *ie* the *i*-umlaut of *ēa* (*OEG* §§200.5, 301)

These forms would appear to indicate that the text of SB was copied by a West-Saxonizing scribe before it was anthologized in the Vercelli Book. The fact that SB2 does not share these forms might suggest that this late W-S influence dates from after the split in the tradition which the two texts represent, though this is uncertain.

§7.6.2 SnS

Both texts of SnS feature forms of a type which the scribes do not favour elsewhere in their work in the same manuscripts. In the B text these are both late W-S and early W-S forms. Two features are late W-S:

> SnS B 61 *hwylū*, 63 *gymmum*, 74 *getymbreð*, 85 *symle*, 88 *gyf*, all with late W-S *y* for earlier *i* (*OEG* §318)
>
> SnS B 68 *synnihte*, with *y* for earlier *i* (an inverted spelling pointing to the unrounding of *y* to *i*; *OEG* §317)

One feature is early W-S:

> SnS B 22 *wesðe* (A *weste*), 36 *eaðusð* (A *eaðost*) are inverted spellings indicating the change of *sþ* to *st* in words like B 18 *gesemesð* (*OEG* §481.1 and note 5).

The A text of SnS has the following features which are atypical of the A scribe in his work elsewhere in the same manuscript:

> SnS A 45, 66 *seofan* with non-W-S *a*-umlaut of *e* to *eo* (*OEG* §210).

> SnS A 87 *gebrengan*, 88 *gebrengest*, 108 *brengeð*, 147 *gebrengan* (cf.
> *bringan* in SnS 234, *gebringeð* in the Prose Dialogue). This word is
> North., possibly also W-S, Kt. or Merc. (*OEG* §753.9.b.5)

There is no significant overlap between the two texts in these forms,
though we should note a sprinkling of early W-S forms in A which may
derive from the same level of transmission as B's early W-S forms. These
are SnS A 85 *siemle* (with *ie* for earlier *i*; *OEG* §300), 88 *ierne* (with *ie*
the product of *i*-umlaut of *io* by fracture of *i* before *r* plus consonant;
OEG §§154.3, 201.1). In the case of 73 *ahieðeð*, *ie* seems to derive from
y, the *i*-umlaut of earlier *u*. It is presumably an inverted spelling, though
if so it would indicate the isolative unrounding of *y* to *i*, for which there is
no good evidence in early W-S (see *OEG* §§315–16).

Chapter 8. The Meticulous Copyist

§8 The reproduction of features of textual presentation

Besides linguistic forms, there are several other features of the written texts of poems which scribes sometimes preserved in the copies they made. The evidence for this comes in the form of textual correspondences that reside in features which are unlikely to have arisen independently in two lines of transmission. The following subsections describe these correspondences and consider their significance.

§8.1 LETTER FORMS

There was considerable variation in the form of some of the letters of the version of the roman alphabet used by the Anglo-Saxons, and it is occasionally possible, either when matches between two texts in unusual letter-shapes occur, or a scribe uses forms in a poem that he tends not to use elsewhere in his work, to be reasonably certain that they originate in some antecedent text. A case of the latter sort is the forms of *a* and *y* that appear in the latter half of the H text of PCE. From line 10, when the minor scribe of the H MS takes over the copying of PCE, to the end of the text, an archaic pointed *a* is used almost invariably,[1] and a distinctive *f*-shaped *y* is used in 22 *dryhten* and 27 *ðyrelne*. The scribe does not use this form anywhere else in his work.[2] These letter-forms therefore

---

[1] The minor scribe of the H text of PCE 10–30 prefers pointed *a* to square *a* in his earlier contributions to the copying of the H text of the *Cura Pastoralis* translation; but in the last passage he copied before his contribution to PCE, which was f. 67ᵛ/13 *herigenne* to f. 69ᵛ/12 *gebrenge* (Sweet 1871: 353/25–363/22), square *a* outnumbers pointed *a* by between three and four to one. In PCE 10–30, however, pointed *a* appears twenty-two times, square *a* only twice, in 13 *gewitlocan* and 22 *hladað* (second instance only).

[2] In *ðyrelne*, the scribe first wrote the rounded *y* he uses invariably elsewhere in his work, but then changed it to *f*-shaped *y*, which tends to suggest that the *f*-shaped form

probably derive from H's exemplar text.

We have already had occasion to mention Cæd L 5 *aeldu*, in which *-u* may be an error for an 'open' *a* in the exemplar (above, §2.1.1.1). In the W text of Cæd, which is the earliest (eleventh century) surviving text of the W-S *ylda* group of texts, certain letter forms — *h* with the second limb turned inwards, rounded *y* in 7 *manncynnes*, 9 *fyrum* (beside straight *y* in other words) — are forms associated with an earlier period (See Ker 1957: xxxi) and therefore noteworthy in a late manuscript. They may derive from W's exemplar, but we cannot be sure. Some striking correspondences between texts of Cæd in forms of *d*, sometimes between texts of different text-families (L, Mg, Hr 1 *weard* with insular *d*; L, Mg, Hr 2 *metudes* with straight *d*; L, Mg 3 *wuldor-* with straight *d*) are unlikely to be anything more than chance coincidences, for obvious reasons.

The case of Brb C 53 *negled-*, in which the first *e* may be an error for the *ę* (a form of *æ*) which occurs in the corresponding form in the A text, has been mentioned earlier (above, §2.1.1.1). The correspondences between the B and C texts of EgD in 24, 26 *hæleþ* with final *þ* and 37 *eorðan* with medial *ð* almost certainly derive from B-C*, their common prototype, for they reside in letter forms less favoured in similar contexts by either scribe.[3] Links between extant texts and their archetype are fairly clear in the case of DEw, where C and D correspond in 15 *-leas* (C *bealuleas*, D *bealeleas*) with tall *s*, a rare form in this position in both scribes' work.[4]

The only correspondence of interest in SnS resides in 70 *gefæstnað* and 80 *ærest*, where both texts feature low *s*, not a common form before *t* in either scribe's work.[5]

§8.2 ACCENT MARKS

Correspondences between texts in the use of acute accents over the vowels of individual words sometimes enables us to establish a literary

---

appeared in his exemplar.

[3] Cf. EgD 13, 31 B *hæleþ*, C *hæleð*, and 1 B *eorðan*, C *eorþan*.

[4] The scribe of the C text of DEw writes low *s* thirty-five times at the ends of words; 15 *bealuleas* is the only example of tall *s* in that position. In the D scribe's work, low *s* outnumbers tall *s* at the ends of words by more than four to one.

[5] Before *t*, the A scribe of SnS normally uses tall *s* (fifteen times in SnS 1–94, with low *s* four times, in 50 *mærost*, 76 *strengra*, 80 *ærest*, and in 70). The corresponding ratio in the B scribe's work is sixteen to eight.

connection between two texts of a poem deriving from an earlier, lost text. It is important, however, to investigate which words or elements are usually given accents elsewhere in other parts of the manuscript written by the same scribes; correspondences residing in such words or elements will obviously lose their value as evidence of textual connections if they are open to interpretation as impositions by any of the latest scribes.

Correspondences in accents between the A and D texts of Brb occur in 2, 19, 30, 37 *eác* and in 64 *-heafóc*. This pattern of agreement seems very distinctive at first sight, but it is difficult to interpret. The A text's usage is not easy to measure against the scribe's normal usages because there is insufficient material available in the manuscript for comparison: his contribution to the copying of the manuscript was very small (ff. 26^r-27^v). The D version of Brb, however, contains other instances of *ea* accented on the second element in 26 *eárgebland*, 35 *cneár*; and the D scribe occasionally writes similarly placed accents in his prose contribution to the D manuscript of the *Chronicle* (*geáre*, *eás*). This makes the four correspondences in *eác* in Brb seem less impressive. On the other hand, the D scribe accents *eac* only once in the prose he writes, beside *eac* unaccented seven times — contrary evidence, tending to suggest that *eác* is reproduced from the text of Brb in D's exemplar. There can be no confusion, on the other hand, about the significance of the accent on the ustressed syllable of 64 *-heafóc*: accents are usually placed on stressed vowels, not unstressed ones, so chance coincidence will scarcely account for the agreement here. There can be little doubt that accented *-heafóc* derives from the archetype of Brb.

In EgC, accents in B and C on 12 *gebýrdtíde* and 15 *fréan* clearly derive from B/C*, for of these accented elements, only *-tíde* can be matched elsewhere in either scribe's work (Brb B 14 *morgentíd*; also *tíd-* once in the *Chronicle* prose copied by the B scribe), and a compound like *gebýrdtíde* with both elements accented is very unusual.

The very high level of correspondence in EgD between texts B and C is impressive; but again, when we attempt to measure them against the scribes' normal practices, their significance seems reduced. B has twenty-one accents in EgD, C seventeen, and thirteen correspondences between them occur (in 7 *rímcræfte*, 8, 14 *gewát*, 9 *lífe*, 11 *cyneríce*, 13 *tírfæst* and *ǽr*, 21 *móde*, 31, 34 *wíde*, 32 *cométa*, 33 *wíse*, 35 *hrúsan*). However, of these, only 11 *cyneríce* and 35 *hrúsan* are really impressive as evidence of links between these texts, because most of the other correspondences reside in words or elements that at least one of the scribes in question commonly gives accents to. The texts of DEw present a similar picture. The degree of overlap between texts C and D seems impressive on the face of it (four out of a possible seven correspondences in 8 *tíd*, 15 *á*, 16 *ǽr*, 23 *gód*); but most of these correspondences are in words which one or other of the scribes accents elsewhere in his work.

Finally, in the W-S *eorðan* group of texts of Cæd, the correspondence between T and O in their accent on T's *ór* and O's *oór,*[d] in 4 probably derives from the group prototype, though unsurprisingly there are no forms of either of these poetic words elsewhere in either scribe's work with which their usage in Cæd may be compared.

§8.3 ABBREVIATIONS

OE scribes sometimes abbreviated certain common words (e.g. *þonne*, *þæt*, *and/ond*) and inflexional endings (especially -*ū* for the masc. or neut. dat. ending -*um* on nouns or adjectives), though usage varied considerably from scribe to scribe. The distribution of abbreviated and unabbreviated forms of words in the extant texts of poems surviving in two or more witnesses can seldom tell us much about the earlier transmission of the poems in question, though evidence from the texts of two poems is worth mentioning. One is SB1 88 *andwyrdan*, corresponding to SB2 82 *ondwyrdan*, both unabbreviated forms: the scribes of the Vercelli and Exeter Books both write abbreviated forms of the prefix *and-/ond-* more often than unabbreviated forms — much more often in the case of the Exeter Book scribe.[6]

More convincing, perhaps, than this correspondence (which does not, admittedly, reside in the same linguistic form: SB1 has *and-*, SB2 *ond-*), is the one between abbreviated *þæt* in SB1 85/SB2 78 and SB1 120/SB2 116 — both, as it happens, places where the texts differ in terms of transposed or displaced verses. In SB1, unabbreviated *þæt* occurs fourteen times, abbreviated forms three times. In SB2 the corresponding figures are twelve and three. The number of possible correspondences in abbreviated forms is five, of which two in fact occur, a remarkable level of agreement which cannot have resulted from chance.[7]

---

[6]   By my count, unabbreviated *ond-* appears only seven times in all: four times in Glc (beside six abbreviated forms), twice in the *Riddles* (no abbreviated forms occur) and SB2 82 (beside one abbreviated form in SB2 100 *&sware*).

[7]   The distribution of abbreviated and unabbreviated forms of *þæt* in the Vercelli and Exeter Books is complex (see Orton 1979a: 175–6 for details), but the broad picture is that in Vercelli the abbreviated forms, though commoner than unabbreviated ones in some

Many of the extant texts of Cæd show an abbreviated dat. pl. ending in 7 *b(e)arnū*, in contrast in most texts with 9 *firum* or *foldum* (or both) unabbreviated.[8] This contrast occurs in M, the earliest of the two texts of the North. *aelda* group (9 *firum*); in T, the earliest text of the W-S *eorðan* group (9 *firum*; the same contrast occurs also in To in this group); in the three earliest texts of the W-S *ylda* group (W, Bd₁, H, all with 9 *firum* (W *fyrum*), and *foldum*); and in Ld₁ (with 9 *fyrum*), one of the two earliest texts of the W-S *eorðe* group. It is likely (not certain) that this distinction is an old one which was preserved in some W-S copies of the poem, perhaps even into the twelfth century.

§8.4 FORMAT

Features of textual presentation sometimes correspond between different versions of the same poem, and in a few cases these correspondences are sufficiently close to point to a common origin in an antecedent text.

The H and Mg texts of the W-S *ylda* group of Cæd are both surrounded by a line-frame in their manuscripts, confirming a close connection between these two texts suggested also by a considerable overlap in punctuation (see §8.5 below). The Mg text could conceivably derive from H, for they share, in addition to the features already mentioned here, overlap in capitalization (see §8.5 below) and the typically eleventh-century spelling 3 *wurc* (W, Ln, Tr₁ *weorc*; Bu has the error *wure*); but they differ in other forms, notably H 2 *myhte*, 9 *ælmyhtig*, both with late OE *y* (*OEG* §§317–18) in contrast to Mg's forms *mihte* and *ælmihtig*, and in 5 H *gesceop*, Mg *gescop*. On the whole, it seems likely that H and Mg descend from a single text, perhaps, in view of their close textual similarities, the exemplar of one or both of them.

Two other texts of Cæd in the W-S *ylda* group, W and Bd₁, exhibit a strikingly similar *signe de renvoi* (visible only in the Latin text in Bd₁, whose text of Cæd itself is badly damaged) which can scarcely be a coincidence;[9] evidently these texts are closely related, though exactly how closely is difficult to judge because of the poor condition of the Bd₁ text.

---

parts of the manuscript, are very rare in the part that contains SB1, and that in the Exeter Book, again, in the part of the manuscript containing SB2, abbreviated forms are rarer than unabbreviated ones.

[8]   For details, see Orton 1998: 159.

[9]   The texts of the Latin Bede in these two manuscripts are closely allied; see Colgrave & Mynors 1969: l-li.

§8.5 CAPITALIZATION AND PUNCTUATION

Systems of punctuation and capitalization in different texts of the same poem are quite often related, pointing unmistakably to a common textual history at some earlier stage in the transmission. Capital letters are seldom used at all frequently in OE poetic texts, so correspondences are conspicuous when they occur.

In SB1 and SB2, the correspondence in capitals in 9 *Sceal* and 15 *Cleopað* (these are the two first small capitals to occur in either text) probably derives from the archetype.[10]

In PCE, correspondences in pointing between the H and D texts in the final part of the poem have already been described in detail (above, §7.2); these must certainly be of common origin. In Brb, the capitalization of B, C 37, 57 *Swylce* (C *Swilce*) clearly derives from B-C*. There is only one other capital in either text, and they correspond in that too, accompanied in this instance by D (53 B *Gewitan*, C *Gewiton*, D *GEwiton*). Campbell is doubtful of the significance of this last correspondence, but in view of the rarity of small capitals in any of these texts, all three correspondences seem to me significant: they derive from the archetype.

In both EgC and EgD, correspondences between B and C, particularly in the pointing of a-verses, evidently derive from B-C*; in EgC, B has three points at the ends of a-verses (5, 15, 18, the second and third after the numeral *xx*) and all of them reappear in C, which has only two additional points after a-verses (10, 16). Pointing of b-verses is fairly regular in both texts, so that correspondences in the omission of points after 4, 17 and 18 are equally conspicuous, indicating that all the pointing in these two texts of EgC derives from B-C*. A very similar picture is presented by the B and C texts of EgD: each text has six points at the ends of a-verses, and there are no less than five correspondences (10, 13, 26, 32, 35). B and C are also linked to B-C* by a shared distribution of capital letters: both distinguish EgD 16 and 24 *Ða* (C *Þa* in both lines), with capitals, from 29 *þa* with lower-case *þ*. In the same poem, a clear division of the text is marked in both A and B at the end of 15, in A by an ornamental point followed by capital, in B by a single point and a capital in the margin. This division must derive from the archetype.

Connections between various texts of the W-S *ylda* group of Cæd are numerous. The *H* of 5 *He* links texts H, Ln and Mg (note also Tr[1]'s

---

[10]   SB1 contains seventeen small capitals, SB2 eight. The two correspondences occur on words that begin new sentences; see Orton 1979a: 176–7.

corruption *Hu*), and *Æ* of 8 *Æfter* links H, Mg and Bu. In punctuation, the pattern in H and Mg is the same (1b, 2a, 2b, 3a, 4b, 6a, 8a), except that Mg has two additional points after 6b *scyppend* and at the end of the text. Ln has the same pattern as Mg except that it omits the point after 8a and has additional points after 3b and 5b. The few points visible in W and Bd₁ make it plain that they both had independent patterns. The historical relationship between the H, Mg and Ln texts is clearly very close.

Evidence for links of a similar kind between the A and B texts of SnS is not nearly so plentiful, but what there is seems to me convincing. It consists solely of the combination, mid-sentence, of point and capital in 23–24 *gewitte. Se*. The A text of the first dialogue (1–178) shows a total of sixteen points, excluding those associated with the presentation of runes. Of these, all but one (149) appear at the ends of b-verses and most of them at the ends of sentences as indicated in Dobbie's edition (Dobbie 1942: 31–38). The nine initial capitals in A are all preceded by points (23, 62, 132, 145, 149, 154, 157, 160, 165) and all *except* 23–24 mark sentence-divisions. The B text of SnS contains a total of eighteen points (excluding points associated with the presentation of letters of the Pater Noster), most but not all of them marking sentence-divisions (exceptions are 3, 15, 23, 63, 75). Of sixteen initial capitals in B, nine are preceded by points (3, 6, 15, 20, 23, 35, 38, 62, 67), of which three involve the name *Salomon* (after 20, 38, 62) and one *Saturnus* (after 35): a new speaker is introduced in these four lines, so the combination of point and capital is appropriate enough. Of the remaining five combinations of point and capital, two involve the word *Swylce* (3, 6), also capitalized without preceding point in 43; one involves *Gif* (15), with which 88 *Gyf* without preceding point should be compared. The fifth is 23–24 *gewitte. Se* in mid-sentence, shared by A. I have gone into detail here in order to show how difficult it would have been to predict this correspondence between the two texts on the basis of a general analysis of the distribution of points and capitals in both manuscripts. The evidence is, as I said above, meagre, but it is difficult to escape its significance: the A and B texts of SnS, despite their numerous variations, retain at least one clear sign of their descent from an earlier written archetype.

Chapter 9. Conclusions

§9 Conclusions

§9.1 THE FAITHFUL REPRODUCTION OF THE TEXT

Few features of OE verse-texts were immune from alteration in the course of transmission, though it is difficult to rank them in terms of their resistance to alteration or removal. It might appear, from the evidence collected in the preceding chapters of this book, that the feature of a text least likely to be transmitted was its letter forms. Certainly one would expect experienced scribes to impose the letter forms they used either by habit or by training, irrespective of those appearing in their exemplars; and in fact there is very little evidence to show that particular forms were ever transcribed faithfully. But the general imposition of their customary forms by individual copyists may not be the only reason for this lack of evidence. It is clear that many OE scribes followed similar practices in their employment of variant letter forms. Even when a letter could have two or even three different forms in Anglo-Saxon script, such as the letters *s* and *y*, scribes very often chose between them according to the same contextual criteria, for example commonly preferring tall *s* before *t* and *w*, but low *s* before vowels or at the ends of words. The chances were slim of the preservation in two or more copies of a rare form, or a common form used in a distinctive context at a particular point in the text. There are a few cases where forms that are rare in a scribe's work may tentatively be traced to his exemplar, but seldom any further than that. An example is the H text of PCE, with its unusual forms of *a* and *y* (§8.1 above). Two cases where the evidence of a literary link between texts is quite good is the agreement between the B and C texts of EgD in the distribution of *þ* and *ð*, and between the C and D texts of DEw in their use of tall *s* in 15 *-leas* (C *bealuleas,* D *bealeleas*). In both these cases, however, it is notable that the archetype cannot be much older than the extant texts. EgD records the death of Edgar in 975; the B text was written, according to Ker, only a few years later, between 977 and 979 (Ker 1957: 249), the C text in the mid-eleventh century (Ker 1957: 253). DEw records the death of Edward in 1065; the palaeography of the C and D texts places both within the next thirty-five years. There are at least two possible factors at work here in favour of the preservation of forms: the lateness of these texts — perhaps the scrupulous reproduction of letter forms from exemplars was characteristic of the end of the Anglo-Saxon period, less so of the earlier centuries — or simply the closeness, in terms of the number of intervening copies, of these texts in particular to their archetypes. The question of the significance of such correspondences in OE generally might bear further investigation. Finally, two correspondences between the A and B texts of SnS that are probably significant are the low *s* that appears in 70 *gefæstnað* and 88 *ærest* in both texts, contrary to the general distribution of forms of *s* in both manuscripts. As we shall see shortly, the evidence of punctuation and capitalization also supports a literary connection between the two texts of SnS.

The poems from the *Anglo-Saxon Chronicle* provide most of the convincing cases of the preservation of accent marks from exemplars (above, §8.2); and a few of these links are traceable to the archetype, as in the case of the A and D texts of Brb (especially 64 *-heafóc*), but not as far back in the transmission in the case of the B and C texts of EgC and EgD. The B and C texts of these two poems are also very alike in their punctuation, their deployment of capital letters, and in EgD at least, as we have just seen, in some of their letter forms. The B and C texts of Brb also show a significant overlap in capital letters — one of several indications of their derivation from a common original, *B-C.

Correspondences in abbreviated or unabbreviated forms are occasionally indicative of a link between texts of poems and their archetypes, but examples are scarce (see above, §8.3). The two texts of SB show correspondences in forms of abbreviated *þæt* that are probably significant, though we should not feel able to place much trust in them were they not supported by other kinds of scribal correspondence between SB1 and SB2, notably in their distribution of capital letters. There is a pattern of abbreviated and unabbreviated forms of the *-um* inflexion in several late versions of Cæd which may go back to the some of the earliest written texts of the poem, but the evidence is not really conclusive.

Correspondences in textual formatting, capitalization and punctuation clearly indicate close connections between texts H, Mg and Ln of the W-S *ylda* group of Cæd, and the W and Bd₁ texts of the same group are linked by the same distinctive *signe de renvoi* that they use to connect the text of the OE poem with the Latin paraphrase of it in the text of Bede's *Historia Ecclesiastica*. Very close correspondences in punctuation between the H and D texts of PCE in the last twenty lines of the poem are strong evidence of the preservation of pointing in the transmission of this poem. Correspondences between the B and C texts of both EgC and EgD obviously derive from *B-C, their common original; and finally, the two texts of SnS, despite showing a very wide range of variation of all kinds, betray their common literary origin in a point and following capital in 23–24 *gewitte. Se*, which could scarcely have originated independently.

Generally speaking, the comparison of texts of the same poem in respect of these scribal features yields a limited range and quantity of information. There are several reasons why this should be so. One is the method I have followed, which relies on the chance survival of significant correspondences against the grain of the scribes' general practices: this alone is enough to ensure that correspondences we can safely identify as significant will be rare. When they do occur, however, they may, on the whole, be relied upon as evidence of literary connections between texts. Such connections, when they exist, rule out the possibility of oral transmission (see further below, §9.7); when significant correspondences in letter forms, accents, abbreviations, capitalization or punctuation occur, we may be reasonably sure that the texts so linked are connected by literary, not oral, transmission, and that therefore *all* the variants they show, of whatever kind, have been generated by the activities of scribes, not by oral performers. This much, at least, can be established in the cases of the B and C texts of EgC and EgD, all the texts of Brb, the W-S *ylda* texts of Cæd, SB1 and SB2, and the A and B texts of SnS. To some extent, of course, this simply confirms what we would have suspected anyway; for instance, it is obviously unlikely that oral performance played any part in the generation of variants between the *Chronicle* poems, because once incorporated as annals in the *Chronicle* their transmission could scarcely be oral from then on. The same is true of Cæd. But oral transmission, which has been suggested as the explanation for variants between SB1 and SB2 (by Gyger 1969), seems to be ruled out for that poem, as well as for SnS.

The view of the second scribe of the H text of PCE as a precise copyist, suggested by his use of variant letter forms, receives confirmation from the Kentish dialectal forms (21 *werð*, 24 *welle*) that probably derive from his exemplar (above, §7.1). Another text in which we have identified (on the evidence of letter forms) signs of very close copying is the D text of DEw; this too shows spellings (*ki-* in the word for 'king') which seem, from what we can deduce from the distribution of comparable forms elsewhere in the D manuscript (see above, §7.2), to derive from his exemplar text, confirming the impression of fine accuracy created by the scribe's use of letter forms. The B and C texts of most of the *Chronicle* poems have many distinctive linguistic forms in common (Brb B, C 40 *maga*, 46 *inwitta*; EgC B, C 2 *kinge* with initial *k*, 4 *egbuend*, 7 *cegeað*, 13 *get*; EgD B, C 12 *aldor*) which are evidently preserved from their common original, *B-C. There are signs of similar links among the W-S *eorðan* texts of Cæd, especially texts T and O; but these are less compelling than the evidence of 2 *metudes* (with early *u*) in the W-S *ylda* texts: no doubt this derives from the original of this group of texts.

In the case of linguistic forms traceable to the archetype of all surviving texts of poems (above, §7.3), the *Chronicle* poems again figure largely: such forms are identifiable in various surviving texts of Brb, CFB, EgC, EgD and DEw. PCP and SnS each contain one such form. Literary transmission is thus indicated for all these poems, and a tolerance of unfamiliar (often dialectal) linguistic forms in the course of it. On the other hand, we have also found clear evidence among the manuscripts of Cæd of the imposition of standard (late W-S) forms on texts even when they were originally written down in dialect (see §1.1 above).

It is difficult to know what to make of linguistic forms which seem to have been imposed on texts against the metre (e.g. CFB C 13b *eadmund cing*, with monosyllabic *cing* where metre requires a disyllabic form; see §7.4 above). Examples are scattered among the texts of several poems (all the texts of Brb, CFB C, SnS B, Gll C, Aza). They are most straightforwardly interpreted as a sign that OE poems were sometimes copied by scribes oblivious to their metrical qualities, though the true explanation may be less simple. Perhaps forms like CFB 13 C *cing*, which are, strictly speaking, unmetrical in their contexts, would not have been so regarded by the Anglo-Saxons because what mattered to them was not conformity to the abstract patterns of permissible metrical types but a less exacting adherence to traditional grammatical and collocational assemblages established by an unconsciously absorbed tradition. Metre was probably only one of several kinds of regularity observed by OE poets (see further

Orton 1994: 10–12).

The texts of the *Chronicle* poems provide the strongest evidence for the scribal reproduction of poetic vocabulary in distinctive (non-W-S) forms, but it is complex evidence and difficult to interpret (see §7.5 above). The spellings of such words in OE generally often identify them as having entered the poetic lexical stock in dialectal form (a clearcut example is Brb 18 A, C, D *ageted* with non-W-S *e* in the stem); but although some of them maintain these forms through several copyings, others appear in W-S form too. Examples (with non-W-S forms followed by W-S ones) are CFB 10 A, C, D *hæfteclommum* with *o* (cf. 9 *norðmannum* and 11 *lange* with *a*) where B has -*clammum*; EgC 9 A *gefrege* with non-W-S *e* where B and C have *gefræge*; EgD 34 A *gefrege*, B, C *gefræge*, 16 all texts *gefræge*; EgD 25 B, C *gewalc*, A *gewealc*; and EgD 26 B, C *gomolfeax*, A *gamolfeax*. Here different texts of different poems show non-W-S or W-S forms in unpredictable distributions, suggesting that the spellings of these words were unstable. Evidently not all exclusively poetic words achieved a fixed form and there are signs that non-W-S and W-S forms may have interchanged in some of them. The evidence (admittedly rather limited in quantity) of the later versions of Cæd suggests, however, that such forms did become fixed eventually (see above, §7.5).

Evidence of scribal tolerance of variety in the forms of words in the texts they copied is limited, but one of the two tenth-century texts of SB (SB1) and both texts (late tenth and early eleventh century respectively) of SnS contain evidence of the faithful preservation of exemplar forms from versions of these poems which probably predate their collection in the manuscripts in which they survive (§7.6 above).

§9.2 ERRORS

Copying errors in the texts of the OE poems examined in this book are mostly easy to identify and quite often easy to explain in terms of the forms likely to have provoked them. Unusual letter forms may occasionally have caused slips, but it is difficult to find convincing examples in the absence of identifiable exemplars of other texts among those that survive. Certain standard features of OE script lie behind many mistakes, e.g. the sequences of identical minims which a letter-combination such as *um* or *nn* or *in* would involve, the similarity of form between *f* and the tall form of *s*, or between the common forms of *c* and *t*, *h* and *b*, or *ð* and *d* (see §2.1.1). In other cases, unfamiliarity with poetic vocabulary probably contributed to the confusion of one letter with another (see §2.1.1.4). Dittography, both retrospective and prospective, is often the only convincing explanation for some of the oddities produced by the scribes, for example EgC A 2 *corðre micelre* for B, C *corðre mycclum*, or EgD B 17 *welhrær* for A, C *welhwær* (see §2.1.1.5). In cases where recognizable words result, as in Cæd 2 O, Ca *wera* for *we(o)rc*, or DEw C 7 *weolm* in place of the non-W-S form *weolan* in the D text, some degree of reflection on the part of the scribe responsible for the resulting form may be assumed, particularly if the word suits the context at all well (as in the case of Cæd 2 O, Ca *wera* but not in DEw C 7 *weolm*); but these are ultimately the results of simple slips, perhaps showing an attempt at repair by a later, more thoughtful, copyist faced with the obscurities created by a predecessor. There is evidence to suggest that quite a few mistakes of this kind were provoked by the occurrence of unfamiliar dialectal spellings in exemplar texts (§2.1.2); but there are many examples of corruptions that, though difficult to explain except as copying errors, seem nevertheless unlikely palaeographically (§2.1.3); in these cases, perhaps other less obvious factors were at work. The D text of Brb and SB2 both contribute several examples in this category. The transposition of letters by mistake seems to have happened only seldom, whereas omission of letters was very common. Haplography is often the cause, and may occasionally account also for the omission of entire words, most often the abbreviation of *and/ond*, 'and'. Dittography produces omissions too, and homoeoteleuton sometimes led to the omission of quite large pieces of text (§2.3.5). SB (both texts) and Aza have suffered most damage from homoeoteleuton. Perhaps the scribe of the Exeter Book, who wrote both SB2 and Aza, was particularly prone to this kind of mistake, though of course the omissions could have occurred in the work of one or several of his predecessors in the handling of these poems.

Small errors were often corrected by the scribes who made them: deletions are commonly prescribed by underdottings or underlinings, insertions by interlinear additions. Large omissions by homoeoteleuton (§2.3.5 above) were seldom corrected so far as we can tell; there is just one passage in SB1 (82–86) where a scribe seems to have been careful to preserve all the exemplar's material after realizing that he had made a slip of this kind. No doubt such omissions, once made, were invisible to later copyists. They would probably be invisible to modern scholarship but for the survival of alternative versions of the poems which have been affected in this way. In the case of individual words, however, scribes might well have been able to see omissions of letters or similar minor mistakes just by looking at their own work, without reference to the exemplar; then, when a small mistake of this kind was noticed, the exemplar would supply the form originally miscopied. If this was the procedure normally followed, it would explain the very numerous instances of the correction of small slips in the manuscripts.

Evidence provided by several examples of the dittographic repetition of alliterating words (§2.4.2 above) is interesting for what it suggests about the way scribes carried the memory of the pieces of text they were copying in their heads. The erroneous repetition of an alliterating word may be a sign of the scribe's expectation of another word with the same beginning in the b-verse; and there is further evidence (rather limited, admittedly) that some scribes, at least, were sensitive to the alliterative and metrical character of the texts they were copying.

§9.3 REPAIRS

When corruptions already existed in scribes' exemplars, they would sometimes transcribe them without change, though convincing examples of this are rather uncommon: there is one good example in the W-S *ylda* texts of Cæd, where a very corrupt text was faithfully transmitted by several late scribes, and SB1 and SB2 have two clear examples in common which must derive from their archetype. Brb 40b–44a shows a sequence of misintepretation (probably of an ambiguous form, 40 *maga*) followed by a number of amendments in different versions to accommodate the new meaning which the original mistake generated. The result of this accumulation of activity is to change the meaning of the whole sentence radically. It is difficult to say how common this sort of amendment by stages might have been, because the survival (as in the case of Brb) of four texts of the same poem constituting three independent witnesses to the archetype is such a rare circumstance. Similar things may have happened to other poems; we are not in a position to tell whether they did or not because we lack the required number of witnesses. The W-S *eorðe* texts of Cæd show a much more modest reaction to an existing corruption in the form of an omission of an entire half-line (4b): the scribe of the Hr text (or a predecessor of his) noticed the imperfect grammar that resulted from the omission of 4b and made a further cut to create a grammatically coherent but even more reduced text. The J text of Gll and (probably) the B text of SnS also show evidence of constructive, though unconvincing, modifications in response to a corruption already established in the text. All these examples show scribes doing their best to repair the damage done by their predecessors, but the results are not very impressive. Some of the scribes involved in the modification of Brb 40–44 do sensible things; but the scribes of the other texts I have mentioned here were clearly not really up to the task they set themselves; they tinker with the text, but they produce either poor sense (Gl1) or poor versification (the Hr text of Cæd). On this evidence, there is little reason to think that scribes possessed any compositional skills.

§9.4 MISUNDERSTANDINGS

One of the major revelations of this study is the extent to which Anglo-Saxon scribes could be confused by the language of the texts they copied. Non-standard spellings in exemplars, unfamiliar items of poetic vocabulary, or words used in unusual senses (a good example is Brb 41 *folcstede*, 'battlefield', misinterpreted as 'dwelling-place' in the C text), often contributed to the confusion, sometimes in combination (e.g. Brb D 38 *hryman* for *hreman*). Individual letters were often misinterpreted as belonging to the following or the previous word in the exemplar, and the text modified in accordance with the misunderstanding (see §4.1). As Campbell remarked, the D text of Brb shows a quite unusual tendency to transform exemplar readings beyond recognition; perhaps D's *dæg gled on garum* for Brb 53 *nægledcnearrum*, 'nailed ships', is the most spectacular of all its examples. In this text, unfamiliarity with poetic vocabulary was obviously a factor behind such corruptions, for the D text often shows the rejection of poetic words in favour of others; but that alone does not explain the radical nature of D's corruptions. In texts of other poems, principal clauses were sometimes mistaken for subordinate ones, and clausal boundaries misconstrued (above, §4.2.1). Poetic syntax, with its common spread of clausal constituents over several lines in an unpredictable order, often led to what are clearly deliberate emendations based on a weak grasp of the shape of the whole clause or, in some cases (e.g. Cæd H 3b *gehwilc*) impatience, when (as in this example) the appearance of a vital element of the clause is delayed (above, §4.2.2). The grammatical function of case-endings within the clause are quite often misconstrued (9 *foldum* in the W-S *ylda* texts of Cæd is a probable example; see §4.2.2.2 above). One part of speech could be mistaken for another when homographs were involved (e.g. the omission of *æt* from

SB1 125), and insensitivity to aspects of poetic style such as variation sometimes led to ill-advised interventions. Unfamiliar proper names could occasionally cause problems for scribes (e.g. Brb 56 *ira*, 'of the Irish', which turns into the gen. pl. 3rd person pronoun *hira* in the A text). Other corruptions, though fairly clearly grounded in misconceptions about the grammar of the received text, are less easy to account for (above, §4.2.3). The D text of Brb and SB1 both show many replacements of poetic words (above, §§4.4.1, 4.4.2), no doubt because they were not understood, though SB1 is distinguished from Brb D by the better integration of its substitutions. The B text of SnS also shows similar amendments (§4.4.3), again mostly quite well integrated. SB1 and SnS B are texts that have clearly been handled by scribes who were relatively competent in producing reasonably good sense and even (sometimes) metre when they amended their received texts.

§9.5 INTELLIGENT MODIFICATIONS

Other changes indicate some level of comprehension of the received text on the part of the scribes who imposed them. There are several examples of probably conscious changes reflecting scribal preferences for one word rather than another of the same, or similar, meaning (above, §§5.1, 5.2). The rejected word is often poetic, its meaning perhaps known or (probably in some cases) guessed by the scribe who replaced it. The B text of Brb, with three substitutions of this kind, has evidently been copied by a scribe willing and able to impose his own preferences on the received text without distorting its meaning. But although many changes in this category suggest a fair understanding of the text, the motive behind them is often unguessable. The reasons for the occasional splitting of compound words, or for the opposite process whereby two simplex words are combined to form a compound (§5.3), are particularly hard to work out. The A text of Brb shows two examples of compound-splitting; instances are rare enough generally to suggest that these were probably the work of a single scribe. The two cases of compound-creation I identify (SnS B 52, SB1 82) both introduce into the text compound words that occur in OE prose as well as in poetry. This distribution is significant, for otherwise these instances of compounding would represent the only clear cases I have seen of what might be called the poeticization of poems during transmission. The general tendency is away from the poetic towards the prosaic rather than vice-versa.

Poetic formulas are very occasionally replaced by others, but clear examples are difficult to pin down (§5.5). Many other substitutions of individual words are difficult to explain, and there are several cases where it seems impossible to say in which direction the substitution operated (§5.6). Examples are particularly numerous in SnS and Aza/Dan (five and six examples respectively); but the very difficulty in determining the direction of these changes argues for a distinctive element of both freedom and competence in the transmission of these poems. There are also signs in both SB and Aza/Dan of the general imposition of preferred forms throughout the text in one or other version (§5.6.2). Again, it seems impossible to say in which direction these changes operated, but the variants show a certain clearness of purpose and consistency on the part of at least one scribe in each poem's history. A fascinating cluster of variants in Aza 46–50/Dan 330–34 (§5.6.3), neither set having any clearcut advantages over the other, is even better evidence of the relatively free, confident and competent transmission of this poem. It sets Aza/Dan apart even from SnS and SB, the only other poems showing reliable evidence for similarly competent initiatives on the part of transmitters. Furthermore, SnS and Aza/Dan are both particularly well represented under §5.6.4, where are listed substitutions that have taken place in one or other direction though it is impossible to say which. This evidence fits in with the general picture of the transmission of these poems that is beginning to emerge. But most startling of all is the evidence of the variants assembled under §5.8, which show cases of grammatical modifications of every kind, though priority cannot be established in any of them: here Aza/Dan is hugely represented, with eighteen examples (the text with the next largest number of examples is SB, with three), marking this poem off quite emphatically from all others. Here is plentiful evidence that transmitters of this poem treated it with exceptional elasticity, and were competent enough in imposing their modifications to disguise their activities from the reader.

§9.6 SCRIBAL ENTERPRISE

Scribes often added structure-words, or other words of minor semantic importance, to the texts they copied. Sometimes a desire to clarify potential obscurities seems to be the motive. The origins of these words as additions is often revealed by appeal, not only to other versions of the poem, but also to metrical laws and the metrical-grammatical conventions of OE verse encapsulated in Kuhn's laws. SB1, Dan and SnS A are all well represented here, with three fairly clear examples in each. The fact that these additions are usually detectable by the breaches of metrical or metrical-grammatical rules that they involve has obvious implications for the attitudes of the scribes who imposed them on the text: they were not poets, and were insensitive to the regularities of verse-composition which OE poets must certainly have taken for granted; but they cared about the communication of verbal meaning. A few of the longer interpolations identified earlier really belong with these minor additions, particularly Gl1 23 J & *on þone*. It results in a breach of Kuhn's law of clause particles, but was probably inspired by a prose translation of the Bible. This is a significant link, for nearly all the minor interpolations I have identified in various poems would be unexceptionable in a prose text. Perhaps we see confirmation of what other evidence has only hinted at: a divergence between the interests and priorities of poets and those of the scribes who processed their work in the manuscripts. Poets, even literate poets, worked in a mode that was historically oral, absorbing the traditional alliterative style by ear and using it in their performances. Scribes, on the other hand, working in a new and essentially literary mode, were inevitably less concerned with this tradition of the voice and the ear than with the communicative power of the text. Here we can see the efforts that some of them made to foster it.

When we look at longer interpolations, involving anything between a single verse and an entire line, certain texts that have already emerged as showing the impact of a free, competent, even adventurous transmission are again prominent in supplying examples. Dan has two (Dan 288a, 343–44) and SB1, three (SB1 111a, 93, 59–60). The two interpolated single half-lines, one in each of these poems, show enterprise on the one hand but indifference to the two-verse structure of the alliterative line on the other. The interpolations in SB1 are particularly interesting, for as a group they convey a sense of opportunistic intervention when easily imitated series of verses of similar grammatical structure invite it (SB1 59–60, 111a), or when familiar contexts offer a chance to contribute a line of conventional formulas (SB1 93); but this interpolator of SB1 (assuming that a single individual was responsible for all these interpolations) was indeed a poetaster; his additions are technically incomplete (111a), poorly integrated into the context (93), or redundant and over-dependent on existing words and ideas (59–60). A much more impressive interpolator was the poet of DrR, who expands on the RCr inscription in the part of his poem that overlaps with it, and may be responsible for much more of the poem as it survives in the Vercelli

Book; but even he leaves his mark in the shape of suspect metrical and stylistic features in the parts of the text he added.

Numerous variants might be interpreted either as additions in one version of the poem or omissions from another. The great majority of these uncertain cases occur in three poems: SnS, SB and Aza/Dan. Here is yet more evidence of the relatively free and confident transmission that these poems in particular have undergone. But the pattern differs from text to text. The A text of SnS has several of these words that are 'extra' in terms of B, and B has none in terms of A. The A text of SnS has already been singled out for the relatively large number of small inter-polations it contains, so it seems very likely that these 'extra' words it contains are also interpolations. Similarly, SB1 has already been distin-guished from SB2 by the number of small interpolations it exhibits; and SB1 has far more 'extra' words than SB2 (twelve and five respectively), making it likely that they too are mostly interpolated. Dan, however, does not follow the trend here, for although it has several small interpolations, Aza has more 'extra' words than Dan (five and three respectively) in cases where there is no obvious priority.

The two extensions of existing poems that I have identified here, SB1 127–66 and DrR 78–156, have certain features in common. Both feed, so to speak, on the original text in terms of borrowed phraseology and ideas, but both also show the clumsy handling of this material which is, of course, what really points to their nature as extensions. The fact that both survive in the same manuscript, the Vercelli Book, may have interesting implications for its history and that of its contents. A similar kind of analysis of other poems in the OE corpus might be revealing.

§9.7 THE NATURE OF TRANSMISSION

The possibility of 'oral transmission' is, perhaps, a distraction in the study of OE poetry. Sisam compared the two texts of three passages, one each from SB, Aza/Dan and SnS, found the number of variants 'very large', and concluded that in comparison with variants in the manuscripts of classical texts 'they show a laxity of reproduction and an aimlessness in variation which are more in keeping with the oral transmission of verse' (Sisam 1953: 34), though he stops short of actually attributing the amount of variation to oral transmission. But what is, or was, oral transmission in the context of Anglo-Saxon alliterative verse? Presuma-bly the verbatim repetition of poems from memory; but the kind of evidence that might indicate this kind of transmission is difficult to envisage. Of the texts of poems that form the subject of this book, the great majority show fairly clear signs of deriving from literary, not oral, archetypes. The only text for which oral transmission seems possible is Aza/Dan; certainly there are no unmistakable scribal links between the two texts. The sheer number of variants (of all kinds) between Aza and Dan is unusually high. Aza/Dan has been identified here on independent grounds as having undergone relatively free, confident and competent transmission. The possibility that there were special factors at work in the transmission of this poem might bear more detailed examination in a separate study. Even now, these two poems have still not attracted the attentions of an editor who is particularly interested in the relationship between them.

The challenge of Sisam's remarks about textual variation in the manuscripts of OE verse has been taken up in Katherine O'Brien O'Keeffe's book *Visible Song* (O'Keeffe 1990; Aza/Dan is not, unfortunately, part of O'Keeffe's study). O'Keeffe's ideas are novel and elaborate, not easily abstracted from the context of her book. At several points, however, she advances a hypothesis of 'formulaic reading' to explain lexical variation between the texts of OE poems. One version of this hypothesis is offered in connection with O'Keeffe's detailed study of the variants between the A and B texts of SnS. She divides these variants into three categories — grammatical, syntactic and lexical. The first two categories contain variants that tend to involve metrical difficulties in one or other version, though both versions are (in her view) acceptable semantically and syntactically; but she identifies ten lexical variations as 'truly alternate readings between which there is no clear choice'. She explains the difference as follows:

> Given the three possible categories of significant variance, the limitation of substantive variants to lexical alternatives is instructive. The poet and audience have active roles in producing and reproducing oral verse. The audience, in receiving such performances, remember, approve or disapprove, but their participation is essentially passive. The scribe, in receiving the text, is a special case of audience, and as reproducer of text is a special case of performer. His performance as a 'formulaic' reader is thus always at odds with his normally passive reception as copyist, and muddles often arise from the conflation of the two roles of language-producer and visual-reproducer. Truly formulaic reading is no more consciously productive of variance than oral performance. In formulaic reading (the hybrid of 'literate' and oral reception), the relative passivity required of a reader/copyist (as against the activity of a poet or performer)

almost guarantees that any modifications other than simple lexical substitution will leave traces of change. Grammatical or syntactic alteration may have wide repercussions within a clause. Simple lexical substitution is the change least likely to affect surrounding context because it is generally containable to the half-line (O'Keeffe 1990: 66–67).

Some of the points made here are elusive. Why, for example, should the 'relative passivity required of a reader/copyist' guarantee that grammatical or syntactical modifications 'will leave traces of change' (presumably meaning that they lead to identifiable corruptions)? What bearing does 'passivity' have on such modifications? It is clear that many of them result from active, even thoughtful, intervention (examples are numerous in Chapters 4 and 5 above). On the other hand, O'Keeffe's hypothesis is impressive for the comprehensive vision it offers of the copyist's role and mentality. There are few loose ends. But is it based upon what is known and what can reasonably be surmised about the transmission of OE poetry?

When a scribe made a lexical substitution, the grammar of the clause in his exemplar and the metrical shape of the word he replaced would provide models to protect him against any serious metrical, grammatical or syntactical disruption of the text; but when he changed the grammar itself, he had nothing to imitate, no model to copy. It goes without saying that a poet would be less likely than a scribe to produce incoherent grammar or metrical irregularities in these circumstances, though of course a poet would never undertake the modification of the grammar of an existing text; he would produce his own version of the story. This is partly why O'Keeffe's attempt to associate scribal with poetic activity runs into difficulties. The scribe who altered the grammar of his exemplar text would be likely (because he was a copyist) to produce results that are less satisfactory than the poet's and so leave his track. I say this only to make the point that there is really no need to think of scribes as alternating in, combining or confusing the roles of 'language-producer' (performer, poet) and that of 'visual-reproducer' (or copyist). Quite apart from the fact that there is no reason to think that Anglo-Saxon scribes regarded themselves, or were regarded by others, as 'language-producers' or performers, the different consequences of the three kinds of variation that O'Keeffe distinguishes could just as well be explained on the basis of the depth of the scribe's engagement with the text he was copying, or his ambitions as a modifier — a quantitative, not qualitative, variation. We have seen plentiful evidence in this book of very varied degrees of engagement with the received text on the part of transmitters. A scribe who found fault with the grammar and syntax of his exemplar text and adjusted it accordingly would have been engaging with the received text at a critical or editorial level; the scribe who simply replaced unfamiliar poetic compounds with more familiar ones with the same metrical contour and grammatical function may have been paying much less attention, or perhaps simply more local attention, to the text he was copying.

As I have pointed out elsewhere in a discussion of variants among the texts of Cæd (Orton 1998), the idea of 'formulaic reading' is not easy to conceptualize. This, in O'Keeffe's view, is where the roles of poet and scribe come together in the period of 'residual orality', after the coming of literacy. Formulaic reading is 'a reading activity [...] which is formula-dependent' (just as poetic composition is formula-dependent), operating 'by suggestion, by "guess" triggered by key-words in formulae.' The formulaic reader 'uses knowledge of the conventions of the verse to "predict" what is on the page' (O'Keeffe 1990: 40). There are several assumptions underlying these remarks which seem to me difficult to substantiate. It is one thing to accept that an oral poet's performance will arouse in his audience unconscious (or, indeed, conscious) expectations of how the story will unfold, even of how it will be expressed — expectations that may be either fulfilled or thwarted. It is another matter to assert that scribes were subject to the same predictive (presumably unconscious) tendencies as the audience and acted upon them, replacing formulas in their exemplars as they copied. The scribe, unlike the reader or hearer, had a specific job to do, a technical job which did not actually require him to read his exemplar with understanding; all he had to do was reproduce it. In view of the nature of their task, it is difficult to accept that scribes would have imposed their predictions or guesses on the text without noticing (as I assume O'Keeffe believes from her statement that 'Truly formulaic reading is no more consciously productive of variance than oral performance'), replacing the poetic formulas of the exemplar with the lines and verses which the context leads them to expect. The concentration of any copyist is bound to wander occasionally, but how far? Not far enough, surely, for him to forget his responsibilities to the very text he is copying.

Given O'Keefe's definition of formulaic reading, the only convincing evidence for its historical existence would be actual instances of formulaic substitution; but I think O'Keeffe may have overestimated the number of clearcut cases of this phenomenon in the extant multiple-copy poems she examines. She tends to rely too heavily, it seems to me, on lexical variants between which there is little to choose in terms of appropriateness in the context, metrical regularity and so on. Such variants show clearly enough that a lexical substitution has taken place in one version or the other; but it seems dangerous to use *our* inability to see why the substitution was made, or to distinguish the substituted word from the original one, as the basic criterion for a categorization of verses that is supposed to reflect historical realities. In practice, the substitution in such verses can only seldom be shown (by reference to parallels in other OE poems) to be formula-based. I have argued elsewhere (Orton 1998: 159–61) that the substantive variants identified by O'Keeffe among the texts of the W-S *eorðan* group of Cæd are mostly, if not entirely, explicable on the basis of difficulties perceived by scribes in the language of the received text which they attempted to overcome by altering the wording. If my interpretation of these variants is tenable, they would appear to be questionable as examples of the kind of unconstrained formulaic fluidity that O'Keeffe seems to have in mind. Despite the large number of examples of lexical substitution among the texts of the poems studied here, and among those studied by O'Keeffe, actual formula-for-formula replacement seems rare, the most convincing examples coming in Aza/Dan, a poem which may, as I have already suggested, be a special case. Among the texts from which O'Keeffe draws evidence is SnS. Of the ten variants in the A and B texts of this poem that O'Keeffe regards as manifestations of formulaic reading by scribes, two, 44 A *dream*, B *dry* and 82 [.]*elm*, B *wlenco*, present severe difficulties of interpretation in both versions (see above, §5.6.4). Two more, 32 A *feohgestreona*, B *fyrngestreona* and 59 A *gemengeð*, B *geondmengeð*, involve hapax legomena (B's readings in both cases; see §5.6.1 above), so that the unfamiliarity of the word could easily have led to its deliberate rejection in favour of a more familiar one. Again, the likely element of constraint involved in the substitution in these cases seems to disqualify them as examples of free formulaic reading and substitution. A fifth variant, SnS 60 A *dreoseð*, B *dreogeð*, is quite likely to be a miscopying of an unfamiliar lexical item (*dreogan* is an item of poetic vocabulary; see above, §2.1.1.4). In the case of 86 A *gæst*, B *gesið*, B's reading only seems acceptable on the assumption that it is ironic, though there is also reason to suspect that its roots lie in a copying error provoked by a dialectal form (see above, §2.1.2). Of the remaining four verses in O'Keeffe's list, two contain the very rare words *ungesibb* and *hædre* (35

A *ungelic*, B *ungesibb*; 62 A *hædre*, B *hearde*; see above, §§4.4.3, 5.6.4) which could well have been consciously rejected in favour of more familiar ones. None of these cases is decisive against formulaic reading in itself; but taken together they show how difficult it is to assemble a significant body of convincing evidence for the sort of unconstrained, speculative, tradition-based guesswork postulated by O'Keeffe. What I find most difficult to square with the idea of formulaic reading is the fact that so large a proportion of the instances in a single poem involve rare or difficult or possibly corrupt forms and readings. If scribes only expressed their formulaic reading in actual substitutions when faced with obscurities in the texts before them, the basis for the idea looks insecure. For some of these substitutions, 'constructive editing' would be a better name for the procedure they exemplify.

As a concept, formulaic reading has its intellectual roots in modern oral-formulaic theorizing. The replacement of one poetic formula by another, or the less drastic modification of exemplar formulas, represents the poetic end of the poet-scribe continuum that O'Keeffe posits. Oral-formulaic theory, as applied to OE verse, originally tended to project an image of the poet as in possession of a sort of mental bag of formulas which he regularly shook and pulled formulas out of. The hypothesis of the formulaic system seemed, when it was first advanced, to obliterate this unlikely image: instead of the bag with its undifferentiated contents, the poet stores chains or networks of concept-based formula-generating systems in his head which enable him to produce (for example) not only the collocation *hwæles epel* (Sfr 60, 'homeland of the whale') for the sea, but all manner of variations on the same model (e.g. Jg1 39 *fisces epel*, 'homeland of the fish', And 293 *fisces bæð*, 'bath of the fish', etc.) in response to the varying alliterative requirements of the lines he composed. If we think about these systems in this way, as data-structures for the generation of formulas, the idea of choice and the mental trying-out and substitution of elements takes hold and is difficult to shake off; but of course no OE poet is likely to have been in a position to think about formulas or formulaic systems in this way. The formulaic system is an unmistakable product of the modern literate intellect. Fully literate persons have no difficulty in conceptualizing it and expressing it linguistically in the shape of lists of formulas merging into each other — the sort of list that O'Keeffe compiles on pp. 96–107 of *Visible Song*. I doubt if anyone would want to quarrel with the view that the OE *scop* would not have known how to make such lists. But literate analysis, and literate expression of analysis, tend to issue in ideas involving behaviour that would only be possible in a fully literate culture. Out of the written formulaic system, I suggest, emerges the idea, not only of formulaic substitution — the replacement of one element of a formula by another (verbal replacement being an essentially literary activity) — but also the notion of formulaic reading which is supposed to make such substitutions possible in the course of the transmission of OE poetry. It is to be doubted if such substitutions were related in any way to the poet's mental activities when he composed, because the poet did not choose. The idea for an expression for (say) the sea would have come to him directly and immediately, because the systems he made use of were carried at an unconscious level and were probably infinitely more complex in their nature, integration and speed of working than the simple list of related formulas which is the modern scholar's formulaic system. Nor, I think, is there any compelling reason for thinking that the audiences for Anglo-Saxon oral poetry were any more inclined than poets to select variants as they listened (or read) on the basis of formulaic systems they had internalized. We shall never understand the way OE verse was composed unless we analyse it from every possible point of view, and the formulaic system has an honourable place in this enterprise; but there is obviously a danger of circularity if we assume too readily that the procedures followed by medieval poets (or their audiences) consisted of putting the schematized products of modern analysis of their work to practical use.

But if formulaic reading is rejected, what is there to put in its place? Why and how did transmission produce such a variety of variants? No single hypothesis can explain all of them. They are varied because they are the products of a variety of attitudes and activities. At one end of the scale there is the simple, mechanical copying mistake, made quite unthinkingly; and at the other end there are the ambitious extensions of the kind which seem to have made SB1 and DrR much longer than they were originally. In between there is a good deal of muddle, but well-intentioned muddle, evidence of concern that texts should be passed on in a comprehensible form. We have found a few hints of knowledge of, and concern for, metrical form on the part of scribes, but little more than that. We have seen much more evidence of an interest in the communication of meaning, irrespective of the technical condition of the verse that expresses it. This leads me to suggest a view which is directly opposed to O'Keefe's: that in the Anglo-Saxon period the copyist and the poet occupied quite distinct worlds. Literacy, after all, was still young at the end of the Anglo-Saxon period. We have seen little here to suggest a phase of transitional literacy or residual orality. The oral poet — and I think this must also have been true of his literate successor — was trained by ear and worked with the voice; the copyist trained and worked with eye and hand. Even poets who transcribed their own compositions must surely have been trained in the traditional way; otherwise it is difficult to see how they could have become alliterative poets. Cynewulf, for example, can scarcely have learnt how to compose alliterative verse from reading books, whatever he may have got from them in the way of material. The scribe, on the other hand, had a much more circumscribed role; he reproduced texts. His job was a new one, and a world away from that of the oral, traditional poet. But just as some poets (Cynewulf, no doubt, among them) will have become writers, so too some professional writers probably became readers. The responsible reader who is also a writer easily becomes an editor; and the amount of editorial work which these critical scribes did on the poems in their care is impressive. But when we are in a position to track them in the modifications they imposed, we can see that their activities amount to a reduction of poetic quality in the texts they received. Despite some successes (among which the full DrR must be counted, whatever reservations we may have about its quality), and some fairly lengthy lists of 'problem cases' (see §§2.1.3, 5.6.4, 5.8 above) in which one variant seems as good as another, it seems fair to say that when a scribe tried his hand at anything approaching genuine composition, the results were often embarrassingly bad.

From the perspective of the general advance of literacy over the history of English, it would be convenient to conclude that this embarrassment is no more than a consequence of a brief but inevitable period of mutual adjustment in which the older world of oral poetry and the new world of books, scribes and scholars were coming to terms with each other; but the apparent decline of vernacular verse composition towards the end of the Anglo-Saxon period suggests that the opposite may be true. Perhaps we owe our knowledge of Old English poetry to an optimistic experiment, based on the understandable but misguided expectation that the oral poetic tradition could adapt to the new literacy and provide the vehicle for a continuity in the verbal arts with the pre-Christian age. In this case, what we see in late OE verse is not the decay of the entire alliterative tradition, but something more in the nature of a rejected graft. Written poetry becomes steadily weaker, prosier, as it loses touch with the oral tradition whose vigour originally sustained it and takes on more and more influences from the new prose writing; but the tradition lives on in the oral sphere, resurfacing before long as Middle English alliterative poetry.

Bibliography

ANDERSON, O. S., 1941. *Old English Material in the Leningrad Manuscript of Bede's Ecclesiastical History.* Kungliga Humanistiska Vetenskapssamfundet i Lund, Skrifter, 31 (Lund: Gleerup).

BESSINGER, J. B., & Philip H. SMITH, 1978. *A Concordance to The Anglo-Saxon Poetic Records* (Ithaca: Cornell UP).

BLISS, A. J., 1967. *The Metre of Beowulf.* 2nd ed. (Oxford: Basil Blackwell).

——, 1971. 'Single Half-Lines in Old English Poetry', *N&Q*, 216: 442–49.

BOSWORTH, J., & T. N. TOLLER, 1898. *An Anglo-Saxon Dictionary* (Oxford: Oxford UP).

BROOKS, Kenneth R., ed., 1961. *Andreas and The Fates of the Apostles* (Oxford: Clarendon Press).

BROWN, Carleton, 1940. '*Poculum Mortis* in Old English', *Speculum*, 15: 389–99.

CAMPBELL, Alistair, ed., 1938. *The Battle of Brunanburh* (London: Heinemann).

——, 1959. *Old English Grammar* (Oxford: Clarendon Press).

CLASSEN, E., & F. E. HARMER, eds., 1926. *An Anglo-Saxon Chronicle from BM Cotton MS. Tiberius B. iv.* (Manchester: Manchester UP).

COLGRAVE, Bertram, & R. A. B. MYNORS, eds., 1969. *Bede's 'Ecclesiastical History of the English People'* (Oxford: Clarendon Press).

CRAWFORD, S. J., ed., 1922. *The Old English Heptateuch, Ælfric's Treatise on the Old and New Testament and his Preface to Genesis.* EETS O.S. 160 (Oxford: Oxford UP).

DEUTSCHBEIN, M., 1901. 'Dialektisches in der angelsächsischen Übersetzung von Bedas Kirchengeschichte', *BGDSL*, 26: 169–244, 266.

DOBBIE, Elliott van Kirk, 1937. *The Manuscripts of Cædmon's Hymn and Bede's Death Song.* Columbia University Studies in English and Comparative Literature, 128 (New York: Columbia UP).

——, 1942. *The Anglo-Saxon Minor Poems*. The Anglo-Saxon Poetic Records, 6 (New York: Columbia UP).

EGER, Otto, 1910. *Dialektisches in den Flexionsverhältnissen der angelsächsischen Bedaübersetzung* (Leipzig: Noske).

FAIDER, P., & P. van SINT JAN, 1950. *Catalogue des manuscrits conservés à Tournai (bibliothèques de la ville et du Séminaire)* (Gembloux: J. Duculot).

FAKUNDINY, Lydia, 1970. 'The Art of Old English Verse Composition', *RES*, n.s. 21: 129–42.

FARRELL, R. T., ed., 1974. *Daniel and Azarias* (London: Methuen).

FRAMPTON, M. G., 1924–25. 'Cædmon's Hymn', *MP*, 22: 1–15.

FRANTZEN, Allen J., 1990. *Desire for Origins* (New Brunswick: Rutgers UP).

FRY, Donald K., 1974. 'Cædmon as a Formulaic Poet', *Forum for Modern Language Studies*, 10: 227–47.

GREIN, C. W. M., ed., 1857. *Bibliothek der angelsächsischen Poesie in kritisch bearbeiteten Texten und mit vollständigem Glossar*. 4 vols. (Göttingen: Wigand, 1857–64), I.

GYGER, Alison, 1969. 'The Old English *Soul and Body* as an Example of Oral Transmission', *MÆ*, 38: 239–44.

HOLTHAUSEN, Ferdinand, 1901. 'Zu alt- und mittelenglischen Dichtungen XII', *Anglia*, 23: 123–25.

HORGAN, Dorothy M., 1973. 'The Relationship between the O.E. MSS. of King Alfred's Translation of Gregory's *Pastoral Care*', *Anglia*, 91: 153–69.

——, 1980. 'Old English Orthography: A Short Contribution', *ES*, 61: 385–89.

HUMPHREYS, K. W., & Alan S. C. ROSS, 1975. 'Further Manuscripts of Bede's *Historia Ecclesiastica*, of the *Epistola Cuthberti de Obitu Bedae*, and Further Anglo-Saxon Texts of *Cædmon's Hymn* and *Bede's Death Song*', *N&Q*, n.s. 22: 50–55.

JONES, Alison, 1966. '*Daniel* and *Azarias* as Evidence for the Oral-Formulaic Character of Old English Poetry', *MÆ*, 35: 95–102.

JUDGE, Cyril Bathurst, 1934. 'Anglo-Saxonica in Hereford Cathedral Library', *Harvard Studies and Notes*, 16: 89–96.

KEMBLE, John M., 1848. *The Dialogue of Salomon and Saturnus, with an Historical Introduction* (London: Ælfric Society, reprinted 1974, New York: AMS Press).

KER, N. R., ed., 1956. *The Pastoral Care: King Alfred's Translation of St. Gregory's 'Regula pastoralis'*. EEMS, 6 (Copenhagen: Rosenkilde and Bagger).

——, 1957. *Catalogue of Manuscripts Containing Anglo-Saxon* (Oxford: Oxford UP).

KLAEBER, F., ed., 1950. *Beowulf and the Fight at Finnsburg*. 3rd ed. (Boston, MA: D. C. Heath)

KRAPP, George Philip, ed., 1932. *The Vercelli Book*. The Anglo-Saxon Poetic Records, 2 (New York: Columbia UP).

——, & Elliott Van Kirk DOBBIE, eds., 1936. *The Exeter Book*. The Anglo-Saxon Poetic Records, 3 (London: Routledge and Kegan Paul).

KROESCH, Samuel, 1928–29. 'The Semantic Development of OE *cræft*', *MP*, 26: 433–43.

KUHN, Hans, 1933. 'Zur Wortstellung und -Betonung im Altgermanischen', *BGDSL*, 57: 1–101.

LUCAS, Peter J., 1987. 'Some Aspects of the Interaction between Verse-grammar and Metre in Old English Poetry', *SN*, 59: 145–75.

LUMBY, J. Rawson, ed., 1876. *Be Domes Dæge*. EETS, O.S. 65 (London: N. Trübner).

MAWER, Allen, 1923. 'The Redemption of the Five Boroughs', *EHR*, 38: 551–57.

MEGGINSON, David, 1995. 'The Case against a "General Old English Poetic Dialect"', in Toswell 1995: 117–32.

MENNER, Robert J., ed., 1941. *The Poetical Dialogues of Solomon and Saturn*. The Modern Language Association of America Monograph Series, 13 (New York: The Modern Language Association of America).

MILLER, Thomas, ed., 1890. *The Old English Version of Bede's Ecclesiastical History of the English People*. 4 vols. EETS, O.S. 95, 96, 110, 111 (London: N. Trübner, 1890–98), I.

MITCHELL, Bruce, 1985. *Old English Syntax*. 2 vols. (Oxford: Clarendon Press).

MOFFAT, Douglas, 1983. 'The MS Transmission of the OE *Soul and Body*', *MÆ*, 52: 300–01.

——, 1987. 'A Case of Scribal Revision in the Old English *Soul and Body*', *JEGP*, 86: 1–8.

——, ed. and trans., 1990. *The Old English Soul and Body* (Woodbridge: D. S. Brewer).

OKASHA, Elisabeth, 1971. *Hand-List of Anglo-Saxon Non-Runic Inscriptions* (Cambridge: Cambridge UP).

O'KEEFFE, Katherine O'Brien, 1990. *Visible Song: Transitional Literacy in Old English Verse*. Cambridge Studies in Anglo-Saxon England, 4 (Cambridge: Cambridge UP).

ORTON, P. R., 1979a. 'Disunity in the Vercelli Book *Soul and Body*', *Neophilologus*, 63: 450–60.

——, 1979b. 'The OE *Soul and Body*: A Further Examination', *MÆ*, 48: 173–97.

——, 1981. 'Aspects of the Transmission of Old English Poetry.' Ph.D. thesis, University of Exeter.

——, 1985. '*The Battle of Brunanburh* 40b-44a: Constantine's Bereavement', *Peritia*, 4: 243–50.

——, 1994. 'On the Transmission and Phonology of *The Battle of Brunanburh*', *Leeds Studies in English*, n.s. 25: 1–27.

——, 1998. 'The Transmission of the West Saxon Versions of *Cædmon's Hymn*: A Reappraisal', *SN*, 70: 153–64.

——, 1999. 'Anglo-Saxon Attitudes to Kuhn's Laws', *RES*, n.s. 50: 287–303.

PAGE, R. I., 1965. 'A Note on the Text of MS CCCC 422 (*Solomon and Saturn*)', *MÆ*, 34: 36–39.

PLUMMER, Charles, ed., 1892. *Two of the Saxon Chronicles Parallel with Supplementary Extracts from the Others: A Revised Text*. Reissued with a Bibliographical Note by Dorothy Whitelock, 1952 (Oxford: Clarendon Press).

ROSS, Alan S. C., 1950. 'Miscellaneous Notes on Cædmon's Hymn and Bede's Death Song', *English and Germanic Studies*, 3: 88–96.

SEDGEFIELD, W. J., ed., 1922. *An Anglo-Saxon Verse-Book* (Manchester: Manchester UP).

SISAM, Kenneth, 1953. *Studies in the History of Old English Literature* (Oxford: Clarendon Press).

SLAY, D., 1952. 'Some Aspects of the Technique of Composition of Old English Verse', *TPS*, 1–14.

SMITH, A. H., 1968. *Three Northumbrian Poems*. 2nd ed. (London: Methuen).

SMYTH, Alfred P., 1975–79. *Scandinavian York and Dublin*. 2 vols. (Dublin: Templekieran Press).

STENTON, F. M., 1971. *Anglo-Saxon England*. 3rd ed. (Oxford: Clarendon Press).

SWEET, Henry, ed., 1871. *King Alfred's West-Saxon Version of Gregory's Pastoral Care*. 2 vols. EETS, O.S. 45 and 50 (London: N. Trübner, 1871–72), I.

THOMSON, E., ed., 1849. *Godcunde Lar and Þeowdom: Select Monuments of the Doctrine and Worship of the Catholic Church in England before the Norman Conquest* (London: Lumley).

THORPE, Benjamin, ed., 1848. *Florentii Wigorniensis Monachi Chronicon ex Chronicis, ab adventu Hengesti et Horsi in Britanniam usque ad annum 1117*, etc. 2 vols. (London: English Historical Society, 1848–49), I.

TOLLER, T. Northcote, 1921. *An Anglo-Saxon Dictionary: Supplement* (Oxford: Oxford UP).

TOSWELL, M. J., ed., 1995. *Prosody and Poetics in the Early Middle Ages: Essays in Honour of C. B. Hieatt* (Toronto: University of Toronto Press).

URE, James, ed., 1957. *The Benedictine Office: An Old English Text* (Edinburgh: Edinburgh UP).

WILLARD, Rudolph, 1935. 'The Address of the Soul to the Body', *PMLA*, 50: 957–83.

WUEST, Paul, 1906. 'Zwei neue Handschriften von Caedmons Hymnus', *ZDA*, 48: 205–26.

Index of Lines Referred To

222